The Cancer

Of

Civilization Jihad

Do Islamic Social norms
oppose
the rest of the world??

By Paul Sutliff

ISBN 978-0-578-88527-8

Dedication

While writing this book, I found myself at times floundering in a sea of overwhelming information, sifting through what seemed like endless material. It is without question that this book could not have come into existence without several supportive people in my life. Many of them are in my church. Pastor Galvano, Pastor Diaz and Pastor Torres, your belief and support for me made this work possible. My father who has never failed to say to me "You can do it!" My sister whose smile and dogged determination to do what is right professionally has never failed to be there to support me. A past student whose love for Jesus has refreshed and encouraged my own love of the great Messiah. My neighbor whose beautiful determination to be the best at playing the piano provided me with musical serenades through a wall that made me feel as if I was home and still living with my parents. Friends like Todd Bensman, and fellow patriots like Patrick Dunleavy may never know how much they encouraged me by just being who they are. My fellow broadcasters on the Global Patriot Radio Network whose love for Truth allows them to empower others with news, analysis, and scriptural truth. Usama and Chris, you helped me finish. You were able to shine a light on the end of the road ahead. THANK YOU ALL!

Table of Contents

Speaking at Kanal D TV's Arena program, Prime Minister **Erdogan** commented on the term "moderate Islam," often used in the West to describe AKP and said, **"These descriptions are very ugly. It is offensive, and an insult to our religion. There is no moderate or immoderate Islam. Islam is Islam and that's it."**

Source: Milliyet, Turkey, August 21, 2007.

"...Islam is a culture that contradicts Western Culture; it contradicts the culture of Western countries, meaning: Europe, North America, Israel or Australia... In fact, you need to know that the original Islam, the paradigm so often mentioned on the TV - the real Islam, is defined by the god, Allah in the Quran; the Quran that was originally transmitted by the Prophet Muhammad. Islam is an Islamic supporter of slavery, an Islamic misogynist, is an Islamic enemy of free speech, of free thought, and that criminalizes freedom of thought. And this is an antithesis of our values and our customs which are inspired by the dominant cultural force in our country [France]; Christian and secular."

Oukacha, Majid, (April 7, 2016) Interview on Livre-Libre by Gilbert Collard, translated by the RAIR Foundation. https://3speak.online/watch?v=rairfoundation/giyzbnai

Why this book?

After my trip to Europe as part of a Fact Finding Expedition on the Islamization of Europe in 2016, I was awed at what I saw of the incredible growth of Islamization - what the Muslim Brotherhood here call Civilization Jihad. I had written two books on the topic of Civilization Jihad. I wrote my third book after the trip, specifically targeting Social Studies Teachers in order to make them aware of the errors in their books. That created an affinity of trust to Islam and a distrust of anything that is of the Judeo-Christian heritage. Yet, I had not addressed what I was seeing, but only a symptom of it - the submission of the American education system to the promotion of Islam.

What that looks like 50 to 100 years down the road was what I saw in Europe in 2016. I have since seen that in the USA, even in my own city. But what exactly am I talking about? The social norms that Western civilization has espoused for hundreds of years is being confronted and opposed on a daily basis by what some claim are social norms of Islam.

This book is not one that looks at individual beliefs. Instead, it examines what has been called mores. Merriam-Webster Dictionary defines this as "the fixed morally binding customs of a particular group." This means that this book examines the Social Psychological principles identified as Social norms.

Baron, Byrne and Suls define Social Psychology as:

'The scientific field that seeks to understand the nature and causes of individual behavior in social situations'[1]

---

[1] Baron, R. A., Byrne, D., & Suls, J. (1989). Attitudes:Evaluating the social world. In R. A. Baron, D. Byrne, & J. Suls, *Social Psychology, 3rd Edition* (pp. 79-101). MA: Allyn and Bacon.

Dr. Saul McLeod defined this further in 2008 when he wrote "Social Roles in Social Psychology":

> "There are many ways that people can influence our behavior, but perhaps one of the most important is that the presence of others seems to set up expectations.

> We do not expect people to behave randomly, but to behave in certain ways in particular situations. Each social situation entails its own particular set of expectations about the "proper" way to behave. Such expectations can vary from group to group."[2]

This book intended to look at a specific group to determine if what is being observed are social norms. Dr. McLeod defines the term "social norm" in the following way:

> "Social norms are the unwritten rules of beliefs, attitudes, and behaviors that are considered acceptable in a particular social group or culture. Norms provide us with an expected idea of how to behave and function, to provide order and predictability in society. For example, we expect students to arrive to a lesson on time and complete their work.

> The idea of norms provides a key to understanding social influence in general, and conformity in particular. Social norms are the accepted standards of behavior of social groups."

The intended purpose of this book was to examine whether what people claim are Islam's social norms are indeed Islamic. If these observed behaviors are exhibits of social norms of a group of followers of Islam, then that would mean they would be defined in their scriptures.

---

[2] McLeod, S. (2008). *Social Roles.* Retrieved April 19, 2021, from Social Psychology: https://www.simplypsychology.org/social-roles.html.

Many people have written about clashes of civilizations, but few have examined what initiated the conflicts. Today, some claim that we are experiencing a clash of civilizations that will lead to an all-out war. I do not intend to look at if the norms examined in this book will cause a war. Instead, I intend to examine each possible social norm of Islam to discover if there are Islamic scriptural backing of the supposed social norm. Then if it is so, how are we seeing this social norm today by an examination of news articles from around the world.

There will be some who claim this book is a book of hate. Yet, this book is one that asks questions and diligently seeks out the answers. Social norms are a valid construct in the academic world. The book is an academic inquiry into supposed social norms of Islam.

The author is a believer of Jesus. He believes that we must love those who do not know Jesus. This includes all Muslims. Does this mean an acceptance of what they believe? No. It means he feels a sense of duty to share what he has learned about Islamic social norms so that Muslims and the rest of the world may see what Islam endorses as acceptable behavior and social constraints.

Chapter 1

Is there an Islamic social norm requiring a Hijrah (Migration) to Western Civilizations?

When I started to have a clue as to what was happening with respect to Civilization Jihad, I was struck by one comment recorded by the FBI; "Stage 1 is complete, we are here."

For a long time, the reasoning behind this statement caused me to be curious. Then I began to read about the hijrah. Sam Solomon was one of the first authors I read on this topic, in his book, Modern Day Trojan Horse: Al-Hijra, the Islamic Doctrine of Immigration, Accepting Freedom or Imposing Islam? After reading this work, I looked deeper into the concept of the hijrah and began to ask my own questions:

1. If the hijrah is an Islamic doctrine, do governments know and acknowledge this?
2. If the hijrah is real, there must be examples throughout history – what are they?
3. If hijrahs have been historically documented and acknowledged before jihads, what is the reason we do not seem to have this information at our fingertips today?

While I had many questions, these three seemed to grab my attention the most. If it is true that the hijrah (Immigration) is an Islamic doctrine, that would make it an Islamic social norm.

Simple, right? How we do find the real answer to that first question? Especially, if the knowledge has been hidden? What do we have to do to learn the truth? These basic simplicities evolved into an acceptance that somehow, in some way, we have been lied to. Who did the lying seemed unimportant at first; the focus was finding the truth regardless of who was hiding it.

I began by looking at the "Islam Question & Answer" website, an online resource where Muslims and non-Muslims ask questions about Islam; questions that are supposed to be answered by knowledgeable Islamic clerics. I found they had answered the question: "Can Muslims settle in kaafir countries for the sake of a better life?"

Interestingly, they started their answer by condemning those Muslims who live amongst non-Muslims:

In the Sunnah, the Prophet (PBUH) said: "I disown every Muslim who settles among the mushrikeen" [non-Muslims]. (Narrated by Abu Dawood, 2645; classed as saheeh by al-Albaani in Saheeh Abi Dawood.)[3]

According to this manner of thought, living in Dar al-Harb is wrong for Muslims. Also, it is not acceptable to live in non-Islamic communities in Muslim lands, according to their prophet. However, the author of this document does make an exception.

Rather, we should say that each Muslim has his own unique set of circumstances and his own ruling that applies to him, and each person is accountable for himself. If he is able to practice his religion in the Muslim country in which he lives more than he can in a kaafir country, then it is not permissible for him to settle in a kaafir country.

But if it is the other way round, then it is permissible for him to settle in a kaafir country, subject to the condition that he is

---

[3] Islam Question & Answer. (2003, April 19). *Can Muslims settle in kaafir countries for the sake of a better life?* Retrieved April 10, 2020, from Islam Question & Answer: https://islamqa.info/en/answers/13363/can-muslims-settle-in-kaafir-countries-for-the-sake-of-a-better-life.

confident that he can resist the desires and temptations to be found there by taking the precautionary measures prescribed in sharee'ah.

Zakriya al-Ansaari al-Shafa'ia said in his book Asna al-Mataalib (4/207):

"It is obligatory to migrate from the kaafir lands to the Muslim lands for those who are able to do that, if they are unable to practice their religion openly."[4]

So why are Muslims coming to non-Muslim countries - what they call Dar al-Harb - if it is forbidden? Is this merely a smoke screen? Are these very words quoted above only for a select few? It makes little sense that they could not practice what they believe in an Islamic country. Or is this a screening out policy? A doctrinal statement that insists Muslims not strong in their faith must stay in an Islamic country. What of those who hold on to their Islamic faith with strength?

Two Hadith passages state what Muhammad said to answer this question:

I charge you five of what Allah has charged me with: to assemble, to listen, to obey, to immigrate and to wage jihad for the sake Allah. (Hadith no. 2863 Kitab al Amthael reported by Timri, also reported by Imam Ahmed Ibn Hanbel as Hadith no 17344.)

This wording implies that migration for the purpose of jihad is not only okay, it is commissioned by the prophet of Islam. But is this the only citation of such a statement?

- Surah 2:218 "Surely those who believed and *those who emigrated and performed jihad.*"
- Surah 8:72 "Surely *those who believed and those who emigrated and performed jihad* with their money and their lives *for the sake Allah*, and those who gave asylum…"

---

[4] Ibid

- Surah 8:74 "And *those who believed and emigrated and performed jihad for the sake of Allah*, and those who gave asylum and help [gave you victory], those are the true believers, they will receive forgiveness and generous provisions."
- Surah 8:75 "And *those who believed afterward and emigrated and performed jihad* with you, those are of you."

The Hadiths also solidify the purpose of Muslim migration to non-Islamic lands (Dar al-Harb); it is for the sole purpose of jihad, war against the infidel.

'A'isha reported that the Messenger of Allah was asked about migration, whereupon he said: There is no migration after the Conquest (of Mecca), but Jihad and sincere intention. When you are asked to set out (for the cause of Islam), you should set out (Sahih Muslim 1864, Book 20, Hadith 4599).

Doesn't this information make you question why non-Muslim countries would accept any Muslims inside their borders? But there is more on this:

Narrated Mu'awiyah: I heard the Messenger of Allah say: Migration will not end until repentance ends, and repentance will not end until the sun rises in the west (Sunan Abi Dawud 2479, Book 14, Hadith 2473).

Clearly, the meaning of "until repentance ends" means when all have turned to Allah. Migration after the conquest of Mecca, if to a non-Muslim land, is for the sole-purpose of conquest! Whether it be an Islamic army crossing a border to wage war, or an individual.

As you can see, the Hadiths and the Quran provide several examples showing that the purpose of migration (al-Hijrah) is to accomplish jihad. Shouldn't Western governments be aware of this? Why aren't they? The US government spends hundreds of millions of dollars researching "violent extremism", trying to determine why some persons become terrorists. But they never examine if the beliefs that are called "extremist" are in any way different or outside the norm of what Islam teaches. I have had discussions with world-renowned expert, Dr. Anne Speckhard on this. She, like many others, does not accept that Islam can be anything but peaceful. The non-peaceful follower of Islam is simply classified as an extremist. But this book is not like those who promote a belief that the term "extremist" clearly defines those who are violent in Islam. This book examines jihad in the last chapter to determine if it is an Islamic social norm.

Khalid Masud wrote "The obligation to migrate: The doctrine of hijra in Islamic law" which is a chapter in Muslim Travellers edited by Dale Eickelman and James Piscatori in 1990.

Masud states:

From the Qur'anic texts, the following significant points about hijra can be inferred: (1) It was an obligation of physical movement towards self-definition in the nascent Muslim society; (2) Hijra was closely associated with jihad; and (3) Hijra established a bond of relationship among Muslims, particularly with the ansar.[5]

Masud's point on hijrah being closely associated with jihad has great significance because what is defined today as Islamic terrorism is often classified as Islamic jihad (holy war) against non-Muslims. Masud did share that there were differing opinions by scholars on whether hijra remained obligatory, and shared that those who do not consider it obligatory believed that after the death of their prophet, Muhammad, hijra ended. But according to Masud, many scholars considered it an important and relevant teaching.

Abu Sulayman Hamid b. Muhammad Khattabi al Busti (AD 931-96/9), a scholar of hadith... argued that hijrah was actually meant to support and strengthen dar al-Islam in its nascent days. After the conquests, dar al-Islam was so strong

---

[5] Eickelman, D. F., & Piscatori, J. P. (1990). *Muslim Travellers: Pilgrimage, Migration, and the Religious Imagination.* Berkeley: University of California, p.32.

and established that migration was no longer required. The hijrah would be required again only and whenever the conditions so demanded (Ibn Hajar 1959; vi, 378).[6]

Masud uses a quick historical examination of the time period of the first few Caliphs to look at the truth of this matter. Masud notes that the cases of opposing Muslim groups (631-632 AD) justified their war, "most often, the ruling group in the centre - in terms of *jihad*. It was therefore necessary to strengthen their camp by asking their followers to migrate from enemy territories."[7]

Masud provides the example of the Khawarij who justified their *jihad and hijra* by stating:

All territories were dar al-kufr until they were brought into the fold of Islam. A territory could turn again into dar al-kufr if its rulers denied the sovereignty of Allah, or committed a major sin, whereby they became kafirs. In these circumstances, hijra from such a territory and jihad against it become obligatory.[8]

This created reasoning for one group of Muslims to declare an opposing Muslim entity to be *mushriks* (polytheists), justifying a *hijrah* for the purposes of strengthening their camp before a *jihad*. There are several historical examples of this. William Hunter recorded examples of hijrahs used by Muslim leaders against other Muslim leaders in <u>The Indian Mussulmans</u> (1871).

Masud quotes Ibn Hanbal as offering a "parallel to the famous five pillars of Islam: 'I convey the following five commandments given by Allah: attention (sawm'), obedience (ta'a), migration (hijrah), struggle (jihad), and organization (jama'a).'"

This quote is actually very important, in that, it refers to the four things that happen when Muslims do migrate to non-Muslim lands. 1) Sometimes, communal prayers are instituted to show strength. 2) Obedience can be a reference to remaining separate

---

[6] Ibid, p. 33.
[7] Ibid, p. 34.
[8] Ibid

from the non-Muslims. 3) Jihad used as "struggle", keeping the hate of the infidel in the heart, which the last caliph defined as the lowest level of jihad in the 1915 fatwa.[9] 4) Organization - this communal obligation to organize encourages the Muslims in their non-integration of their community into their new homeland. This creates a division and separation of cultures and laws.

It's time to step back and analyze what is happening around the globe in light of massive Muslim migration. Are Muslims making a hijrah today in accordance with Islamic scholars? If so, these migrations en masse are only for one purpose…Islamic conquest.

Organization

Perhaps we simply need to listen to what Muslims are saying to other Muslims. Dr. Ismail al-Faruqi gave a talk to the UK Islamic Mission in 1986. He said:

We are here to stay, we are here to plant Islam in this part of the world and we must utilize everything in our power to make the word of Allah supreme…In the presence of living here, we can become ambassadors of Islam… Allah … has carved out a vocation for you, a new mission, and this mission is to save the West, to save the humanity of the West, by converting that humanity to Islam… we want to live henceforth as if we were muhajjirs, Companions of Muhammad from Makka to Madina … And so, let us invest our Hijra with this new meaning, let us appoint ourselves as ambassadors of Islam in this country and let us begin a pramme, a programme of real action.[10]

Dr. Patrick Sookhdeo, wrote the report, Islam in Britain, in 2005. In this, he identified two major problems with Islamic immigration: self-imposed segregation or separation from the native culture of the new country, and the Islamic requirement to organize. In the USA, there had not been enough Muslims outside of major cities to identify self-imposed segregating groups. However, there has been evidence of organization since the

---

[9] Appendix B

[10] al-Faruqi, I. (1986). The Path of Da'wah In The West. London. 19-26.

Muslim Brotherhood's first legal organized entity. The Muslim Student Association began in 1963 and was founded by documented members of the Muslim Brotherhood.

In the United Kingdom, this self-imposed segregation and organization revealed a definitive goal and plan. Srdja Trifkovic wrote in 2002 of a 1982 Declaration by the Islamic Foundation in Leicester that claimed the Islamic movement;

> *...is an **organised struggle** to change the existing society into an Islamic society based on the Qur'an and the Sunna, and make Islam, which is a code for entire life, supreme and dominant, especially in the socio-political spheres. ...that the ultimate objective of the Islamic movement shall not be realized unless the struggle is made by locals. For it is only they, who have the power to change the society into an Islamic society.*[11]

This statement reveals that Muslims, who appeared to come to the UK in the 1960s and 1970s "for a better life"[12] actually came with the intention of making the United Kingdom into an Islamic country. This is subversive. It is seditious. It is a hijrah.

Dr. Sookhdeo states that "because of Islam's history of political dominance during most of which shari'a was enforced, and because of its theology based on political power, Muslims have difficulty adapting to life as minorities in a non-Muslim environment. Traditionalists develop strategies to help Muslims maintain their Muslim identity and resist secular temptations."[13]

---

[11] Trifkovic, S. (2002, December 20). The Islamic Conquest of Britain. Retrieved August 2, 2019, from Chicles Magazine: https://web.archive.org/web/20040710081633/chroniclesmagazine.org/news/trifkovic/newsst122002.html.

[12] Al-Munajiid, M. S. (2003, April 29). *Can Muslims Settle in Kaffir Countries for the Sake of a Better Life".* Retrieved March 28, 2020, from Islamqa.info: https://islamqa.info/en/13363. Accessed March 28, 2020. http://islamqa.info/en/13363.

[13] Sookhdeo, D. P. (2005). *Islam in Britain.* London: The Institute for the Study of Islam and Christianity, p.9

The organization of Muslims is seen as a religious obligation. Dr. Sookhdeo noted that Islamic scholar Mawdudi, whom Jihadists refer to often, talked about da'wa and its inability to be effective if there is no organization. He said this about a Muslim's duty to organize:

> *These aims cannot be realized so long as power and leadership in society are in the hands of the disbelieving rulers, and so long as the followers of Islam confine themselves to worship rites ... Only when power is in the hands of the Believers and the righteous, can the objectives of Islam be realized. It is therefore the primary duty of all those who aspire to please Allah to launch an organized struggle, sparing neither life, nor property, for this purpose. The importance of securing power for the righteous is so fundamental that, in neglecting this struggle, one has no means left to please Allah.*[14]

Dr. Sookhdeo also observed that Professor H. Ali Kettani, believed that organization was the key to Muslim Minority group's survival:

> *The secret of the Muslim communities which have been able to survive across the centuries and generations lies in one word: organization. Islam cannot survive if individual Muslims believe it is a personal affair... When a group of Muslims is formed, the first thing they should do to keep Islam among themselves is to organize themselves on an Islamic basis. To keep Islam alive from one generation to another, they should establish two basic Islamic Institutions: the mosque and the school.*[15]

---

[14] Mawdudi, S. A. (2007). *The Islamic Movement: Dynamics of Values, Powe and Change.* London: The Islamic Foundation, p. 79.

[15] Kettani, M. (1986). *Muslim Minorities in the World Today .* London: Mansell Publishing , p. 25.

With this point of view that organization is required and needed for the faith structure to survive in a non-Muslim land, it is not surprising that the first organization are mosques and schools in most countries. It is interesting that both Mawdudi and Kettani express a belief that Islam alone is not able to keep a Muslim from straying. He needs to be organized into resistance to his new country and its government. That organization will not be viewed as successful until the day the government submits to Islam as its authority alone.

These organizations have helped create the possibility of parallel lives rather than assimilation into a new host country. Muslims in the UK can be born into a Muslim family, go to a Muslim school, go to Muslim Community Centers and then work in exclusively Muslim work environments. These organizations allow and encourage the Muslim to remain separate from the Christians and Jews.

Is immigration a national security threat?

Because there are some who do not see a threat from the first stage of Civilization Jihad, it is time to look at Islamic immigration in terms of it posing a possible threat to our national security. Immigration in the United States of America, has been studied in light of being a national security threat for a long time. This study is much broader than a singular view of Islam alone. Leo Lucassen wrote The Immigrant Threat in 2005. His book addresses immigrants that come in large numbers, "hundreds of thousands rather than tens of thousands." His book sees an immigration threat of such large groups existing on three levels: religious, national, and social. But let's not forget that this is an - intentional infiltration and take over, via a massive population expansion through migration and child rearing.

Dr. Patrick Sookhdeo states in his book, Dawa: The Islamic Strategy for Reshaping the Modern World, (2014) that "most Muslim countries regard their large populations as a political weapon and are glad to send their citizens to settle in Europe,

America, Canada, Australia, Latin America, Japan, South Korea and other Non-Muslim countries."[16]

Recent news events have shown that this is more than true. On October 7th[th] of 2019, Erdogan threatened to open the Turkish border into Europe.[17] Only a month earlier on September 5th, Bilder[18] reported a new threat from Turkey's president Erdogan. He was demanding even more money than what the willing European Union had already agreed to pay. According to Bilder, the EU had paid out €5,600,000,000 ($6.21 billion) out of an agreed €6 billion ($6.65 billion). Erdogan wanted an additional amount immediately, to build housing facilities; not in Turkey, but 30 miles into Syria, or else!

On July 21, 2019, "Turkish Interior Minister Süleyman Soylu accused European countries of leaving Turkey alone to deal with the migration issue. In comments published by the state news agency Anadolu Agency,[19] he warned: "We are facing the biggest wave of migration in history. If we open the floodgates, no

---

[16] Sookhdeo, P. (2015). *Dawa: The Islamic Strategy for Reshaping the Modern World*. London: Isaac Publishing, p. 42.

[17] ABC News Australia. (2019, October 10). *Turkey's Erdogan threatens to send Syrian refugees to Europe*. Retrieved May 30, 2021, from ABC News Australia: https://www.abc.net.au/news/2019-10-10/turkish-president-erdogan-threatens-to-flood-europe-refugees/11591930.

[18] Bild.de. (2019, September 5). *Turkey President Demands Help With The Care Of Syrian Refugees: Erdogan Threatens Eu With Border Opening! "Either That Happens - Or We Open The Gates"*. Retrieved May 30, 2021, from Bild.de: https://www.bild.de/politik/ausland/politik-ausland/erdogan-will-hilfe-fuer-syrische-fluechtlinge-und-droht-eu-mit-grenzoeffnung-64440610.bild.html.

[19] Soylu, Süleyman. 2019. *Interior Minister Soylu: When we open the doors, their government cannot last 6 months*. July 21. Accessed March 28, 2020. https://www.aa.com.tr/tr/politika/icisleri-bakani-soylu-kapilari-actigimizda-hukumetleri-6-ay-dayanamaz/1537340.

European government will be able to survive for more than six months. We advise them not to try our patience."[20]

Keep in mind that Turkey was providing medical and other logistical support to the terror group known as ISIS or the Islamic State that "created" this migration crisis.

Only a few months earlier on April 16, 2019, the Libyan Prime Minister Fayez al-Sarraj said, "What's going to happen with this security breakdown is that 800,000 illegal migrants on Libyan ground will have to leave Libya and will cross the sea towards Europe. Amongst these 800,000, there are terrorists and criminals. This will be disastrous."[21]

These threats are pretty constant. It shows just a glimmer of a belief in Islamic supremacy, which will be tackled in the next chapter.

Religious Threat

A different religion could have a differing and competing worldview that may not be compatible with those in the country they emigrated to. On top of this, religion could have a long history of conflict with the religion of those already in the country, dating back centuries. Lucassen states that in some respects, a competing religion of migrants could be against the religion of those who started the country. It could even be a causative factor of the country being created and separated from others. A massive group of persons from such a religion would indeed pose a threat to the nation under this view.

United States of America: It is no secret that the Navy and Marine Corp were first formed under the US Constitution to war

---

[20] Kern, S. (2019, July 21). *Turkey Threatens to Reignite European Migrant Crisis*. Retrieved August 22, 2019, from Gatestone Institute: https://www.gatestoneinstitute.org/14624/turkey-threatens-migrant-crisis.

[21] Hayward, J. (2019, April 16). *Libyan PM: Siege of Tripoli Could Drive 800,000 More Migrants into Europe*. Retrieved 22 2019, August, from Breitbart News: https://www.breitbart.com/national-security/2019/04/16/libyan-pm-siege-of-tripoli-could-drive-800000-more-migrants-into-europe.

against the Barbary States, the first official enemy of the constitutional government of the United States of America. In the US, we refer to them as the Barbary Pirates. The Barbary States were Islamic ruled states in what is now referred to as Libya. These states functioned as independent governments ruled by a despotic caliph. These states waged war against vessels that passed within their reach, thus the label, pirates fits. The pirates, following shariah, captured goods, and people. They then chose to either keep them or sell them back at a ransom. Some people were kept as slaves, some were ransomed. These actions are still legal under shariah, thus, allowing for the Muslim pirates near Somalia to continue to exist.

So, is there a long standing enmity between Muslims and the Judeo-Christian heritage of colonial America under the US Constitution? Cultural divides are shown in the recordings of the war from the Islamic belief that lying is permissible to non-Muslims. There was a time when Lieutenant Andrew Sterrett, commanded the frigate *Enterprise* in battle against the Tripolitan 14-gun galley, commanded by Admiral Rais Mahomet.

In a three-hour battle, the outgunned galley lost sixty men, while the Enterprise, incredibly, lost none. The Tripolitans twice lowered their colors, only to resume fighting when the Americans approached to take possession of the surrendered vessel.[22]

During this time period, a ship's flag was only lowered as a sign of surrender. To say deception is not a part of war would be insane; but at the time, to make a declaration of surrender and then fire on those who seek to end the conflict peaceably, was a stance against the rules of warfare on the seas. It endangered every ship's ability on the high seas to surrender after a battle, and their captain's ability to save the remaining crew.

This belief that it is permissible to deceive or lie to non-Muslims so permeates Islamic culture, that the term *taqiyya*, is known widely known in counterterrorism circles. This belief runs

---

[22] Toll, I. W. (2006). *Six frigates: The Epic History of the Founding of the US Navy*. New York City, NY: W. W. Norton & Co., Inc., p. 171.

counter to a belief in the concept of the importance of communication amongst men and women of the United States of America. The Constitution allows for freedom of speech; however, the concept of lying and deceiving others is not a protected form of speech. We have terms such as slander, defamation of character, and perjury that declare that this belief is dangerous to the American way of life.

National Security Threat

According to Lucassen, a threat can also exist in taking in large numbers of low or non-skilled persons. Doing this creates conflict with those who are already within the country and are also low-skilled. This conflict exists primarily as low-skilled jobs become fewer in a world filled with technology.

Not stated in Lucassen's initial review of national threats are differing political ideologies that may be entirely opposed to the political beliefs and practices of their new homeland. If large groups of immigrants enter a country with this conflict, it becomes a viable threat to the governing philosophy of the current governmental structure.

Social Threat

Lucassen viewed this threat as, primarily, criminal activities, and the growth of poverty and low-income housing.

Some of this threat extends not only from the first generation, but from the second generation and their difficulties in life, starting with their ability or inability to attain success in an academic environment. Yes, this is a look at whether they are successful in integrating by learning the language and social structure of the community where their parents have chosen to live.

If we look at countries where a hijrah is seemingly changing the social fabric and structure, such as Sweden, Denmark and the UK, do we see the criminal activity that Lucassen warns about?

The very week I was writing this, I was notified by a person from Sweden that one of my hashtags on LinkedIn could not be accessed in their country. #MuslimMigrantCrime, was the hashtag I started to use to document the numerous crimes that I was discovering in relation to the hijrah in Europe. Sweden is a country that has moved from protecting its citizens to protecting Islam. This very month, August 2019, several sad crimes have been noted in Sweden.

It is time to ask if there are vast differences between social norms from Islam and social norms from Judeo-Christian heritage.

Chapter 2

Do all Muslims believe the same things?

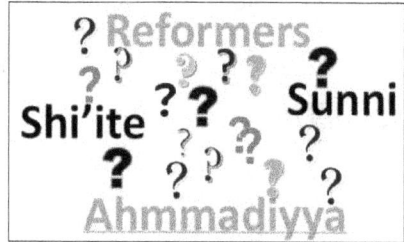

? Reformers
Shi'ite ? ? Sunni
Ahmmadiyya

WARNING READ FIRST

This chapter was started when I began to think about how to communicate what I was seeing in the news every day without sounding crazy. *What can I do to make people see what I am seeing?*

I began to think about what I was seeing in terms of crimes and offences, and then the elements that could explain these crimes. I have done the research into this for far too long to be able to answer my own questions. It put to rest my own disbelief about what is true regarding Islamic culture and social norms. My research, over the years, has included interviews, numerous hours of reading and researching, and then keeping fresh with what is in the news daily. I thought long and hard about the New York State's Regents statement that religions all have rules for behavior. These are rules that should be followed or, by not following, cause the person definite trouble.

How do we look into these behaviors, which are social norms? How do we prove they are real and not imagined by people who are not Muslims? Most adherents to Islam accept the entire Quran along with the Sunnah, (the Hadiths, and Sirats). Understanding the need for more than the Quran is important, because the followers of Muhammad, the devout followers, desire to emulate Muhammad their prophet. This means, in order to provide a good understanding of Islam acceptable to a devout Muslim, we need to

20

look at both the Quran and the Sunnah. We also need to consider Islamic law, called Shariah.

But to start this topic, it is important to understand the concept of duality which exists within Islam. This means that two messages are often given. When the topic of separation is discussed, alliance will also be an important topic. When love is discussed, expect hate to also be a topic. Expect to learn about what is deemed an acceptable lie when the topic of telling the truth comes up.

This section and the entire book does not address all Muslims. There are some Muslims who want to create a new religion and consider themselves Muslim Reformers. There are also some called Meccan Muslims who do not accept anything from Muhammad since he departed from Mecca. In addition, there are Ahmmadiyya Muslims. This, in truth, is not a Muslim sect, as they claim to have a new prophet. This negates some of the most basic teachings of Islam. What the Ahmadiyya will not tell you is that they accept all the Islamic sources that Sunni Muslims accept.

It is important to understand that Muslims who do not necessarily want shariah are submissive to those who do want shariah. An example of this was seen recently in Toronto, Canada when a Muslim proprietor who allowed parties with alcohol at his restaurant, insisted a non-Muslim party with alcohol, would have to remove the alcohol or leave, since a Muslim group was coming soon.[23] The Muslims coming insisted there be no alcohol at all on the premises. The non-shariah adherent Muslims quickly submitted to their shariah adherent customers' requests, forcing non-Muslims to submit to shariah.

The only remaining difference between Muslims are the Sunnis and the Shi'ites. Doctrinally, there is almost no difference in belief. Their major issue is not doctrine, but the form of government. The belief that their belief cannot be questioned is what makes this a violent issue. Only one possibility is allowed in their belief structure. This makes the other guilty of heresy. To

---

[23] Lagace, P. (2020, February 9). *Four bottles of wine*. Retrieved February 28, 2020, from La Presse:
https://www.lapresse.ca/actualites/202002/08/01-5260172-quatre-bouteilles-de-vin.php.

question, disagree, or not accept even a small part of the belief of Islam is in itself a violation of the belief in Islam. Entering this realm makes you subject to the accusation of Apostacy which shariah imposes a death sentence on. With a death sentence weighing heavily on all those who would dare to question anything about Islam, intellectual inquiry finds itself largely forbidden. It is the one thing that could and would unite both Sunni and Shi'ite. But that type of inquiry is forbidden, and attracts a death penalty; the results of which have been what seems to be endless wars between the two factions.

It is what both Sunnis and Shi'ites accept that we must pay attention to; that will cause us concern. Both accept the Quran, the hadiths, and the Sirats. There are some Shi'ite hadiths that Sunnis do not accept. But in general, this is the same. They are united in their refusal to accept intellectual inquiry of their faith and its claims. Both are united in their refusal to accept textual criticism and historical evidence that questions much of what has been taught, that often comes from hadiths. Both believe in the Islamization of Knowledge, a term proposed by Ismail al-Faruqi, which is now a graduate level discussion.

Chapter 3

Do Muslims have a social norm of Islamic Supremacy?

"Supremacy is supremacy. Whatever group is striving for supremacy, the end result is the same: a protected class with special privileges that others don't enjoy. This is quintessentially anti-American."

--Pamela Geller[24]

Islamic supremacism as a belief can be found in the Islamic doctrine known as *"Al-Wala' and Al-Bara'."* Shaykh Muhammad Saeed al-Qahtani is an Islamic scholar based in Saudi Arabia who is the author of <u>Al-Wala' Wa'l-Bara'</u>, published in 1999 in English by Al-Firdous Publications and is considered the leading authoritative book on the subject today.[25] Al-Qahtani states that in knowing what *Al-Wala'* truly means, you have to understand that:

---

[24] Merse, J. (2017, September 27). *Why Can't We Talk About Muslim Supremacism?* Retrieved August 14, 2019, from Daily Caller: https://dailycaller.com/2017/09/27/why-cant-we-talk-about-muslim-supremacy.

[25] Advice for Paradise. (2019). *Muhammad Saeed al-Qahtani.* Retrieved March 28, 2020, from Advice for Paradise: https://www.adviceforparadise.com/profiles/12.

Al-Muwaalaat refers to "support" in Islam, as Imam Shafi'i explained with regards to the Hadith of the Prophet Muhammad: "Whomsoever I am his supporter, Ali is also his supporter."

Likewise, Allah states in the Qur'an: *(That is because Allah is the Mawla' (ally) of those who believe, and the disbelievers have no Mawla' (ally)). [Quran 47:11]*[26]

Al-Qahtani says of the reference to an ally, "the ally is the opposite of the enemy."[27] This is important to acknowledge as it places all non-Muslims as enemies.

According to this author, "Al-Bara' in Arabic language means Severance; severance is to leave off something; it is to walk away from something or to distance oneself from it."[28]

Thus, what is the Muslim severing from himself in this belief! It is the things and people that are not of Islam! Al-Qahtani refers to Quran 2:257 to clarify this:

Allah is the ally of those who believe. He brings them out from darkness into the light. And those who disbelieve - their allies are Taghut. They take them out of the light into darkness. Those are the companions of the Fire; they will abide eternally therein.

Tagut is a reference to those who do not worship Allah — non-Muslims. We, the non-Muslims are seen as the "companions of the Fire." The Quran here, says Non-Muslims will abide in hell fire, hence the reference to "eternal fire."

---

[26] Al-Qahtani, M. S. (1999). *Al-Wala' Wa'l-Bara Part 2* (Vol. 2). New York City: Al-Firdous Publications Ltd. Retrieved August 14, 2019, from http://tawheednyc.com/aqeedah/al%20walaa%20wal%20baraa/alwala walbara2.pdf. p. 11.

[27] Ibid

[28] Ibid, p. 12.

Al-Qahtani also believes Muslims must be separate from disbelievers in every way. He quotes from the Quran to prove his point:

And if you turn away, He will exchange you for some other folk. [Quran 47:38]

And whoever turns towards them in alliance is one of them. [Quran 5:51]

It is interesting that al-Qahtani does not cite the full verse here, so I will provide it for you below:

O, you who have believed, do not take the Jews and the Christians as allies. They are [in fact] allies of one another. And whoever is an ally to them among you - then indeed, he is [one] of them. Indeed, Allah guides not the wrongdoing people.

Now you can see that Jews and Christians are specifically named as not being allies, which, under Islamic teaching makes them enemies. There is no in-between. No space for remaining neutral.

Some of the verses in the Quran are well-known, but only portions of them. Take Surah 2:256 for example. Many people have heard "there is no compulsion in religion", but that is only a part of the verse.

There shall be no compulsion in [acceptance of] the religion. The right course has become clear from the wrong. So, whoever disbelieves in Taghut and believes in Allah has grasped the most trustworthy handhold with no break in it. And Allah is Hearing and Knowing.[29]

Tagut is the reference to non-Muslim beliefs. The statement of "no-compulsion" is paired with a statement that reminds Muslims

---

[29] From Quran.com

of who and what they are to be separated from. "The right course has become clear from the wrong." They are willing to take converts to Islam, but stand against those who do not have Allah as their ally.

Surah 3:103 talks about the "rope of Allah" as being unifying. But if you read this closely, it is the actions of those who believe in Allah, not Allah himself that is unifying.

And hold fast by the rope of Allah all together, and do not divide it. And remember Allah's grace on you when you were enemies, so he attuned between your hearts. So you became brethren by his grace. And you were on the edge of the pit of Fire, so He delivered you from it. Likewise, Allah clearly showed you his verses, perhaps, you may be guided.

This unifying is for the purpose of uniting a people who should be superior to others. That is what the pit of fire is for. The others who disbelieve in Allah will burn in that fire.

Surah 6:71 is seemingly like other religions that believe in their version of what is right. However, there is a significant difference.

Say, "Shall we invoke instead of Allah that which neither benefits us nor harms us and be turned back on our heels after Allah has guided us? [We would then be] like one whom the devils enticed [to wander] upon the earth confused, [while] he has companions inviting him to guidance, [calling], 'come to us.' "Say, 'Indeed, the guidance of Allah is the [only] guidance; and we have been commanded to submit to the Lord of the worlds.'"

Note the reference, those who are not Allah's followers are compared to confused devils. Hence, non-Muslims are demonic. They are not only demonic, but also confused devils.

Surah 98:6 calls Jews and Christians and polytheists the "worst of creatures." Think of what this creates in terms of

26

permissibility with the faith structure known as Islam, whether Sunni or Shi'ite. It does not get much more supremacist than this;

> *Indeed, they who disbelieved among the People of the Scripture and the polytheists will be in the fire of Hell, abiding eternally therein. Those are the worst of creatures.*

Islamic supremacist belief is preached in mosques all over the globe. One supremacist message was given in a Friday sermon, in Jatt, Israel, by Sheikh Ahmad Badran on June 28, 2019, that was uploaded to the internet in hopes of reaching Muslims around the world. It was captured and translated by the Middle East Media Research Institute (MEMRI):

> *We should say to the infidels that when we rule according to Islam, there will not be a single law that will not be Islamic. That's not all. **We will never allow a non-Muslim to rule over Muslims**. We should be clear about it.*
>
> *Some of our brothers say: **'We exploit democracy in order to come to power.'***
>
> *I am saying to the infidels: Don't let yourselves be fooled. Our Muslim brothers – although we think they have chosen a wrong path - **If they rise to power through democracy, and manage to consolidate their power, they will not allow an infidel to rule over them ever again. You can be sure about it.** I am referring to Erdogan or Mohamed Morsi, may Allah have mercy on his soul. It's all the same. Anywhere that Muslims come to power, by any method, they will not allow an infidel to rule over Muslims ever again. We do not accept a pluralistic system that combines Islam and heresy. There is only Islam.*[30]

---

[30] Badran, S. A. (2019, June 28). *Clip No: 7350 Friday Sermon in Jatt, Israel by Sheikh Ahmad Badran: Once Muslims Come to Power, They Will Never Allow Infidels to Rule over Muslims*. Retrieved August 19, 2019, from Middle East Media Research Institute: https://www.memri.org/tv/israel-

The short and sweet on the Islamic supremacy is that they believe Islam is a political structure as well as a religious structure. That belief means that absolutely everyone must obey Islamic law whether they are Muslim or not. This belief leads to conflict with countries who have their own laws that oppose shariah. Some of these will be addressed in this chapter.

One of the most shocking Islamic supremacist statements I have found is in Shariah. In 'Umdat al-Salik aka Reliance of the Traveller, the passage (o1) on the penalty for murder (o1.1) states: "Retaliation is obligatory against anyone who kills a human being purely and intentionally and without right." There are then listed exceptions to the rule (o1.2):

(1) A child or insane person, under any circumstances...

(2) A Muslim for killing a non-Muslim.

Some of these things you must see for yourself in print. I had heard about this, but it was so hard to accept as truthful. Believe me, I know! I have been researching the topic of Islam for about 10 years now.

This aspect of Islamic supremacy, where a non-Muslim's life is viewed as less than equal to that of a Muslim's is absolutely essential to grasping the differences in social norms between the rest of the world and Islamic civilization. It explains why beliefs in Islamic conquest such as the terror groups - Al-Qaeda and ISIS - gave the claim that they would have victory through jihad. These supremacists' claims continue to be heard around the world, even here in America.

Taiseer Hussein, gave a speech on January 19, 2020 at a conference held by Hizb ut-Tahrir America in Glendale Heights, IL where he emphasized that Islam will conquer Spain, Rome and India. Since Islamic civilization had conquered a large portion of

---

jatt-sheikh-badran-muslims-come-power-never-allow-infidels-exploiting-democracy.

Spain and India, the references to those conquests are called liberations.[31]

This Islamic sense of superiority has led to problems, after migrations (hijrahs) into European countries. In some cases, the superiority goes so far as to have Islamic youths robbing natives, making them strip naked and peeing in their mouths.[32] If this is shocking and offensive to you, it should be!

[31] Hussein, T. (2020, January 19). *Taiseer Hussein of Hizb ut-Tahrir America: We Will Conquer Rome and Liberate India and Spai.* Retrieved February 28, 2020, from MEMRI: https://www.memri.org/tv/taiseer-hussein-hizb-ut-tahrir-america-conference-islamic-nation-establish-caliphate-conquer-rome.

[32] R., E. (2020, February 11). *Foreign robbers peed in Swedish teenager's mouth while shouting racist slurs.* Retrieved February 28, 2020, from Voice of Europe: https://voiceofeurope.com/2020/02/foreign-robbers-peed-in-swedish-teenagers-mouth-while-shouting-racist-slurs.

Chapter 4

Is there an Islamic social norm against telling the truth?

One of the major components of trust in Western society is based on a belief that those you know and are friends with you, will tell you the truth. We also expect a person who is sworn into a court of law to tell the truth. We expect people under oath to tell nothing but the truth. This is a Western cultural norm. It is common sense not to expect criminals to tell the truth, when lying can get them out of trouble. Sadly, in today's world we expect politicians to lie to us. But this also is a statement that they are going against the norm. When politicians get caught lying, we call it scandalous. They get exposed for telling lies. But is this the same for people who believe in Islamic supremacy?

Under Islam, there are five Arabic words that have to do with lying to Non-Muslims. We need to start with the most basic understanding of this concept which can be found in the Hadiths. Bukhari gives several examples of what Muhammad said regarding war and lying. This is important to grasp, as Islam has no problem with the deceit of those they are at war with; this means all those within lands classified as Dar al-Harb. Dar al-Harb means the land of constant warfare. The following are three examples from Bukhari about the legitimacy of deceit during war. This is not to say that deceit is of no importance during war. This lays a frame work for understanding, particularly considering the fact that an area, which is not actively engaged in a war is considered at war with Islam for not being Islamic.

Narrated by Abu Huraira:

*The Prophet said, "Khosrau will be ruined, and there will be no Khosrau after him, and Caesar will surely be ruined and there will be no Caesar after him, and you will spend their treasures in Allah's Cause." He called, "**War is deceit'**. (Volume 4, Book 52, Number 267)*

Narrated by Abu Huraira:

*Allah's Apostle called, "**War is deceit.**" (Volume 4, Book 52, Number 268)*

Narrated by Abu Huraira:

Allah's Apostle called, "War is deceit." (Volume 4, Book 52, Number 269)

If Islam claims that it is at war with Dar-al Harb, Muhammad justifies lying to non-Muslims based on his statement that "War is deceit." This creates an environment for deceit to be justified by every Muslim when interacting with non-Muslims in places where Islam is not the majority, and/or shariah is not the law of the land.

Taqiyya (Ta-Key-Ya): This word means it is permissible to lie to non-Muslims in order to protect Islam or to save your life. This lying may also be done to further Islam by deceiving others. This belief in lying to Non-Muslims is based in Sura: 3:28:

Let not believers take disbelievers as allies rather than believers. And whoever [of you] does that has nothing with Allah, except when taking precaution against them in prudence. And Allah warns you of Himself, and to Allah, is the [final] destination.

31

This verse tells Muslims not to take non-Muslims as friends unless they are in the minority and have reason to fear them. In fact, under Islam, unlike Christianity, one is allowed to deny that he is a Muslim according to Quran 16:106:

Whoever disbelieves in Allah after his belief... except for one who is forced [to renounce his religion] while his heart is secure in faith. But those who [willingly] open their breasts to disbelief, upon them is wrath from Allah, and for them is a great punishment.

According to the Bible, if you deny Christ before men, you will be denied by Jesus before his father, according to Matthew 10:33:

But whosoever shall deny me before men, him will I also deny before my Father which is in heaven.

Perhaps the strongest example of deceit allowed by Muhammad was deceit in order to kill Al-Ashraf for him. This man had simply offended Muhammad with his words. Nothing more. This is recorded in Bukhari:

Narrated by Jabir bin 'Abdullah:
Allah's Apostle said, "Who is willing to kill Ka'b bin Al-Ashraf who has hurt Allah and His Apostle?"

Thereupon, Muhammad bin Maslama got up saying, "O Allah's Apostle! Would you like that I kill him?"

The Prophet said, "Yes," Muhammad bin Maslama said, "Then allow me to say a (false) thing (i.e. lie in order to deceive Kab)."

The Prophet said, "You may say it."

Then Muhammad bin Maslama went to Kab and said, "That man (i.e. Muhammad) demands Sadaqa (i.e. Zakat) from us, and he has troubled us, and I have come to borrow something from you."

On that, Kab said, "By Allah, you will get tired of him!"

Muhammad bin Maslama said, "Now, as we have followed him, we do not want to leave him unless and until we see how his end is going to be. Now we want you to lend us a camel load or two of food." (Some difference between narrators about a camel load or two.)

Kab said, "Yes, (I will lend you), but you should mortgage something to me."

Muhammad bin Mas-lama and his companion said, "What do you want?"

Ka'b replied, "Mortgage your women to me."

They said, "How can we mortgage our women to you and you are the most handsome of the 'Arabs?"

Ka'b said, "Then mortgage your sons to me."

They said, "How can we mortgage our sons to you? Later they would be abused by the people's saying that so-and-so has been mortgaged for a camel load of food. That would cause us great disgrace, but we will mortgage our arms to you."

Muhammad bin Maslama and his companion promised Kab that Muhammad would return to him. He came to Kab at night along with Kab's foster brother, Abu Na'ila. Kab invited them to come into his fort, and then he went down to them. His wife asked him, "Where are you going at this time?"

Kab replied, "None but Muhammad bin Maslama and my (foster) brother Abu Na'ila have come."

His wife said, "I hear a voice as if dropping blood is from him."

Ka'b said. "They are none but my brother Muhammad bin Maslama and my foster brother Abu Naila. A generous man should respond to a call at night even if invited to be killed."

Muhammad bin Maslama went with two men. (Some narrators mention the men as 'Abu bin Jabr. Al Harith bin Aus and Abbad bin Bishr). So, Muhammad bin Maslama went in together with two men, and said to them, "When Ka'b comes, I will touch his hair and smell it, and when you see that I have got hold of his head, strip him. I will let you smell his head."

Kab bin Al-Ashraf came down to them wrapped in his clothes, and diffusing perfume. Muhammad bin Maslama said. "I have never smelt a better scent than this."

Ka'b replied. "I have got the best 'Arab women who know how to use the high class of perfume."

Muhammad bin Maslama requested Ka'b "Will you allow me to smell your head?"

Ka'b said, "Yes."

Muhammad smelt it and made his companions smell it as well. Then he requested Ka'b again, "Will you let me (smell your head)?"

Ka'b said, "Yes."

When Muhammad got a strong hold of him, he said (to his companions), "Get at him!" So they killed him and went to the Prophet and informed him. Abu Rafi was killed after Ka'b bin Al-Ashraf." (Volume 5, Book 59, Number 369)

There are a lot of Islamic statements that taqiyya is only practiced by Shi'ites versus Sunnis. In my research, I found this to be untrue. In fact, there is a section of Shariah on this very topic. Shariah law under Sunni law has four schools of thought; Hanafi, Maliki, Shafi-I, and Hanibal. In *'Umdat al-Salik* aka Reliance of the Traveller, is shariah in English; this particular translation has statements of approval of accuracy in translation by groups of the Muslim Brotherhood and trusted sources in Sunni Islamic scholarship. r.8.0-8.2 it states:

r8.0 LYING

r8.1 (Nawawi:) Primary texts from the Koran and sunna that it is unlawful to lie (dis:p24) are both numerous and intersubstantiative, **it being among the ugliest sins and most disgusting faults.** Because of the scholarly consensus of the Community (Umma) that it is prohibited and the unanimity and amount of the primary textual evidence, there is little need to cite particular examples; thereof, out only concern here being to explain the exceptions to what is considered lying, and apprise of the details.

PERMISSIBLE LYING

r8.2 The Prophet (Allah bless him and give him peace) said, ``*He who settles disagreements between people to bring about good or says something commendable is not a liar."* This much is related by both Bukhari and Muslim, with Muslim's version recording that Umm Kulthum added, ``*I did not hear him permit untruth in anything people say, except for three things: war, settling disagreements and a man talking with his wife, or she, with him (A:in smoothing over differences)."*

This is an explicit statement that lying is sometimes permissible for a given interest, scholars having established criteria defining what types of it are lawful. The best analysis of it I have seen is by Imam Ghazali. **If something is attainable through both telling the truth and lying, it is unlawful to accomplish it through lying because there is no need for it. When it is possible to achieve such an aim by lying but not by telling the truth, it is permissible to lie if attaining the goal is permissible** (N:i.e. when the purpose of lying is to circumvent someone who is preventing one from doing something permissible), **and obligatory to lie if the goal is obligatory.** When for example one is concealing a Muslim from an oppressor who asks where he is, it is obligatory to lie about his being hidden. Or when a person deposits an article with one for safekeeping and an oppressor wanting to appropriate it inquires about it, it is obligatory to lie about having concealed it, for if one informs him about the article and he then seizes it, one is financially liable (A: to the owner) to cover the article's cost. **Whether the purpose is war, settling a disagreement, or gaining the sympathy of a victim legally entitled to retaliate against one so that he will forbear to do so; it is not unlawful to lie when any of these aims can only be attained through lying. But is religiously more precautionary (def:c6.5) in all such cases to employ words that give misleadng impression, meaning to intend by one's words something that is literally true, in respect to which one is not lying (def:r10.2) while the outward purport of the words deceives the hearer, though even if one does not have such an intention and merely lies without intending anything else, it is not unlawful in the above circumstances.** 'This is true of every expression connected with a legitimating desired end, whether one's own or another's. An example of a legitimating end of one's own is when an oppressor intending to appropriate one's property inquires about it, in which case one may deny it. Or if a ruler asks one about a wicked act one has committed that is solely between oneself and Allah Most High (N: i.e. it does not concern the rights of another), in which case one is entitled to disclaim it, such as by saying, 'I did not commit fornication, 'or' I did not drink.' There are many well known hadiths in which those who admitted they deserved punishment were given prompting (A: by the Prophet (Allah bless him and give him peace)) to retract their confessions. An example of a legitimating desired end of another is when one is asked about another's secret and one disacknowledges it. And so on. One should compare the bad consequences entailed by lying to those entailed by telling the truth, and if the consequences of telling the truth are more damaging, on is entitled to lie, though if the reverse is true or if one does not know which entails more damage, them lying is unlawful. **Whenever lying is permissible, if the factor which permits it is desired end of one's own, it is recommended not to lie, but when the factor that permits it is the desired end of another, it is not lawful to infringe upon his rights.** Strictness (A: as opposed to the above dispensations (rukhsa, def:c6.2)) is to forgo lying in every case where it is not legally obligatory."

If this doesn't have you shocked, you're probably one of the few readers out there who stays informed. The question that has to be asked is, "is this not an irreconcilable difference with Western Civilization?" Can we even trust answers on an application to immigrate to a Western country? This social norm is an affront to Western Civilization as a whole. Being that it is part of Shariah, it becomes a documented doctrinal belief.

Now let's examine the concept of permissible lying with the shariah concept *Darura*. According to the Oxford Islamic Studies Online Dictionary, *dura* means:

In legal terminology, a state of necessity on account of which one may omit doing something required by law or may do something illegal. The conditions allowing this license and the extent of the license are stipulated variously by different legal scholars. Most legal theorists agree that murder or other gross physical harm is never legitimate.[33]

According to *Darura*, a Muslim may break the law, including giving false testimony if a state of necessity exists. This tells us that Muslims can believe such a state exists, and it allows them to commit crimes, such as perjury, filing a false police report, falsely accusing people of Islamophobia and more.

According to Dr. Patrick Sookhdeo, the term "*darura* is used by many Islamic scholars to justify Muslim minority adaptation to western norms in western states, compliance to western legal systems, and loyalty to western states and governments. Sheikh Tantawi of al-Azhar used this argument to justify Muslims in France, obeying the new prohibition on wearing veils in public institutions (especially schools)." [34]

Using *darura* to justify complying with the law of a non-Muslim country also implies that they will as soon as possible refuse those laws when they are numerous enough to change them.

Several examples exist of Muslims lying, to non-Muslims. But what is not noticed enough is when they say one thing to the non-Muslim, then say the opposite to their Muslim friends. The concept of *darura* completely accepts this.

Anjem Choudhary, a leader of the Al-Muhajiroun, was on the BBC claiming he condemned the actions of the 9/11 terrorists shortly after the event. But not even up to two years later, he was exposed[35] as supporting those actors of terror against the USA. A recording was made of Anjem Choudary, calling the hijacker

---

[33] Esposito, J. (2004). *The Oxford Dictionary of Islam.* NYC: Oxford University Press . Retrieved from The Oxford Dictionary of Islam.

[34] Sookhdeo, D. P. (2005). *Islam in Britain.* London: The Institute for the Study of Islam and Christianity, p. 25.

[35] Evening Standard. (2003, September 9). *Extremist Muslims praise the 9/11 killers.* Retrieved November 14, 2019, from Evening Standard: https://www.standard.co.uk/news/extremist-muslims-praise-the-911-killers-6962609.html.

terrorists, the "Magnificent 19." He also said, "We are here today, to talk about the Magnificent 19. Those who, two years ago, split the world today into two camps, the camp of Islam and the camp of non-Islam, the Kuffar; those who revived again the obligation of jihad worldwide."

On September 12, 2019 Lars Weinand's article[36] on what was supposed to be a horrid example of "Islamophobia" was published with t-online.de. This article states that the picture below had already circulated, showing pages of a Quran in a toilet, along with several other pieces of the Quran shredded and used for toilet paper. The concept of *Darura*, would say that it's ok to lie and not tell that a Muslim committed this act. Did the Imams of the mosque know who committed the crime? We may never know.

This event in a mosque in Schleswig, Germany actually took place much earlier on July 5, 2019. It was claimed that this event was an "Islamophobic" hate crime. But an Iraqi migrant in France was caught and pled guilty to the crime. By the time the police had discovered that a Muslim had committed the supposed "hate

---

[36] Wienand, L. (2019, September 12). *Koran pages in the toilet: Iraqi caught red-handed.* Retrieved November 14, 2019, from t-online.de: https://www.t-online.de/nachrichten/deutschland/gesellschaft/id_86435956/koran-im-wc-iraker-als-verdaechtiger-in-schleswig-gefasst.html.

crime" against his faith, pictures of this event had spread into Turkey, angering many.

I have had encounters with Muslims openly lying to me and others. Dr. Muhammad Shafiq a former professor at Nazareth College, and the former Imam of the Islamic Center of Rochester, NY and I have met three times, and each time, I have asked the same question and received the same answer. He tells everyone "Islam means peace." I ask him during the Q and A time, "What does Islam mean in Arabic?" He responds, "Submission." I then respond, "So, you were lying to us when you told us it meant peace?" The last time, he went so far as to say that the Arabic word *Salaam* (Islam) means the same thing as *Shalom* (Peace) in Hebrew. He did not know I took 12 undergraduate credits in Hebrew. I got so angry at his lie, I could not speak. Instead, I wrote to the Board of Trustees at Nazareth College, and asked that he never be allowed to teach there again since he was lying to the public, using his title as a professor emeritus from Nazareth as part of his qualifications to speak. Submission is as far from peace as you can imagine. Lying to the general public while claiming to be an expert educator from an institution, whether retired or not, is academic malfeasance and grounds for dismissal or removal of credentials!

One of my most recent encounters with Muslims came as a result of using Uber to get to church. I rode with a Muslim driver who said he was an Imam at his mosque. He told me Christians were deceived and they did not have the truth about Jesus. I said to him, "So, you want me to read about Jesus in the Quran? You do know the Quran states the gospels are accurate, right?" He lied to me saying that was not true. My claim that he lied is based on the Quran:

> *[He] has sent down on you, the Book with the truth, confirming what is between his hands, and has sent down the Torah and the injeel {Gospel}.* (Surah 3:3)

> *And He will teach him the book and the wisdom and the Torah and the Gospel.* (Surah 3:48)

As stated previously, this misinformation to Christian and Jews and all non-Muslims is part of their doctrinal belief that they are at war (*jihad*) with non-Muslims. People who live in lands and areas that are not Dar-al Islam can be deceived. The Imam I spoke of above, was not happy when I let him know I was aware that he considered this Dar-al Harb, and thought deception was justified to bring people to Islam. I told him, when I wanted to know about Muhammad, I went to the Quran and the Sunnah. I read the *Sirat al-Rasul*. So why is it wrong to go to the Christian sources that Quran states are legitimate to learn about Jesus?

Sadly, this brings me to the problem that deceit creates when used too often – it messes with your logic center. When you are deceitful on a regular basis, in order to justify your lies, you have to contradict the laws of logic. Many law enforcement personnel are experts at detecting deception.

As shown above, deceit is such a ruling way of life under Islam that it is even used to trick people into becoming Muslims. Stories about this type of deceit being used for what Muslims call *dawa* are abundant. One of the most recent ones came across my desk as I was doing my daily news share.

AsiaNews.it ran a story May 15, 2019 about a 13-year old boy being tricked on TV into converting to Islam.[37] A few days earlier, on May 11, Nihat Hatipoğlu, a theologian and the rector of Gaziantep University of Science and Technology, went on an ATV television show and introduced a boy, Arthur, as someone who wanted to become Muslim with the statement, he had the permission of the parents. This was a lie. This means the boy stated the *shahada*. There is nothing in it that says I now believe in Islam. According to Arthur's mother, "A Syrian friend of his told him: 'Come, we'll talk on live TV. They will give us toys, and we will eat with the stars.' And my son went with him. He's a child, he made a mistake, but he did not convert nor was he

---

[37] Demir, M. (2019, May 15). *A 13-year-old Armenian boy tricked into converting to Islam on live TV*. Retrieved December 2, 2019, from Asia News: http://www.asianews.it/news-en/A-13-year-old-Armenian-boy-tricked-into-converting-to-Islam-on-live-TV-47021.html.

circumcised." Alina, the boy's mother took the matter to court, because this "conversion" violated the Lausanne Treaty, as forced conversions are a breach of its clauses on the rights of ethnic and religious minorities. The absence of the parents and the absence of their consent make this a forced conversion.

Muslims even lie to other Muslims when *darura,* a state of necessity exists. On October 2, 2019, a retired General of Egypt, Fouad Fayoud was on Channel 1 and told the people of Egypt that Hasan al-Banna, the founder of the Muslim Brotherhood had been a Jewish man.[38] For those who are unaware, the Muslim Brotherhood is a banned entity in Egypt. It is labelled a terrorist entity. Hasan al-Banna was a very charismatic teacher who began the movement to strengthen Islam in Egypt. To Fayoud, it was more important that Muslims be deceived and not join the Muslim Brotherhood, rather than joining them and becoming an enemy of Egypt. The Muslim Brotherhood had attempted to kill Egypt's second president Gamal Nasser on October 26, 1954. It was thought that President Nasser was inspiring Egyptians to be proud of their heritage. However, the Muslim Brotherhood was against nationalism, but in favor of pride in being Muslim which was why an assassin was sent.

This religious permissive lying has become a system of lying or deceit that is practiced to all, and well-known. The problem that may be even deeper, is the dangers this systematic method of lying cause to local societies, to nations, and to the world in general. With systematic lying as an accepted social norm, why does anyone trust what is said to them by those who profess Islam?

I asked William Bradford, a former DHS official for a comment on lying and how it effects the logic center of the brain. Mr. Bradford is a notable lawyer who has published on the Rules

---

[38] Fayoud, F. (2019, November 25). *Retired Egyptian General Fouad Fayoud: MB Founder Hassan Al-Banna Was a Jew.* Retrieved November 26, 2019, from MEMRI.org:
https://www.youtube.com/watch?v=FK5gnFHnqJM&feature=emb_title.

of Engagement and has served the USA with honor as a Marine. His response was:

> "Any time a person lies, s/he experiences cognitive dissonance because the **brain cannot hold two completely contradictory propositions at once without turmoil.** Behavioral detection of lies, which is optimally done by experienced interrogators and not by a polygrapher, can reveal certain physical manifestations of cognitive dissonance."

As a researcher, this response set off all sorts of bells and whistles. Islam as a religion teaches duality as a religious concept. Their god, Allah says one thing then later contradicts it. Hence, the truth becomes a problem. Muslims address contradictions in the Quran through the process of Abrogation. Basically, that which was said last can and does negate what was said previously. The Quran itself says it is inconsistent and has contradictions. For this reason, abrogation exists as stated in the Quran:

> "We do not abrogate a verse or cause it to be forgotten except that we bring forth [one] better than it or similar to it. Do you not know that Allah is over all things competent?" (Quran 2:106)

> "And when We substitute a verse in place of a verse - and Allah is most knowing of what He sends down - they say, "You, [O Muhammad], are but an inventor [of lies]." But most of them do not know." (Quran 16:101)

Holding two opposing beliefs by giving priority to one over the other is another method of deception. Unless you know the correct chronological order of the Quran, you cannot know which passages supersede others. This also creates deception for many Muslims who read the Quran simply because they may be unaware of its chronological order. In case you do not know, the Quran is ordered by length, not by chronology.

Thus, a culture of holding two opposing positions is ingrained in Islam. They teach that the later teaching is true, allowing for the earlier teaching to be easily dismissed.

Children who become aware of the doctrine of Islam that allows contradictions to stand create a routine of teaching Muslims to accept that their god allows them to hold to two opposing positions at one time.

With all this lying being permissible, and the planned and expected deceiving of non-Muslims, should non-Muslim societies be open to receiving those who plan to deceive them? This concept of deceit and lying is doctrinal to Muslims. It is part of their culture so much so that *daruda* even allows them to lie to other Muslims as shown above. What do you think? Is this an irreconcilable difference between cultural norms of Islam and the rest of the world?

Chapter 5

Is slavery legal under Islamic social norms today?

Under Western Civilization, slavery, which had existed for centuries no matter the race, was outlawed in the mid-19th century. It is now the 21st century. Throughout the world, slavery is considered to be one of the most heinous crimes. Prostitution is often seen as a form of slavery, when someone controls how much the woman/man sells their body for and determines how much they will give them, if anything at all. But is actual slavery of a person akin to the 19th century slaves on American plantations permissible under Islam today? Read on for the answer.

The Quran has several references to slaves, and the treatment of them in it. Most of these references are to those serving as sex slaves:

> *Surah 23:1-6:* *"Certainly will the believers have succeeded: They, who are during their prayer humbly submissive And they who turn away from ill speech And they who are observant of zakah And they who guard their private parts Except from their wives or **those their right hands possess**, for indeed, they will not be blamed."*

> *Surah 33:52:* *"Not lawful to you, [O Muhammad], are [any additional] women after [this], nor [is it] for you to exchange them for [other] wives, even if their beauty were to please you, except **what your right hand possesses**. And ever is Allah, over all things, an Observer."*

Surah 70:29-31: *"And those who guard their private parts Except from their wives or* **those their right hands possess,** *for indeed, they are not to be blamed, but whoever seeks beyond that, then they are the transgressors –*

The phrase, "right hand possess", refers directly to the female slaves owned by Muslims. Muhammad was a slave owner. He had numerous slaves, both white and black. They are recorded in the Hadiths.

> Narrated `Umar: "I came and behold, Allah's Apostle was staying on a Mashroba (attic room) and **a black slave of Allah's Apostle** was at the top if its stairs. I said to him, "Tell the Prophet that here is `Umar bin Al- Khattab (asking for permission to enter)." Then he admitted me. (Bukhari 7263).

> Allah's Messenger was on a journey, and **he had a black slave called Anjasha**. He was driving the camels (very fast, and there were women riding on those camels). Allah's Messenger said, "Waihaka (May Allah be merciful to you), O Anjasha! Drive slowly (the camels) with the glass vessels (women)!" (Bukhari 6161)"

> **It was narrated that Abu Hurairah said: "We were with the Messenger of Allah in the year of Khaibar, and we did not get any spoils of war except for wealth, goods and clothes. Then a man from Banu Ad-Dubaib, who was called Rifa'ah bin Zaid, gave** the Messenger of Allah a black slave who was called Mid'am. **The Messenger of Allah set out for Wadi Al-Qura. When we were in Wadi Al-Qura, while Mid'am was unloading the luggage of the Messenger of Allah,** *an arrow came and killed him. The people said:*

> *'Congratulations! You will go to Paradise,'* but the Messenger of Allah said: 'No, by the One in Whose hand

is my soul! The cloak that he took from the spoils of war on the Day of Khaibar is burning him with fire.' **When the people heard that, a man brought one or two shoelaces to the Messenger of Allah, and the Messenger of Allah said: 'One or two shoelaces of fire.'" (Sunan an-Nasa'i 3827)**

In Pakistan on May 31, 2010, talk show host Mubasher Lucman, interviewed Islamic clerics Maulana Naeemi, Mohammed Siddiqui, and Allama Zaheer on Pakistani television channel Express News on various topics. Amongst them, the topic of slavery came up.

Mubasher Lucman: "I have a question. I will move to the details later. Does Islam allow slave trading?"

Allama Zaheer: *"Islam allows to trade slaves where there are established markets for this purpose. Taking new [i.e. free] men as slaves is neither allowed in Islam nor does Islam encourage it."*

Mubasher Lucman: "The offspring from a slave is a slave, isn't it?"

Allama Zaheer: *"No. There are a number of conditions under which an offspring of a slave is free. If the owner wants to set him free, he is... If somebody marries a concubine and she gets pregnant, the offspring is not a slave. After marrying a concubine, either the master can set her free or can marry her to another man, but cannot sell her again...It's not that slave of a child is always slave..."*

Mubasher Lucman: "What are the conditions in your eyes?"

Maulana Naeemi: *"...First, it is important to note that slaves were sold and markets were established even before*

Islam... How were they enslaved? They were captured in conditions of wars; were abducted from roadsides; children were kidnapped by force and sold; slaves were leading a miserable life before Islam.

"The conception of slavery in Islam is not to continue its practice, but the concept of slavery was allowed because it existed at that time; ending it suddenly could have resulted in a host of problems. Therefore, the concept of slavery was adopted, but a number of steps were stipulated so that it is not thought that slavery is permitted in Islam, that slavery will continue; rather, along with those steps, slavery began moving toward its end from society."

"Insofar as the question is how the people were enslaved... and how those slaves were treated is concerned; during the times of the prophet (peace be upon him), a battle was fought from where war booty was brought; among them was a beautiful lady. She was given to a companion of the prophet (peace be upon him). The prophet took her back from him, sent her to Mecca, and a few Muslim prisoners there were gotten for free in exchange for her. There are a number of similar examples where slaves brought from wars were used for prisoner exchange, or were set free against some payment, or most importantly, were set free as a goodwill gesture."[39]

This interview included a question about how they would get slaves since many believed if they had signed an alliance with the United Nations, that they would be forbidden from taking slaves from any country that had also become part of the UN. This left many questions indeed. There was also an exception to this rule. That will shock you!

---

[39] Point Blank with Luqman. (2010, June 28). *Pakistan TV Debate on Concubines and Slavery in Islam*. Retrieved August 24, 2019, from Middle East Media Research Institute:
https://www.memri.org/reports/pakistan-tv-debate-concubines-and-slavery-islam.

Mubasher Lucman: *"Suppose today, if we go to war against Kufr [infidel world] on the Kashmir issue, win it, and bring slave men and women..."*

Mohammed Siddiqui: *"You should consult religious scholars; they are of the opinion that the countries which have signed the Charter of the United Nations Organization are not permitted to take the citizens of other member countries as slaves."*

Mubasher Lucman: *"I am talking about the perspective of Islam, not of the UN as the UN is not following Islam."*

Mohammad Siddiqui: *"Why are you arguing about it?"*

Mubasher Lucman: *"I am not arguing about it. I am trying to understand it."*
[Interruptions...]

Mubasher Lucman: *"How are UN and Islam linked?"*

Mohammed Siddiqui: "The link between the UN and Islam is that we have been ordered by the Koran to keep our accords. If an accord is not against Islam, we are bound by it."

Allama Zaheer: "Maulana Mohammed Siddiqui has rightly said that we cannot take the citizens of the countries as slaves who have diplomatic relations with us."

Mubasher Lucman: *"What if we go to a war against Israel, can we take slaves and concubines as we don't have diplomatic relations with them...?"*

Allama Zaheer: *"Yes, we can. It is permitted to have concubines [from Israel]."*

49

Mubasher Lucman: *"What do you say Maulana Aslam Siddiqui? Did you listen to Maulana Ibtisam Zaheer?"*

Mohammed Siddiqui: *"No, I could not."*

(Mubasher Lucman repeats the statement by Ibtisam Elahi)

Mohammed Siddiqui: "We do not have any accord with the countries with which we have no diplomatic relations..."
[Interruptions...]

Mubasher Lucman: *"So, we can take [slaves] from Israel, if we achieve victory over Israel and get manpower?"*

Mohammed Siddiqui: "Imagine! I am surprised how far-fetched you think..."

[Interruptions and laughter...]

Maulana Naeemi: "Islamic laws are very old and true. The law from the times of the caliphs is that you have to keep your promises. If you have an accord of prisoner exchange with a country, you have to give the war captives back to them."

Allama Zaheer [interrupts]: "You gave the example of Israel very positively. They are Jews. We could have married with their women in case of a victory, but we don't need that as we don't have diplomatic relations; so if we win and get slave women, and if the emir of the army distributes concubines, we can keep them as concubines if we get some of our share of war booty. And we should be thankful to Allah for that. But we cannot steal a woman from war booty..."
(Break)

Mubasher Lucman: *"I have an important question that demands a detailed answer... any of you can answer it... It appears that there is a grey area where we are no defining zina [rape/adultery] as zina, as it is."*

Maulana Naeemi: "No, it's not so..."

Mubasher Lucman: *"You said, it can be without nikah."* [Interruptions...]

Maulana Naeemi: "We have to follow Koran. We cannot question the Koran. If the Koran says it is black, we have to say it is black; we cannot think if it is black or not. If the Koran says it is white, it is white. The Koran says when you have women in war booty, you are allowed to have sexual relations with them. This is what the Koran says, not you and I."

Allama Zaheer: "There is no grey area. What the Koran allows is allowed, what the Koran forbids us from is forbidden..."[40]

In 2011, Salaw al-Mteiri, a Kuwaiti political activist woman discovered an issue she wanted to push. She made not one video to express her opinion on the issue, but two! The Middle East Media Research Institute translated these speeches and shared them. In 2011, the world that saw the video translated was horrified. Those who understand Islam were not surprised about anything except that a Muslim woman was on video and talking politics. In her first video which aired on May 25th, 2011, she said:

I asked [a Saudi mufti]: What is the law with regard to slave girls? The mufti told me that the law requires there

---

[40] Point Blank with Luqman. (2010, June 28). *Pakistan TV Debate on Concubines and Slavery in Islam*. Retrieved August 24, 2019, from Middle East Media Research Institute:https://www.memri.org/reports/pakistan-tv-debate-concubines-and-slavery-islam.

to be a Muslim country raiding a Christian country – sorry, a non-Muslim country – and taking POWs. I asked him whether it was forbidden [to turn them into slaves], and he said that Islam does not prohibit keeping slave girls – on the contrary.

The law pertaining to slave girls is not the same as for free women. Free women must cover their bodies, except for their hands and faces. The slave girl must cover up from the belly button down.

There is a big difference between slave girls and free women. With a free woman, the man must make a marriage contract, but with a slave girl – all he has to do is buy her. It's as if he married her. So there is a difference between slave girls and free women.

Here in Kuwait too, I asked religious scholars and experts about this, and they said that for the average, good religious man, the only way to avoid forbidden relations with women is to purchase slave girls.[41]

Later in July, she was interviewed on July 1 on Al-Hayat TV. Her political activities seemed to fascinate the interviewer. His first question addressed her opinion and research on slavery.

Salwa Al-Mteiri: *"I thought that if the age of slave-girls was restored in a proper legal fashion, it could be a solution [to many problems], Allah willing."*

Interviewer: *"Will women and wives in Kuwait welcome the idea of slave-girls, and have their husband go to some*

---

[41] Al-Mteiri, S. (2011, May 25). *Kuwaiti Political Activist Salwa Al-Mteiri Calls for a Law Permitting the Purchase of POWs in Order to Turn Them into Slave Girls.* Retrieved August 24, 2019, from Middle East Media Research Institute: https://www.memri.org/reports/kuwaiti-political-activist-salwa-al-mteiri-calls-law-permitting-purchase-pows-order-turn.

office and buy a slave-girl or two? How will they accept it?"

Salwa Al-Mteiri: *"The believing woman is content with the law of Allah, and with what her religion requires her to do. In my opinion, this is the best solution to reduce the rate of marital betrayal and the spread of disease. This is a problem not only in Kuwait, but throughout the world."*[42]

Keep in mind, this is before ISIS became the Islamic State and enslaved hundreds of Yazidi and Christian girls as sex slaves. There are literally hundreds of articles out there from those who survived and were freed somehow, either by their own escape or the military squashing of the Islamic State.

Remember the reason slavery is still legal under Islam is because Muhammad owned slaves. Muslims must imitate Muhammad in every way, so this is one thing that is currently not permissible in most non-Islamic countries. Some Islamic countries also do not permit slavery — according to their posted laws. But keep in mind that each Islamic country states in their constitution that the country is subject to shariah, so while a law may exist banning slavery, under shariah, it is permissible.

---

[42] Ibid

Chapter 6

Are their Racist Social Norms Within Islamic beliefs Against Black People?

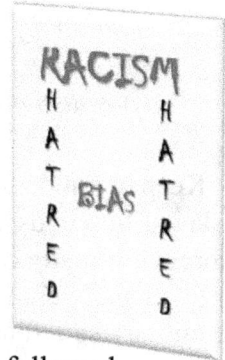

RACISM
H   H
A   A
T BIAS T
R   R
E   E
D   D

I met many students and parents who followed Elijah Muhammad as a young teacher. I found their belief system interestingly different from what I knew of Islam, and that surprised me. I had a difficult time trying to figure out how some of these teachings could easily be accepted when this is the Age of Information. The Quran, Hadiths, and Sirats are easily accessible via the Internet on reliable Islamic sites. But then, I learned more about how few actually read the Quran, and met others who called themselves "Five Percenters." All of this built off Islam, and I had not met one person who had actually read the Quran while espousing these views.

A serious study of the Quran and Hadiths would change the minds of any serious researcher into Islam if they had been members of what is called the Nation of Islam. I found a like for Malcolm X as I learned about his choosing to leave the Nation of Islam after a hajj. His reasoning appeared sound and scholarly. At the time, I did not look more into what he what he must have found. I have always found the topic of racism repugnant -- beneath that of people who have any humanity.

To combat things we wish not to exist, we need to define what we are combatting.

Racism is a topic that has to be viewed academically when it can. Racism is defined by Dictionary.com as: "a belief or doctrine that inherent differences among the various human racial groups determine cultural or individual achievement, usually involving the idea that one's own race is **superior** and has the right to dominate others or that a particular racial group is **inferior** to the others."[43]

Let's start by looking at Arabic language. I defer to my colleague Usama Dakdok who has a ministry to Muslims and hosts a weekly show on Blog Talk Radio.com's Global Patriot Radio network. Usama Dakdok's knowledge of Arabic is extensive. He was born in Egypt and raised with Arabic as his native tongue. Usama states that there are two words for "black" in Arabic - "*aswad* (means the color black) and *"abd"* (which means slave)." This means that the Arabic culture Islamic social norms are reflected in their use of vocabulary. The choice of *abd* over *aswad* when discussing the black race is the employment of what is defined in Western culture as racist terminology. This is no different than using the "n-word" in English language.

Now, we can ask if Islam is racist. Does it have a racist stand at its core? Is Islam a racist faith structure? Using only Islamic sacred texts, the facts will be presented.

> On the Day [some] *faces will turn white and [some] faces will turn black. As for those whose faces turn black, [to them it will be said], "Did you disbelieve after your belief? Then taste the punishment for what you used to reject.*" (Quran 3:106)

> And on the Day of Resurrection, you will see *those who lied about Allah [with] their faces blackened. Is there not in Hell a residence for the arrogant?* (Quran 39:60)

If the Quran portrays racist views, was Muhammad a racist? It has been said to me that "only white people can be racist"; I find

---

[43] Dictionary.com. (2019). *Racism*. Retrieved August 24, 2019, from Dictionary.com: https://www.dictionary.com/browse/racism.

that a racist statement in itself. I thought it important to share that the Hadiths state that Muhammad was a white man.

Narrated Anas bin Malik: "While we were sitting with the Prophet in the mosque, a man came riding on a camel. He made his camel kneel down in the mosque, tied its foreleg and then said: "Who amongst you is Muhammad?" At that time, the Prophet was sitting amongst us (his companions) leaning on his arm. We replied, "**This white man** reclining on his arm." The man then addressed him, "O Son of 'Abdul Muttalib." The Prophet said, "I am here to answer your questions."" (Sahih Bukhari 63)

It was narrated that 'Abdullah said: "The Messenger of Allah used to say the salam to his right so that the **whiteness of his cheek** could be seen, and ... to his left so that the **whiteness of his cheek** could be seen." (Sahih Sunan an-Nasar'i 1323)

(He would then raise [his hands] high enough) that the whiteness of his armpits became visible. ... 'Abd al-A'la said that (he was in doubt whether it was) the **whiteness of his armpit** or armpits. (Sahih Muslim 1953)

Sa'd reported: I saw the Messenger of Allah (may peace be open him) pronouncing taslim on his right and on his left till I saw the **whiteness of his cheek.** (Sahih Muslim 582)

Abu Juhaifa reported: I saw Allah's Messenger that had **white complexion and had some white hair**, and Hasan b. 'Ali resembled him. (Sahih Muslim 243a)

Jurairi reported: I said to Abu Tufail: Did you see Allah's Messenger? He said: Yes, **he had a white handsome face.** Muslim b. Hajjaj said: Abu Tufail who died in 100 Hijra was the last of the Companions of Allah's Messenger." (Sahih Muslim 2340a)

Now, since we know that Muhammad had slaves, and that he had both white slaves and black slaves, did he treat or value his slaves differently based on race alone?

"A slave came and gave his pledge to the Messenger of Allah to emigrate, and the Prophet did not realize that he was a slave. Then his master came looking for him. The Prophet said; 'Sell him to me.' **So he bought him for two black slaves**, then he did not accept until he had asked; 'Is he a slave?'" (Sunan an-Nasa'i 4621)

Jabir (Allah be pleased with him) reported: "There came a slave who pledged allegiance to Allah's Apostle on migration; he (the Holy Prophet) did not know that he was a slave. Then there came his master who demanded him back, whereupon Allah's Apostle said: Sell him to me. **And he bought him for two black slaves**, and he did not afterwards take allegiance from anyone until he had asked him whether he was a slave (or a free man)." (Sahih Muslim 3901)

Let's give Muhammad the benefit of the doubt. So he valued white slaves above black slaves. Maybe he never used racist descriptive words.

Narrated Anas bin Malik: The Prophet said to Abu-Dhar, "Listen and obey (your chief) even if he is an Ethiopian with a head like a raisin." (Sahih al-Bukhari 696)

Perhaps the most damning thing Muhammad did to declare his racist views was to describe Satan as a black man. This is recorded by Muhammad's first biographer Ibn Ishaq, who was born 85 years after the hijrah. Best estimates place his writing of the *Sirat al Rasul* at when he was about 31 years old. To date, this biography of Muhammad is the most extensive one written. The English translation was written by Guillaume, who cited his sources. As you see below from page 243:

"From B. Dubay'a b. Zayd b. Malik b. 'Auf b. "Amr b. Auf: Bijad b. "Uthman b. "amir. From B. Laudhan b. "Amr b. 'Auf: Nabtal b. al-Harith. I have heard that it was of him that the apostle said, '**Whoever wants to see Satan, let him look at Nabtal b. Al-Harith! He was a sturdy black man with long flowing hair, inflamed eyes, and dark ruddy cheeks.** He used to come and talk to the apostle and listen to him and then carry what he said to the hypocrites. It was he who said: 'Muhammad is all ears: if anyone tells him anything, he believes it.' God sent down concerning him: 'And of them are those who annoy the prophet and say he is all ears. Say: Good ears for you. He believes in God and trusts the believers and is a mercy to for those of you who believe; and those who annoy the apostle of God, for them there is a painful punishment.'"

On May 18, 2017, Mansour Jamal Ibrahim wrote a piece titled, "Racism in The Muslim Community: Are We Really One?" for Mvslim.com. This article exposes that there is indeed racism within Islamic communities against people who are black. Mansour does not see any basis for the racism and seeks to expose it as a wrong. Here is what he says:

"When non-Muslims are racist towards black Muslims, it's quite predictable and somehow easier to deal with. We are taught to ignore these racist and forgive them for their ignorance. **But when your own "brothers and sisters" reject you and your blackness, it's quite sad and problematic.** Where do you go to? Where do you belong? **Are the days of Arab supremacy towards black people still not passed? Has there ever been a unified Muslim community?**

The most well-known Black Muslim (and one of the Companions of the Prophet, peace be upon him) has to be Bilal Ibn Rabaah. He was an Abyssinian slave who lived in Mecca and embraced Islam in its very beginning. Almost every Muslim knows about this black slave who was freed by the help of the other companions and became the first caller to the congressional prayers. There is no racism in Islam. An Arab has no superiority over a non-Arab and a non-Arab has no superiority over an Arab. Those were the exact words of the Prophet Mohammed.

So where did it go wrong? Why do so many Muslims speak highly of Bilal yet dehumanize black Muslims of this time? Why are intercultural marriages looked down upon, and mixed babies praised? Muslims are not perfect, but aren't we taught that brother- and sisterhood is the key to a strong and unified Muslim community?[44]

I give Mansour Jamal Ibrahim credit for calling out the racism in Islam. I applaud him for standing up to this injustice. But he does not see how it is inherent in Islam due to Muhammad's own racism. Racism, no matter who it is from, is indeed in conflict with Western Civilization's social norms today. Mansour did open another question of possible conflict with Western Civilization.

---

[44] Ibrahim, M. J. (2017, May 18). *Racism in The Muslim Community: Are We Really One?* Retrieved April 2, 2020, from https://mvslim.com/racism-in-the-muslim-community-are-we-really-one/

Chapter 7

Is there ethnic prejudice with Islam giving Arabs superiority?

In Western Civilization, we joke and make claims of superiority of one ethnicity over another using humor. It's totally natural and normal to want whatever nationality you are to be better, and to expect more from your own ethnicity. However, as a social norm today, this is frowned upon and can lead to dismissal in a work environment and social isolation for being too offensive.

One of the interesting things a person faces when they start to learn about Islam is the claim that, if you can't read Arabic, you can't know anything about Islam; as if translations inherently are wrong if they are of the Quran or Hadiths, or Sirats. This statement raises a larger concern, not only for a serious student of Islam who does not wish to convert, but for all the Muslims of the world who do not understand one word of Arabic. According to *Encountering the World of Islam*, "only 20% of the world's Muslims speak Arabic."[45]

I tried finding the stats of what percentage of Muslims can read Arabic. For some reason, that statistic is very hard to locate. What does this mean? If 80% of the Muslim world can NOT read Arabic, it means that Muslims whose native tongue is Arabic are

---

[45] Encountering Islam. (2018). *Muslim World Facts*. Retrieved August 24, 2019, from Encountering the World of Islam: https://www.encounteringislam.org/muslim-world-facts.

given a sense of superiority, and those who do not read Arabic are imbedded with a sense of inferiority.

A simple online search on the topic "Arab superiority in Islam," resulted in a few interesting results. Islamic Virtues has an article titled, "Superiority of the race of Arabs over non-Arabs." This site lists several hadiths to enforce the belief that Arabs are superior to non-Arabs in Islam.

> Narrated Wathilah bin Al-Asqa': that the Messenger of Allah said: "Indeed Allah has *chosen* Isma'il from the children of Ibrahim, and He *chose* Banu Kinanah from the children of Isma'il, and He *chose* the Quraish from Banu Kinanah, and He *chose* Banu Hashim from Quraish, and He *chose* me from Banu Hashim." (Jami` at-Tirmidhi, Vol. 1, Book 46, Hadith 3605)

Islamic Virtues has a slightly different wording switching out "chosen" for "granted eminence." This may have been so that it flows better with the hadith below:

> Wathila b. al-Asqa' reported: "I heard Allah's Messenger as saying: Verily, Allah granted eminence to Kinana from amongst the descendants of Isma'il, and he *granted eminence* to the Quraish amongst Kinana, and he *granted eminence* to Banu Hashim amonsgst the Quraish, and he *granted me eminence* from the tribe of Banu Hashim." (Sahih Muslim 2276)

Some may see this as "tribalism." But it is important to keep in mind that Muhammad is claimed to be the messenger of Allah (a god he claimed was the only god), and that he was the prophet. Additional hadiths support this superiority of Arabs and show tribalism. This next one is considered a weak hadith. It is not necessarily considered as authentic as the two above. However, the site does state there is authentication and provides what it believes to be so below the hadith on the site.

> Narrated Al-Muttalib bin Abi Wada'ah: "Al-Abbas came to the Messenger of Allah, and it is as if he heard

something, so the Prophet stood upon the Minbar and said: 'Who am I?'

They said: 'You are the Messenger of Allah, upon you be peace.'

He said: 'I am Muhammad bin 'Abdullah bin 'Abdul-Muttalib, indeed **Allah created the creation, and He put me in the best [group] of them, then He made them into two groups, so He put me in the best group of them, then He made them into tribes, so He put me in the best of them in tribe**, then He made them into houses, so **He put me in the best of them in tribe and lineage**.'" (Jami` at-Tirmidhi, Vol. 1, Book 46, Hadith 3608)

Islamic Virtues also recommends an Imam agrees with the belief that there is an ethnic superiority of Arabs. The article refers to Shaykh Amjad Rasheed of SunniPath.com. A special notation is given that the site is down, and a reference is given to the Internet Archive for sites that disappear as long as someone asks for it to be noted for history purposes. This was found on Archive.org. The title of the website says it all: "Arabs preferred over other nations."[46] What you will see here is that this Muslim was even more forthright about a tribe being chosen and the Arabs being chosen over all.

The fact that Allah Most High has chosen the Arabs over other nations is affirmed in rigorously authenticated hadiths of the Prophet, may Allah bless him and give him peace; related by Bukhari and Muslim in their "Sahih" in the beginning of the chapter of merits, #5897, on the authority of Wathilah ibn al-Asqa` who said, "I heard the Messenger of Allah, may Allah bless him and grant him peace, say, 'Verily, Allah has chosen Kinanah from the son of Isma`il, and He has chosen Quraysh

[46] Rasheed, S. A. (2008). *Arabs preferred over other nations*. (U. S. Ahmad, Editor) Retrieved August 25, 2019, from Sunni Path: https://web.archive.org/web/20140201113831/http://qa.sunnipath.co m/issue_view.asp?HD=7&ID=9427&CATE=1.

from among Kinanah and He has chosen Hashim from among Quraysh and He has chosen me from the Bani Hashim.'"

So this hadith is a primary text about the preference of Arabs over others, and the preference of some Arabs over other Arabs. And this is what the Imams have chosen from the.........[47] of their books, and even in individual books such as the book of Qurb about the merit of Arabs, authored by the great Imam al-Hafiz Zayn al-din al-`Iraqi. And it was summarized by Shaykh al-Islam Ibn Hajar al-Haytami and others.

Therefore, **the preference of Arabs over other nations, and the preference of some Arabs over other Arabs is affirmed in the Sacred Law.** Allah has even preferred some months over other months and some days and nights over others, as well as places. So in the same way, Allah Glorious and Exalted is He, has chosen some men over others, such as the prophets over others and even some prophets over other prophets. Muslims should not have any objection to this, because all of this returns to the wisdom of the Most Wise, Glorious is He, who is not asked about what He does, but rather, they are the ones who are asked;

… **It is obligatory on a Muslim to believe that Arabs are preferred over other nations because there is a proof for it.** However, this is not one of the pillars of our religion such that if someone rejected this, they would be considered outside of Islam. But if one does reject this, one has sinned for not believing in it because it is an affirmed matter according to a clear rigorously authenticated hadith. Also, **this issue is not something that is commonly known among most Muslims, so for this, one should not hasten to blame one who disagrees with it. It is necessary, rather, to tell him about the issue.**[48]

---

[47] ibid
[48] ibid

As stated at the beginning of this chapter, it is not believed that all Muslims believe these things. This is due to them not knowing about their faith, and their scriptural references that prove their social norms. So, in some sense, they are unfamiliar with Islamic social norms.

Chapter 8

Are Women Considered Less Than Equals in Islamic Social Norms?

One of the great privileges I have had as a talk show host is to talk with people like Dr. Phyllis Chesler, who put me on to the term, *Islamic Gender Apartheid*. It is the name of one of her books. Western Civilization Social Studies textbooks claim that women receive equality in Islam. Women wearing hijabs go to various places to speak of the greatness of Islam and how it gives them freedom and equality. But are they telling the truth? This is a question Dr. Chesler asks. As a well-known Feminist, she also asks why feminists won't do academic studies on the lack of freedom and equality given to women in Islamic social norms.

Dr. Chesler says in her book, Islamic Gender Apartheid:

> "The plight of both men and women in the Islamic world (and increasingly in Europe) requires a sober analysis of reality and a heroic response. World events have made feminism more important, yet, at the same time, feminism has lost much of its power. To my horror, most Western academic and mainstream feminists have not focused on what I call **gender apartheid** in the Islamic world or in its steady penetration of Europe."

It has to be asked, "Is there an Islamic scriptural basis for what Dr. Chesler calls Islamic Gender Apartheid?" If so, that would mean that Islamic social norms are exceedingly opposed to that of Western ones regarding women. The Hadiths reveal a surprising amount of information on this:

> **Narrated by Ibn 'Abbas:** The Prophet said: "**I was shown the Hell-fire, and that the majority of its dwellers were women who were ungrateful.**" It was asked, "Do they disbelieve in Allah?" (or are they ungrateful to Allah?) He replied, "**They are ungrateful to their husbands and are ungrateful for the favors and the good (charitable deeds) done to them.** If you have always been good (benevolent) to one of them and then she sees something in you (not of her liking), she will say, 'I have never received any good from you." (Sahih Bukhari Volume 1, Book 2, Number 28)

> **Narrated by Abu Said Al-Khudri:** Once Allah's Apostle went out to the Musalla (to offer the prayer) o 'Id-al-Adha or Al-Fitr prayer. Then he passed by the women and said, "**O women! Give alms, as I have seen that the majority of the dwellers of Hell-fire were you (women).**" They asked, "Why is it so, O Allah's Apostle?" He replied, "You curse frequently and are ungrateful to your husbands. **I have not seen anyone more deficient in intelligence and religion than you.** A cautious sensible man could be led astray by some of you." The women asked, "O Allah's Apostle! What is deficient in our intelligence and religion?" **He said, "Is not the evidence of two women equal to the witness of one man?" They replied in the affirmative. He said, "This is the deficiency in her intelligence. Isn't it true that a woman can neither pray nor fast during her menses?" The women replied in the affirmative. He said, "This is the deficiency in her religion."** (Sahih Bukhari Volume 1, Book 6, Number 301)

It is shocking to say that Islam recorded these things for posterity. It is actually recorded and written down, preserved as something to be revered under Islam.

When a girl is born to Islamic family, it can be viewed as less of a blessing than that of a boy. This can be seen in the Islamic practice of 'Aqiqiah (Aqee-Qa). *'Umdat al-Salik* aka Reliance of the Traveller, records the differences in sexes as significant under this section.

j15.0 SACRIFICE FOR A NEWBORN ('AQIQA) AND NAME GIVING

(O: Lexically, 'aqiqa means the hair on a baby's head at birth. In Sacred Law, it means the animal sacrificed when the baby's hair is cut, which is a confirmed sunna (def: c4.1).)

SUNNAS AFTER BIRTH

j15.1 It is recommended for anyone to whom a child is born to shave its hair on the seventh day thereafter (O: meaning any newborn, whether male or female; a baby girl should also have her hair shaved) and give away in charity gold or silver equal to the weight of the hair. It is also recommended (N: when the baby is first born) to give the call to prayer (adhan, def: f3.6) in its right ear and the call to commence (iqama) in its left.

THE SACRIFICE

j15.2 **If the baby is male, it is recommended to slaughter two shahs** (def:h2.5) that meet 'Eid Sacrifice specifications (def:j14.2), while **if the baby is female, it is recommended to slaughter one.**

(O: The person called-upon to slaughter for a newborn is the one obliged to support the child (dis: m12.1).) After slaughtering, the shah is cooked (O: as at any feast) in sweet sauce, but none of its bones are broken (A: it is cut at the joints), and it is recommended to distribute the meat to the poor.

There exist some who try to claim that Islam is a feminist religion. In making this claim, they state that Surah 2:228 claiming that "the rights of the wives [with regard to their husbands] are equal to the [husbands'] rights." However, they do not share the context of the verse, nor the entire verse. This verse is about divorced women. The entire verse says something quite different.

> And the divorced women shall undergo, without remarrying, a waiting-period of three monthly courses: for it is not lawful for them to conceal what God may have created in their wombs, if they believe in God and the Last Day. And during this period, their husbands are fully entitled to take them back, if they desire reconciliation; *but, in accordance with justice, the rights of the wives [with regard to their husbands] are equal to the [husbands'] rights* **with regard to them, although men have precedence over them [in this respect].**

Also, from the same chapter of the Quran, verse 282 tells us how unequal women are to men.

> And bring to witness two witnesses from among your men. And if there are not two men [available], then a man and two women from those whom you accept as witnesses - so that if one of the women errs, then the other can remind her. And let not the witnesses refuse when they are called upon.

This speaks of women not having the same memory capacity as the male counterparts. It is demonstrative of how women are thought of in Islamic cultures.

In 2016, Dispatches, a British based television show shared their undercover discovery in one of the United Kingdom's largest mosques. This was a return to see if the mosque first shown in Dispatches 2007[49] and its bookstore and several of its speakers had cleaned up their act. They showed a video of Murtaza Khan who attacked the idea that women could be independent from men. According to him, when a woman believes she does not need

---

[49] Dispatches. (2007, January 15). *Dispatches - Undercover Mosque.* Accessed March 29, 2021
https://www.newenglishreview.org/Miscellaneous/Dispatches_-_Undercover_Mosque.

a man to survive, and believes she can get her own job, her own education, her own place, or even her own welfare, she is deceived. He says that belief is of the devil, and that "man is stronger than woman. But men today do not know how to take care of their families. That is why their women walk loose. Their women speak loose -- and that's their evil society that the Muslim society has become like today."[50]

This is what is being taught consistently over a period of 9 years in one of the United Kingdom's largest mosques; the belief that women are lesser beings, a belief that they must be controlled by men. Does this not show an Islamic social norm with respect to their thoughts on women?

Court of Law

Under Sharia, a woman is counted as less than a man as you read in the Hadith above. In the Quran, this is stated very clearly:

*O you who have believed, **when you contract a debt for a specified term, write it down. And let a scribe write [it] between you in justice.** Let no scribe refuse to write as Allah has taught him. So let him write and let the one who has the obligation dictate. And let him fear Allah, his Lord, and not leave anything out of it. But if the one who has the obligation is of limited understanding or weak or unable to dictate himself, then let his guardian dictate in justice. **And bring to witness two witnesses from among your men. And if there are not two men [available], then a man and two women from those whom you accept as witnesses - so that if one of the women errs, then the other can remind her.** And let not the witnesses refuse when they are called upon. And do not be [too] weary to write it, whether it is small or large, for its [specified] term. That is more just in the sight of Allah and stronger as evidence and more likely to prevent doubt between you, except when it is an immediate transaction which you*

---

[50] Dispatches. (2016, April 23). *Dispatches: Undercover Mosque | The Return | Real Stories*. Retrieved March 29, 2020, from: https://www.youtube.com/watch?v=3WgVa3VRFb4.

conduct among yourselves. For [then] there is no blame upon you if you do not write it. And take witnesses when you conclude a contract. Let no scribe be harmed or any witness. For if you do so, indeed, it is [grave] disobedience in you. And fear Allah. And Allah teaches you. And Allah is Knowing of all things. (2:282)

Shariah is a bit more explicit, limiting what a woman can do by herself to almost nothing. An individual woman's legal ability to act as a witness are half that of a man, this includes the signing of contracts, such as witnessing the validity of a marriage.

m3.3 The second integral is that the marriage have witnesses, it not being valid unless two witnesses are present who are:

(a) male (O: since a **marriage witnessed by a man and two women would not be valid (A: though it would be valid in the Hanafi school))**

o24.7 The testimony of the following is legally acceptable when it concerns cases involving property, or transactions dealing with property, such as sales:

(1) two men;

(2) **two women and a man;**

(3) or a male witness together with the oath of the plaintiff.

024.10 If testimony concerns things which men do not typically see (O: but women do), such as childbirth, **then it is sufficient to have two male witnesses, a man and two women, or four women.**

If women are not considered equals in a court of law held by Islamists, people who want shariah, what does that mean about how they view women as a whole? Many years ago, I had a house mate from Nigeria who worked as a doctor at a local hospital. One day, one of his nurses appeared and asked me to teach him how to treat women in America, or he would soon be shipped home for his sexist treatment towards women as a whole. The nurses of the hospital were going to file a complaint against him as a group unless he made a drastic change. I sat down with this doctor, and talked to him about how women are valued in America, and what happens to those in the work environment who do not catch on quickly; more specifically, that they get fired. This was around 1986; today, persons who commit such vulgar acts would be charged in a court with sexual harassment which would follow them for the most of their lives.

Chapter 9

Are Muslim Women required to wear the hijab or is it a choice?

This question is asked for several reasons, amongst them are the differing claims of Muslim women that is a choice, and a requirement. If it is required, why would some make the claim? This must be examined.

Women's magazine *Cosmopolitan* decided it was important to ask this question on July 4, 2016:

> *While Islam as a religion often comes under heavy scrutiny for its oppression of women, given many wear a hijab around their face or a burqa to cover their full body, isn't it worth hearing how the women themselves feel?*

> *We think so, which is why this Reddit thread, which invites women who do wear a traditional garments to cover themselves up either fully or partially in public, was so interesting to read. How does it feel to wear it?* **Is it a choice or, is there pressure from within their family or their community?** *Do they feel sidelined in public because of their burqa?*[51]

---

[51] Harvey-Jenner, C. (2016, July 4). *Muslim women explain how they feel about wearing a hijab: Mainly it's their choice.* Retrieved from Cosmopolitan: https://www.cosmopolitan.com/uk/reports/news/a44416/muslim-women-explain-how-feel-wearing-burqa-hijab/.

Sadly, this article talks about how a woman feels, addresses the head scarf (hijab) only as a family tradition, but never explores if it is required by Islam. It is as if the brief article asks the question fairly from women who like and hate the hijab. In this, it appears unbiased, unless you ask why they addressed the question about pressure from a family versus a religious requirement. The article, in truth, never addresses who or what places the requirement on the family. Is it not Islam that places this requirement or choice on a family? What does Islam say about the Hijab? Is it a choice?

The Quran states in 33:59 that Muslim men must tell their wives and daughters to cover-up for their own safety. Below is the verse. The reasoning for covering pretty much means, if you do not obey, a severe punishment follows.

O Prophet, tell your wives and your daughters and the women of the believers to bring down over themselves [part] of their outer garments. That is more suitable that they will be known and not be abused. And ever is Allah Forgiving and Merciful.

This is not clearly stating to cover the hair. But notice the reasoning behind it. If they are not covered, they will be abused. This a reference to sexual abuse. Who would do the abusing? Considering this passage was given inside an Islamic community, it would be Muslim men doing the abuse. This included daughters. So little girls also had to be cautious of men seeking to sexually abuse them AND WERE TOLD TO COVER THEMSELVES TO KEEP FROM BEING MOLESTED.

The Quran also says in 24:31:

And tell the believing women to reduce [some] of their vision and guard their private parts and not expose their adornment except that which [necessarily] appears thereof and to wrap [a portion of] their headcovers over their chests and not expose their adornment except to their husbands, their fathers, their husbands' fathers, their sons, their husbands' sons, their brothers, their brothers' sons, their sisters' sons, their women, that which their right hands possess, or those male attendants having no physical desire, or children who are not yet aware of the private aspects of women. And let them not stamp their feet to make known what they conceal of their adornment. And turn to Allah in repentance, all of you, O believers, that you might succeed.

Some say this stomping was to show cleavage that their garments did not cover, but the shawl/head gear draped over them to provide extra protection. Some say that it is indeed a covering over the hair because 'adornment' is a direct reference to the hair. A slight reference is made to women stomping so they could show someone their pretty hair, by causing their cover to slip. This has evolved to a tight wrap of the hair not allowing any of it to appear in public. Does this seem optional? Is there a choice given? Remember, from the above statement, the citation states the purpose is to protect the women and daughters from sexual attacks.

In the Islamic countries like Pakistan, the head covering of a hijab can also be a chador. One official in the Haripur district of Pakistan in September 2019, made it mandatory for all school age girls to wear a head covering and gown to dress "in order to protect them from any unethical incident,". This official deemed it "necessary to protect girl students from a growing number of complaints of eve-teasing and harassment."[52]

Here, they are saying that the hair of school girls (ages 5 to 18) are tempting men to sexually molest girls, so it is their fault if this happens, WHEN THEY ARE NOT COVERED. Of course, if they are, their word only counts as half a man in a court of law so they can never bring charges against their molester.

The question of whether the hijab is mandatory has been a central theme wherever Islam wanders today. On August 7, 2019, Al-Qaeda's Al-Sahab media wing released a video of Al-Qaeda leader Ayman Al-Zawahiri titled "The Battle of the Hijab." The Middle East Media Research Institute caught this, translated it and released a summary of it to the public within a week. According to this lover of shariah, western countries are doing everything they can to destroy Islamic women's modesty and morals. This is

---

[52] Sirajuddin. (2019, September 16). *KP govt makes it mandatory for schoolgirls across the province to 'cover up'.* Retrieved September 30, 2019, from Dawn: https://www.dawn.com/news/1505542.

how Islamic women are warned against Western cultural values. It is deemed as an attack on their modesty.

France has had a law forbidding the displaying of religion for a hundred years. It is called, Laïcité (Lah-Cee-Tay). They have been fighting to keep French culture which a hijrah is working to dismiss. France passed a law in 2010[53] to ban the face veil as part of keeping French culture and Laïcité. Granted, this is not about the hijab, but a more restrictive requirement placed on Islamic women by stricter observance of Islam seen in many Islamic countries.

This law passed the French Senate with 46 votes and had already passed the upper house of the parliament in July of that year. Justice Minister, Michèle Alliot-Marie stated, "the full veil dissolves a person's identity in that of a community. It calls into question the French model of integration, founded on the acceptance of our society's values. Living with one's face uncovered was a question of dignity and equality."[54]

In the USA, the Democratic Party took it upon themselves to lift a 181-year-old law forbidding hats in the House of Representatives so that Ilhan Omar would not have to remove her hijab in order to serve in her role as a representative of Minnesota. A hijab is not a hat, but a head covering. She is one of two Muslim women elected. Rep. Rashida Tlaib does not wear a hijab, so they simply could have enforced the rule, showing that not all Muslims follow this rule. Rep. Ilhan Omar has made bold statements about her hijab and her reasons for wearing it. In March 0f 2019, she told *Vogue* magazine, that:

Wearing her hijab allows her to be a 'walking billboard' not only for her faith, but also for representing something different

---

[53] Davies, L. (2010, September 14). *France: Senate votes for Muslim face veil ban.* Retrieved October 1, 2019, from The Guardian: https://www.theguardian.com/world/2010/sep/14/france-senate-muslim-veil-ban.

[54] Ibid

from the norm. 'To me, the hijab means power, liberation, beauty, and resistance. '[55]

This is the same rule that several Democrats violated, by wearing hoodies on March 28th, 2012, when trying to show they were standing with Trayvon Martin who was killed in Florida.

In 2007, Quebec Canada's Bouchard-Taylor Commission created recommendations, which became policies for the province. Amongst them was:

Judges, Crown prosecutors, police officers, prison guards and the president and vice-president of the National Assembly be prohibited from wearing religious signs.[56]

This recommendation was for government employees alone. It, in effect, banned the Christians from wearing of a cross, the Sikhs from wearing a turban, Jew from wearing yarmulkes, or Muslim women from wearing a hijab to work in a government post. There is no religious prejudice involved as it does not address any one religion.

Tarek Fatah, a Canadian Muslim "reformist" sees the hijab a little differently than many do today. He wrote of it:

The fact is that while the Sikh turban, Jewish yarmulkes and the Catholic crucifix are definitely religious symbols, the hijab is not. Rather, it is a political symbol that until the late 1970s, was unheard of in Pakistan, India, Indonesia, Bangladesh,

---

[55] Gouveia, A. (2019, March 28). *Ilhan Omar: "To Me, the Hijab Means Power, Liberation, Beauty, and Resistance"*. Retrieved October 1, 2019, from Vogue Magazine: https://en.vogue.me/culture/ilhan-omar-first-somali-american-hijabi-congresswoman.

[56] Global News. (2013, October 13). *Fact file: 10 Bouchard-Taylor report recommendation*. Retrieved October 1, 2019, from Global News: https://globalnews.ca/news/880174/fact-file-10-bouchard-taylor-report-recommendation.

Turkey, Somalia and Nigeria. It was the uniform of the Muslim Brotherhood in the Arab world.[57]

Fatah also made mention of Ferid Chikhi who lives in Quebec and agrees with him that the hijab is a political symbol more than a religious one. Chikhi stated:

... the hijab, conceals in itself the idea, the representation or the thought of a first generic sense which is ignored by all, and which conveys a double meaning: translated in French or in other languages, this word wants say curtain, separation, hanging ... or even storefront and not dress or scarf that covers the head of women. He simply referred to a separation of the space into two; the foreign men to the Prophet's house and that of his women.

Then, history reminds us, after the death of the Prophet, the male power extended the territory hijab, imposing it as a separation between the spaces of all men and all women. Finally, at those generally Islamic and not Muslims, citing verses al-Ahzâb (33 e sura), the khimar is a shawl and djilbab or thaûb are shawls, worn by the women of the time in these same Arab Gulf countries. They did not have the function of covering as they would like to make us believe the head, but the shoulders and the chest.[58]

This is the reason why some ambiguity exists as to whether a hijab is required or not. The Quran refers to covering. It refers to shawls and more. But the specific item of a hijab is not mentioned. It is why Iran has a chador and not a hijab.

---

[57] Fatah, T. (2019, June 18). *FATAH: Why some Canadian Muslims celebrated the Quebec hijab ban.* Retrieved October 2, 2019, from Toronto Sun: https://torontosun.com/opinion/columnists/fatah-why-some-canadian-muslims-celebrated-the-quebec-hijab-ban.

[58] Cikhi, F. (2019, March 28). *State secularism: veil or hijab, the real meanings and their scope.* Retrieved October 2, 2019, from Huffington Post: https://quebec.huffingtonpost.ca/ferid-chikhi/laicite-etat-voile-hijab-veritables-significations-portees-quebec_a_23702059.

If required, a woman is often left without a choice to wear the hijab. Youness Moussaid, left little doubt of this in December 6, 2019 in Bismark,[59] North Dakota, when school officials reported the abuse he had done to his step-daughter. His step-daughter was refusing to wear the hijab and dresses when at school. She snuck in a change of clothing.

Moussaid, in response, struck the teenage girl with a broom stick, causing bruising on the top of her right hand and on the front of her thighs. He grabbed her hair and struck her head against the wall, causing a quarter-sized bump.

Moussaid admitted to this crime. Perhaps he did not see it as a crime, nor did he understand that females are considered equals under the law.

The girl now has an order of protection from her step-father. He faces 5 years if convicted. Moussaid felt justified by the Islamic social norm he believed in to demand his daughter wear a hijab.

---

[59] Svihovec, T. (2019, December 6). *Man accused of abusing stepdaughter with broomstick over religious beliefs.* Retrieved March 30, 2020, from The Bismark Tribune: https://bismarcktribune.com/news/local/bismarck/man-accused-of-abusing-stepdaughter-with-broomstick-over-religious-beliefs/article_4d95d50a-95c1-555f-a2bb-cca8e84dd7d1.html.

Chapter 10

Do Islamic social norms make men see women as intellectual equals or as sexual objects of pleasure?

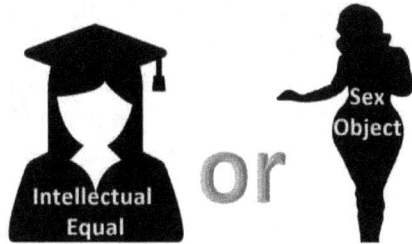

As I started to put this section together, I also thought about how some women are objectified as being nothing more than pleasure toys for some men. They seem like extreme opposites. On one side, a woman is appreciated because of her intellect. On the other side, a woman is only good for how she can please a man; no intellect needed.

In the 1990s, when the Taliban started to make the news, it became known that they said women did not need an education, and objected to schools for girls. In 2009, the Taliban issued a statement that no girls would go to school. The Mullah Shah Doran, second in command in the Swat Valley announced, "From January 15, girls will not be allowed to attend schools."[60] Mullah Doran also said educating girls is "un-Islamic."[61]

In 2018, Radio Free Europe and Radio Liberty's Gandhara[62] ran a story on the Taliban, stopping education of girls in the birthplace of its current President, Ashraf Ghani, who states he advocates for girls' education and gender equality.

---

[60] Washington Times. (2009, January 5). *Taliban bans education for girls in Swat Valley*. Retrieved October 4, 2019, from Washington Times: https://www.washingtontimes.com/news/2009/jan/05/taliban-bans-education-for-girls-in-pakistans-swat.

[61] Ibid

[62] Shafaq, N., Parsa, N., & Siddique, A. (2018, June 20). *In Afghan Leader's Home District, Taliban Ban Girls From Education*. Retrieved October 23, 2019, from Gandhara: https://gandhara.rferl.org/a/afghan-leader-home-district-taliban-ban-girls-from-education/29306920.html.

Which is true? Do those who want shariah believe women are equal in intellect? Keep in mind here that we have already addressed the Islamic social norm that accepts lying to non-Muslims.

What do Muslims say to each other on this topic? Saudi Cleric Abd Al-Aziz Al-Fawzan, gave a speech entitled, "Husbands Should Put Up with Their Wives' Slips and Errors, Because the Twisted Nature of Women Stems from Their Very Creation" on June 11, 2007.

These hadiths provide some of the most decisive evidence that Islam protects women and guarantees their rights. Islam has surrounded the woman with a fence of compassion and mercy. **It has shown that the twisted nature of women stems from their very creation. This is how Allah wanted a woman to be. Therefore, the husband must adapt himself to her and be patient with her. He should not giver her too many things to do, or things that she is incapable of doing. He should not make her do anything that is contrary to her nature, and to the way she was created by Allah. In addition, he should turn a blind eye to her mistakes, he should tolerate her slips and errors, and put up with all the silly ignorant things she might say, because this constitutes part of the nature of her creation.** *In addition, women have surging emotions, which in some cases, might overpower their minds.* **The weakness with which women were created is the secret behind their attractiveness and appeal to their husbands. It is the source of women's seduction of men, and one of the elements strengthening the bond between husband and wife.** *This is one of the wondrous miracles of Allah: The strength of a woman lies in her weakness. Her power of seduction and appeal lie in her emotions, which might overpower her mind at times.*[63]

---

[63] Al-Fawzan, A. A.-A. (2007, June 11). *Saudi Cleric Abd Al-Aziz Al-Fawzan: Husbands Should Put Up with Their Wives' Slips and Errors, Because the Twisted Nature of Women Stems from Their Very Creation.* Retrieved

*Both husband and wife should satisfy their spouse's natural urges, and should try to gratify their desires, as long as nothing prevents this. This is why the Prophet said: "**When a man calls his wife to fulfill his needs, she must go to him, even if she is busy with the oven.**" Imagine this: There is fire in the oven, and she wants to bake bread. But even if she's busy with this work that cannot be neglected, when he calls her, she must leave the oven and go to her husband. Another hadith says: "She must go to him, even if she is on the back of a camel." She must go to him, even if she is riding.*[64]

It is important to keep in mind this is not something all Muslims believe. It however, is very encouraged in Islamic countries. Although, the lack of males attaining college degrees in countries like Saudi Arabia may have something to do with more women going to college today.

Bukhari, Volume 1, Book 6, Number 301, records a hadith of a woman asking why Muhammad considers them deficient in intelligence. His answer demonstrates a use of circular logic, something the western culture calls fallacious (false) reasoning.

Narrated Abu Said Al-Khudri:

A cautious sensible man could be led astray by some of you." The women asked, "O Allah's Apostle! What is deficient in our intelligence and religion?" He said, "Is not the evidence of two women equal to the witness of one man?" They replied in the affirmative. He said, "This is the deficiency in her intelligence."

In the discussion about the hijab, Pakistani leaders ordered children to cover up from head to toe to keep them from being lusted after. This demonstrates that it is not wrong for Muslim men

---

October 4, 2019, from Middle East Media Research Institute: https://www.memri.org/tv/saudi-cleric-abd-al-aziz-al-fawzan-husbands-should-put-their-wives-slips-and-errors-because/transcript.

[64] Ibid

to lust after little girls. But it is wrong for a little girl to allow the man to lust after her because she has not covered up. The sexualization of girls over their intellectual capability is what contributes to the next issue, Child Marriage.

Dr. Wafa Sultan is one of those rare women who was able to become a medical doctor in an Islamic country. When she became a fourth year medical student, she was asked to work in a Gynecologist practice. She shares in her book, <u>A God Who Hates,</u> that her work was "confined in most cases, to diagnosing pregnancies and confirming the virgin status of young girls."[65]

Dr. Sultan described her travels to and from school on a bus in this Islamic culture of Aleppo, Syria:

The journey, which took about an hour by bus, was a cruel one. The bus route passed through many neighborhoods and, only ten minutes after leaving campus, the vehicle would already be packed with passengers like sardines. Most of the women on the bus, who never made up more than a quarter of the total number of passengers, were students, and their movements resembled those of mice trying to flee from a malicious cat. No sooner did a man get the opportunity to press up against a woman than his penis would poke into her back like an iron bar. Shrieked complaints could be heard. But the sad fact of the matter was that the residents of the town regarded the female students as prostitutes, plain and simple.[66]

Sadly, this is not unlike many buses now in Europe where Muslim men press upon European females. In Germany alone, sex crimes have escalated exponentially since the hijrah started. What does this social norm impose upon women in non-Muslim countries? What does this bus event above say about how Islamic social norms like this are changing cultures and nations towards

---

[65] Sultan, W. (2009). *A God Who Hates.* New York City: St. Martin's Press, p. 27.

[66] ibid, p. 29.

Islamic social norms? Should we be accepting of this or should we simply reject it in every way possible? Acceptance means dhimmitude. Women should be standing up everywhere and shouting, "NO!"

Chapter 11

Is child marriage and forced marriage part of Islamic social norms?

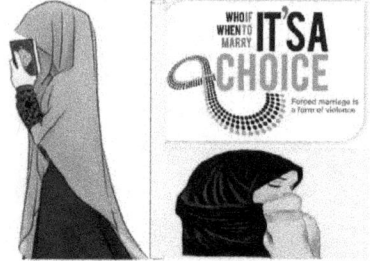

While child marriage is not an issue for Islam alone, it is however, the only religion that endorses the practice on religious grounds. Other issues with child marriage are cultural. While some may even be fringe cultic groups, they are not accepted by any major religious group today. Islam remains the only religion that gives religious reasoning for not outlawing child marriages.

Children are not considered mature enough to make lifelong decisions, so, these are forced marriages. Children will obey the adults out of respect or fear of disobeying. This leaves no choice to a child bride.

Child marriage is endorsed by Islam because Muhammad married a girl at the age of 6 and consummated the marriage when she was 9. Aisha herself is recorded as having stated she was 9 years old. This is in lunar years not solar years, so Aisha may have still been 8 solar years old. It is one thing to hear that Muhammad had sex with a child bride who was 9 lunar years old, but when you start to look at the evidence for it in the Hadiths, you learn that it is Aisha herself who says she was 9 years old.

'A'isha (Allah be pleased with her) reported that Allah's Apostle married her when she was seven years old, and he was taken to his house as a bride when she was nine, and her dolls were with her; and when he (the Holy Prophet) died she was eighteen years old. (Sahih Muslim Book 16, Hadith 83)

Narrated `Aisha:
that the Prophet married her when she was six years old and he consummated his marriage when she was nine years old.

Hisham said: I have been informed that `Aisha remained with the Prophet for nine years (i.e. till his death). (Sahih al-Bukhari 5134)

The fact that dolls were with Aisha tells us that she had not yet entered puberty. In Islamic culture, girls are allowed to play with dolls until they enter puberty. Girls Health.gov states that girls begin puberty between the age of 8 and 12.[67] So it is entirely possible that she had entered puberty. But the fact that she was still playing with dolls calls this into question.

According to the Bukhari, Muhammad exhorted his followers to marry young virgin girls as he did. The following hadith has Muhammad talking about playing with them.

> **Narrated Jabir bin `Abdullah:**
> *When I got married, Allah's Messenger said to me, "What type of lady have you married?"*
>
> *I replied, "I have married a matron.'*
>
> *He said, "Why, don't you have a liking for the virgins and for fondling them?"*
>
> *Jabir also said Allah's Messenger said, "Why didn't you marry a young girl so that you might play with her, and she, with you?" (Sahih Bukhari Vol. 7, Book 62, Hadith 17)*

Devout Muslims require more than the Quran in order to copy what Muhammad did. This imitation aspect of Islam is complete, from the exact copying of the movements and words said in prayer, to every aspect of his life.

Attempts to outlaw the behavior of marrying prepubescent girls and consummating the marriage have been tried in Islamic

---

[67] Girls' Health. (2014, May 23). *Timing and stages of puberty*. Retrieved October 23, 2019, from Girls Health.gov: https://www.girlshealth.gov/body/puberty/timing.html.

countries like Pakistan. In 2016, the country attempted to raise the minimum age for marrying to 16. "A representative from the Council of Islamic Ideology (CII) had dubbed the amendment to the Child Marriage Restraint (Amendment) Bill 2014 as "anti-Islamic" and "blasphemous" during the committee meeting."[68]

In Iraq in 2017, parliamentarians drafted a law that would allow children as young as nine to marry.[69] This is based on Bukhari's hadiths given by Aisha that were cited earlier in this chapter.

The differences shown here in the legal marrying age has to do with what Muslims state about - whether or not - Aisha entered puberty at the age of nine. Some believe, yes, she had started puberty, while others say no.

In the Philippines, the marriage age is codified in the Code of Muslim Personal Laws, which was originally written in 1977. A Primer on the Code of Muslim Personal Laws of the Philippines states:

*Any Muslim male at least fifteen years of age and any Muslim female of **the age of puberty** or upwards and not suffering from any impediment under the provisions of this Code may contract marriage. A female is presumed to have attained puberty upon reaching the age of fifteen. (Art. 16.1)*

This looks like marriage is something equally agreed to by both the male and female. However, that is not entirely true. It is also not true that a female must have started puberty. The Primer proposes two questions that address this.

---

[68] AFP. (2016, January 15). *Pakistani clerics block 'un-Islamic' child marriage bill.* Retrieved from Al Arabiya:
http://english.alarabiya.net/en/News/asia/2016/01/15/Pakistani-clerics-block-un-Islamic-child-marriage-bill.html.

[69] Maclean, R. (2019, June 21). *Senior Islamic cleric issues fatwa against child marriage.* Retrieved October 21, 2019, from The Guardian:
https://www.theguardian.com/global-development/2019/jun/21/senior-islamic-cleric-issues-fatwa-against-child-marriage.

CAN A FEMALE BELOW FIFTEEN YEARS OF AGE CONTRACT MARRIAGE?

Yes. The Shari'a District Court may, upon petition of a proper *wali*, order the solemnization of the marriage of a female who, though less than fifteen but not below twelve years of age, has attained puberty. (Art. 16.2)

IF ANY OF THE CONTRACTING PARTIES IS BELOW THE PRESCRIBED AGE, WHAT HAPPENS TO THE MARRIAGE?

Marriage through a *wali* by a minor below the prescribed age shall be regarded as betrothal. It may be annulled upon the petition of either party within four years after attaining the age of puberty, provided no voluntary cohabitation has taken place, and the *wali* who contracted the marriage was other than the father or paternal grandfather. (Art. 16.3)[70]

A *Wali* is a guardian. The male parent/guardian may arrange a marriage of a child bride after she is 12. It is stated that the bride may annul the marriage four years after, provided there has been no cohabitation.

In *'Umdat al-Salik* aka Reliance of the Traveller, which is shariah in English, we learn that marriage AND consummation of the marriage to prepubescent girls are permissible:

e10.3 When a woman who has been made love to performs the purificatory bath, and the male's sperm afterwards leaves her vagina, then she must repeat the ghusl if two conditions exist:

---

[70] Muslim Mindano. (2005). *A Primer on the Code of Muslim Personal Laws of the Philippines.* Retrieved May 29, 2021, from Muslim Mindano: https://web.archive.org/web/20200424141448/http://www.muslimmin danao.ph/shari'a/pesonal_laws.pdf.

(a) that she is not a child, but rather old enough to have sexual gratification (A: as it might otherwise be solely her husband's sperm);

Whether or not Islamic communities define the marrying age by the concept of puberty or not, there are several news stories of women and children who have escaped the confinement of child marriage within Islamic communities. One of them is Scholastica Nacap in Nigeria, who was orphaned at the age of 9. When she was 13, "she was told by her father's relatives [that] she must marry a much older wealthy man." Nacap's answer was to run. She ran 60 kilometers before she stopped. "I had to escape. I couldn't accept [becoming] a wife and mother at 13," said Nacap.[71]

It must be said that Islamists have the only religion that defends child marriage. But, it is not the only culture to have child marriages. It was only a few years ago that Tennessee outlawed child marriage.

What about other forms of forced marriage? While doing research on this topic, I typed into Google, "forced marriage" and Islam. The most prominent result took me to Discover-the-truth.com, where Kaleef K. Karim had written a brief piece alleging that Islam requires consent of both the woman and the man. He began by giving a passage from the Quran 4:19, showing that women are considered property and can be inherited.

O you who have believed, it is not lawful for you to inherit women by compulsion. And do not make difficulties for them in order to take [back] part of what you gave them unless they commit a clear immorality. And live with them in kindness. For if you dislike them - perhaps you dislike a thing and Allah makes therein much good.

---

[71] Okiror, S. (2018, June 26). *The Ugandan girl who trekked barefoot to escape marriage at 13*. Retrieved October 24, 2019, from The Guardian: https://www.theguardian.com/global-development/2018/jun/26/uganda-girl-trekked-barefoot-escape-marriage-13.

But in this sense, women as property must consent to being married. This speaks of women, not child brides. Kaleef considers this strong enough evidence to state: "So the above passage from the Quran is crystal clear that men cannot inherit women against their will. This passage alone is enough evidence that Islam forbids it, but we will go further." Sadly, Kaleef misses that this passage is specifically talking about inheritance.

The next passage Kaleef offers is indeed troublesome.

Abu Hurairah narrated that:

The Prophet said: "A matron should not be given in marriage until she is consulted, and a virgin should not be given in marriage until her permission is sought, and her silence is her permission." (Jami` at-Tirmidhi 1107)

Equating silence to consent is problematic! What if the bride to be is scared for her life? What if she has been told if she says no, her family will be killed? But in Islam, this is OK? Silence equals consent? It becomes twice as problematic when the Islamic marriage ceremony is looked at. Unlike, Judaism and Christianity, consent is measured in a contract signed by 4 witnesses, 2 for the bride and two for the groom. If the bride is pressured to sign and the witnesses are provided by the groom, a forced marriage can occur easily. Remember here that the silence of the bride to be is seen as consent.

Kaleef did not address other passages which refer to marrying a slave. Slaves do not get choices.

*'If you fear that you shall not be able to deal justly with the orphan girls, then marry (other) women of your choice, two or three or four; but if you fear that you shall not be able to deal justly (with them), then only one, **or (the captives) that your right hands possess**. (Sahih Bukhari Vol. 7, Book 62, Hadith 2)*

Narrated Abu Burda's father:

*Allah's Messenger said, any man **who has a slave girl whom he educates properly, teaches good manners, manumits and marries her**, will get a double reward.*

(Sahih Bukhari Vol. 7, Book 62, Hadith 20)

This allows Muslim men to take a captive woman as a slave and marry her. Of course, she must convert to Islam first. Historically, Islam has forced conversions through threats during conquests.

Muhammad himself presided over a marriage where the woman was given no chance to consent. In fact, she offered her consent in marriage to Muhammad, not to someone else!

Narrated Sahl bin Sa`d As-Sa`idi:

A woman came to Allah's Messenger ((and said, "O Allah's Messenger (!(I have come to give you myself in marriage (without Mahr)." Allah's Messenger ((looked at her. He looked at her carefully and fixed his glance on her and then lowered his head. When the lady saw that he did not say anything, she sat down. A man from his companions got up and said, "O Allah's Messenger (!(If you are not in need of her, then marry her to me." The Prophet ((said, "Have you got anything to offer?" The man said, "No, by Allah, O Allah's Messenger ("!(The Prophet ((said (to him), "Go to your family and see if you have something." The man went and returned, saying, "No, by Allah, I have not found anything." Allah's Apostle said, "(Go again) and look for something, even if it is an iron ring." He went again and returned, saying, "No, by Allah, O Allah's Messenger (!(I could not find even an iron ring, but this is my Izar (waist sheet)." He had no rida. He added, "I give half of it to her." Allah's Messenger ((said, "What will she do with your Izar? If you wear it, she will be naked, and if she wears it, you will be naked." So that man sat down for a long while and then got up (to depart). When Allah's Messenger ((saw him going, he ordered that he be called back. When he came, the Prophet ((said, "How much of the Qur'an do you know?" He said, "I know such Sura and such Sura," counting them. The Prophet ((said, "Do you know them by heart?" He replied, "Yes." The Prophet ((said, "Go, I marry her to you for that much of the Qur'an which you have."
(Sahih al Bukhari Vol. 7, Book 62, Hadith 24)

If Muhammad required no consent in a marriage he performed how many Imams who are eager to copy him, will require consent? These passages explain some of the forced marriages that are now monthly making the news.

In October 2020, Huma Younus, a Christian girl who was 14 years old in Pakistan was kidnapped. A few days later, her parents received documents that she had converted to Islam and had married. The parents went to court to fight the forced marriage of their teen daughter to an abductor. The girl, fearing for her life, did not appear in court. The "Sindh High Court dismissed a petition to have the marriage and forced conversion of a Catholic girl overturned because both are valid under Islamic law, since a girl can marry after she has her first period." [72] The parents are still fighting for their daughter, even after the province passed a law against child marriage. But as you can see, it is not being enforced.

Pakistan regularly makes the news on the topic of forced marriages. The UK also made the news recently on this topic. The Foreign and Commonwealth Office of the UK had been charging women forced into marriages approximately €740 as the cost of bringing them home safely by the government.

An article by the Guardian in January of 2019 stated there had been 82 victims from the UK who had been forced into marriage and requested assistance being returned to the country. [73] This article mentions four British teens who had been brought to

---

[72] AsiaNews.it. (2020, February 5). *Court rules that a girl who's had her first period can marry, thus backing Huma Younus's kidnapper. For girl's lawyer, this is shameful.* Retrieved February 28, 2020, from AsiaNews.it: http://asianews.it/news-en/Court-rules-that-a-girl-whos-had-her-first-period-can-marry,-thus-backing-Huma-Younuss-kidnapper.-For-girls-lawyer,-this-is-shameful-49220.html?fbclid=IwAR3RhQZCEvTFUSz_mNQzYib12uCJg1NCugUnRLE9aVe7rTZDq_hS6pIlq1w.

[73] Busby, M., & Perraudin, F. (2019, January 2). *Women forced into marriage overseas asked to repay cost of return to UK.* Retrieved January 28, 2020, from The Guardian: https://www.theguardian.com/society/2019/jan/02/women-forced-into-marriage-overseas-asked-to-repay-cost-of-return-to-uk.

Somalia for a forced marriage and were being tortured and kept at a "correctional" religious school while awaiting the ritual.

The UK government has had to address so many forced marriages that it created the Forced Marriage Unit within the Foreign & Commonwealth Office and Home Office in 2013. Statistics indicate it has been addressing hundreds of complaints a year now. Not all of the cases it addresses are of Muslims, but the vast majority of cases indicate they are Muslims. Interestingly, the UK stats also state that 20% of the forced marriages they address are for males while 80% of the cases are for women.

Year	Cases
2012	1,485
2013	1,302
2014	1,267
2015	1,220
2016	1,428
2017	1,196

Source: https://www.gov.uk/ guidance/forced-marriage#history

France also has a Forced Marriage Unit. In Germany, a study was conducted in 2011 by the women's rights organization Terre des Femmes and the Hamburg-based Lawaetz Foundation for the Ministry of Family Affairs, senior citizens, women and youth. This study found that in 2008, two counseling centers in Germany reported 3,443 forced marriages.[74] That is within Germany alone. With the large Muslim migration over the last 12 years, this number may have tripled. Family Minister Kristina Schröder said of the study, "it is important to be aware that 'only the brave' actually seek help. Those who are threatened with forced marriage risk being isolated from their own family if they try to resist. The real number of people who are

---

[74] Ripperger, S. (2011, November 10). *Study finds thousands of forced marriages in Germany*. Retrieved February 29, 2020, from DW.com: https://www.dw.com/en/study-finds-thousands-of-forced-marriages-in-germany/a-15522401.

intimidated into marriage is much higher, but it's impossible to accurately quantify the scale of the issue."[75]

In the USA, Dave Gaubatz, a retired Federal Agent with the U.S. Air Force Office of Special Investigations (AFOSI), investigates mosques undercover to discover if they are promoting shariah and Islamic social norms. Dave Gaubatz has written many affidavits on the literature found in mosques in the United States; some called Islamic Centers that support child marriage.

On March 6, 2020 Dave Gaubatz went undercover to the Islamic House of Wisdom mosque in Dearborn Heights, Michigan. Here, "he found literature he says legitimizes child marriage, jihad and Sharia-compliant "temporary" sex marriages."[76]

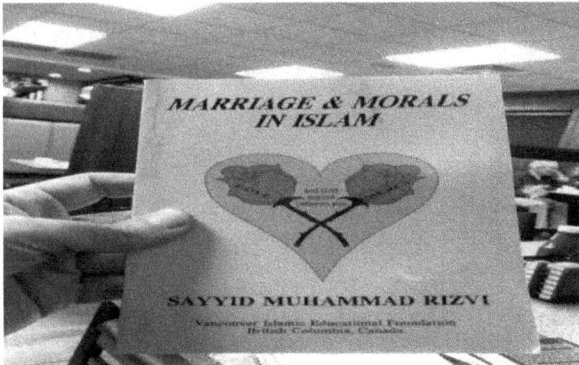

Picture by Leo Hohman

Dave Gaubatz went to a mosque in Nashville, Tennessee in 2012 with one of his female researchers, to conduct firsthand

---

[75] Ibid

[76] Hohman, L. (2020, March 9). *Undercover agent: Michigan mosques promoting child marriage, openly campaigning for Bernie Sanders.* Retrieved June 10, 2020, from LeoHohman.com: https://leohohmann.com/2020/03/09/undercover-agent-michigan-mosques-promoting-child-marriage-openly-campaigning-for-bernie-sanders/.

research at a Somalian Islamic mosque. This is what he discovered:

*Allegedly, a group of Somalians had left MN, and subsequently formed a mosque in Nashville. During the research, I observed numerous books in the mosque library pertaining to the marriage of young girls. In addition, we observed small children being hit with sticks during Sharia classes. During one such sharia class, a young girl began speaking to my female researcher. The girl told my researcher her arms, back, and legs were hurting because Islamic leaders hit the children during classes. Then the young girl, who said she was 7 (seven) years old started talking about what her **HUSBAND** did to her. I immediately informed law enforcement at various levels, senior politicians, and even CAIR requesting assistance to help this innocent child. They all refused, stating it was a religious and culture matter and they could not intervene.*[77]

It took several months to get the state Child Protective Services involved to protect that young girl.

As recently as April 22, 2021 Algeria[78] sentenced Said Djabelkhiran "academic" to 3 years in prison for offending Islam. Said had questioned Islam's social norm in the marrying of pre-pubescent girls and continuing a practice of sacrificing sheep that existed before Islam in Arabia. This shows that the social norm of marrying pre-pubescent girls is not only a social norm, it is not permitted to question it.

---

[77] Ibid

[78] AFP. (2021, April 22). *Algerian academic gets 3 years for 'offending Islam'.* Retrieved April 25, 2021, from Daily Mail: https://www.dailymail.co.uk/wires/afp/article-9499693/Algerian-academic-gets-3-years-offending-Islam.html.

Chapter 12

Is there an Islamic social norm requiring Female Genitalia Mutilation (FGM)?

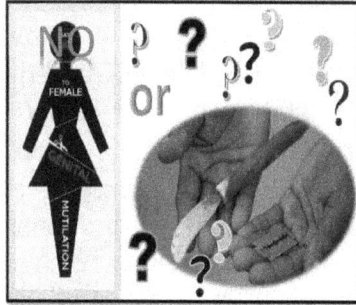

According to Ian Askew, World Health Organization Director for the Department of Reproductive Health and Research:

> *FGM describes all procedures that involve the partial or total removal of external genitalia or other injury to the female genital organs for non-medical reasons. It has no health benefits.*
>
> *More than 200 million girls and women alive today are living with FGM, and many are at risk of suffering the associated negative health consequences as a result.*
>
> *These include death, severe bleeding and problems urinating. Longer-term consequences range from cysts and infections, to complications in childbirth and increased risk of newborn deaths.*
>
> *FGM is a grave violation of the human rights of girls and women.*[79]

---

[79] Askew, I. (2016, May 16). *It's our job as health workers to 'do no harm'*. Retrieved December 11, 2019, from World Health Organization: https://www.who.int/mediacentre/commentaries/fgm-do-no-harm/en/.

Female circumcision is FGM. In some countries, a preferred reference to this horror is called FGC as it is seen as "more neutral." The "C" being a reference to "cutting."[80] This "more neutral" term allows their medical personnel to package FGM into the "birth package."[81]

Ebony Ridell Bamber, the head of advocacy and policy at Orchid Project, a UK-based NGO working towards ending FGM, states that, "It really contributes to legitimizing and entrenching the practice even further."[82]

In Islam, legitimization comes through when Shariah, Islamic law, endorses and promotes a practice. Under Shariah, female circumcision is required of Muslim females. This is documented in <u>Reliance of the Traveller</u> which is *Umdat al Salik*, in English.

> e4.3   Circumcision is obligatory (O: for both men and women. For men, it consists of removing the prepuce from the penis, and for women, removing the prepuce (Ar. Bazr) of the clitoris (n: not the clitoris itself, as some mistakenly assert). (A: Hanbalis hold that circumcision of women is not obligatory, but sunna; while Hanafis consider it a mere courtesy to the husband.)"

I found Islamic scholars using this piece to declare to non-Muslims that shariah does not agree with FGM going so far as to claim it is "un-Islamic" if carried out to the extreme, by totally removing the clitoris. An example follows:

> *Female circumcision, known pejoratively in its extreme form as female genital mutilation or cutting, is not prescribed in the Quran, and there are no authentic prophetic traditions*

---

[80] Wright, L. (2020, February 6). *Why do so many girls still face FGM?* Retrieved February 11, 2020, from DW.com: https://www.dw.com/en/female-genital-mutilation-why-do-so-many-girls-still-face-fgm-a-52265630/a-52265630.

[81] Ibid

[82] Ibid

recommending the practice. The basis in Islamic law is that it is not permissible to cause bodily harm, and any such practice of female circumcision proven to be harmful would be unlawful[83]

This is very deceptive. Let's look at what the abbreviations mean in the above section of shariah:

A: ... comment by Sheikh 'Abd al-Wakil Durubi.
Ar.   Arabic.
n: ... remark by the translator.
O: ... excerpt from the commentary of Sheikh 'Umar Barakat.
Taking the commentary of the translator out, the passage now reads:

> e4.3   Circumcision is obligatory (O: for both men and women. For men, it consists of removing the prepuce from the penis, and for women, removing the prepuce (Ar. Bazr) of the clitoris.

Abu Amima Elias would have us believe that the hadiths that refer to FGM are weak and unreliable. He claims that Sunan Abi Dawud is not authentic, but weak.

لَا تُنْهِكِي فَإِنَّ ذَلِكَ أَحْظَى لِلْمَرْأَةِ وَأَحَبُّ إِلَى الْبَعْلِ

Do not cut severely, as it is better for the woman and more desirable for the husband.

Source: Sunan Abu Dawud 5271, Grade: *Da'eef* (weak)

(Screen pic of https://abuaminaelias.com/islam-female-genital-mutilation/)

But if you actually look up the Hadith for yourself at Sunnah.com, you will find that this was just more deception.

---

[83] Elias, A. A. (2014, April 24). *Does Islam support female genital mutilation (FGM)?* Retrieved December 16, 2019, from Faith in Allah: https://abuaminaelias.com/islam-female-genital-mutilation/.

SUNNAH.COM

Home » Sunan Abi Dawud » Book of General Behavior (Kitab Al-Adab)

Narrated Umm Atiyyah al-Ansariyyah:

A woman used to perform circumcision in Medina. The Prophet (ﷺ) said to her: Do not cut severely as that is better for a woman and more desirable for a husband.

Abu Dawud said: It has been transmitted by 'Ubaid Allah b. 'Amr from 'Abd al-Malik to the same effect through a different chain.

Abu Dawud said: It is not a strong tradition. It has been transmitted in mursal form (missing the link of the Companions)

Abu Dawud said: Muhammad b. Hasan is obscure, and this tradition is weak.

Grade	: **Sahih** (Al-Albani)
Reference	: Sunan Abi Dawud 5271

(Screen pic of https://sunnah.com/abudawud/43/499)

Sahih is the highest claim for hadiths; meaning that, it has been judged to be authentic by a consensus of Islamic scholars).

Many other hadiths also back up the obligation for FGM under Shariah. For example:

- Jami` at-Tirmidhi Vol. 1 Book 1 #109
  Aishah narrated that the Prophet said: "When the circumcised meets the circumcised, then Ghusl is required." (Grade: Sahih)

- Muwatta Malik Book 2, Hadith 73
  Yahya related to me from Malik from Ibn Shihab from Said ibn al- Musayyab that Umar ibn al-Khattab and Uthman ibn Affan and A'isha, the wife of the Prophet, may Allah bless him and grant him peace, used to say, "When the circumcised part touches the circumcised part, ghusl is obligatory."

- Sahih al-Bukhari 6599-6600
  Narrated Abu Huraira: Allah's Messenger said, "No child is born but has the Islamic Faith, but its parents turn it into a Jew or a Christian. It is as you help the animals give birth. Do you find among their offspring a mutilated one before you mutilate them yourself?" The people said, "O Allah's Messenger! What do you think about those (of them) who die young?" The Prophet said, "Allah knows what they would have done (were they to live).

To say that FGM only happens in third-world countries would be ignorant. It ignores the sad and sorry truth that several countries have passed laws forbidding this cruelty to their children. Egypt passed a law stopping FGM in 2008. But by 2015, a "government survey discovered that 87% of Egyptian women and girls aged between 15 and 49 have been mutilated, or as the Egyptian government put it, "circumcised."[84] This information was in the news on January 31, 2020, because a 12-year old school girl was brought to the doctor by her parents to have the illegal butchery done. That little girl is now dead. As a result, the parents have been arrested and charged with crimes related to FGM.

On February 1, 2020, Egyptian Islamic scholar Salama Abd Al-Qawi was interviewed on Elsharq TV talking about FGM. MEMRI caught this and translated it.

> **Interviewer:** "It is said that expert doctors have determined that female circumcision is harmful and that it might even lead to death. One of the goals of *shari'a* law is to keep people out of harm's way. You told me so yourself."
>
> **Salama Abd Al-Qawi:** "Yes of course."

---

[84] Nsubuga, J. (2020, January 31). *Girl, 12, dies after undergoing female genital mutilation in Egypt.* Retrieved February 5, 2020, from Metro News: https://metro.co.uk/2020/01/31/girl-12-dies-undergoing-female-genital-mutilation-egypt-12161820.

Interviewer: "Therefore, every action that threatens this principle is *haram*, according to Egypt's Dar Al-Ifta. As you can see on the screen, they wrote that [female] circumcision can lead to death. I believe that this is the thing that people are most worried about or afraid of."

Salama Abd Al-Qawi: "[Female] circumcision can lead to death? Well, riding the train can also lead to death. Flying in a plane can lead to death. Drinking water can lead to death. Eating eggplant can lead to death."

Interviewer: "How are these relevant?"

Salama Abd Al-Qawi: "They all [can lead to death].
[...] "Who said this?"

Interviewer: "Expert doctors."

Salama Abd Al-Qawi: "Who are these expert doctors? My mother, my sister, my daughter, and my wife [have all gone through this], and so have the mothers, sisters, and wives of those 'expert doctors,' and they did not die from it. According to our customs, and you are a village man like I am... Have we ever heard of a girl who died during circumcision? You are familiar with the village customs. They make a celebration out of it."

Interviewer: "True."

Salama Abd Al-Qawi: "Who has ever died? The expert doctors and the people at Dar Al-Ifta should tell us how many girls have died during circumcision. Tell me another thing. Giving birth can lead to death, right? How many women have died during child birth? Many more than have died during [female] circumcision, by the way... So should women stop giving birth?" [85]

Sadly this fallacious reasoning avoids discussing the dangers and also ignores the topic using the strawman fallacy, and the Big Band fallacy. No medical professional is sought out to refute the doctor's comments. This is a poor display of reasoning, but it seems like the best this Islamic scholar could give. The importance is that this verifies that Muslim Brotherhood stands behind the practice of FGM as this particular TV station is a well-known entity of theirs.

It is interesting to note that a news station ignored that a month earlier, international news carried a story about a 12-year-old dying as a result of FGM. This was done because it did not allow their narrative to have any strength. It negated everything they said!

Perhaps, Salama Abd Al-Qawi needed to actually talk to women who had undergone this mutilation, who described the misery and danger of it. The German news site, DW, ran an article titled "Female genital mutilation feels 'like living in a dead body'" on February 6, 2020. In the article, Shadia Abdelmoneim describes how a midwife performed FGM on her without her consent, after the birth of her third child in Sudan:

It led to a lengthy period of shock thereafter, where she found it difficult to trust anybody, but Shadia also vividly recalls the moment she realized what had happened.

"I wanted to go to the toilet, but something wasn't right. I couldn't walk and was in considerable pain. When I saw what

---

[85] Elsharq TV. (2020, February 1). *Egyptian Islamic Scholar Salama Abd Al-Qawi Defends FGM on Muslim Brotherhood TV: Drinking Water and Eating Eggplants Can Also Lead to Death*. Retrieved February 10, 2020, from Middle East Media Research Institute: https://www.memri.org/tv/egyptian-islamic-scholar-salama-qawi-defends-fgm-air-travel-drinking-water-eggplants-birth-also-lead-death.

she had done, I was shocked. She'd cut everything open and then sewn it closed. I had no idea what to do."

Shadia, already fighting against female genital mutilation and for women's rights as an activist in Sudan, was in her mid-30's at the time. She started living in a constant state of fear for her three daughters; she could barely let them out of her sight.

"How could women do something like that to one another, how?" she asked, her eyes welling up with tears. "Being circumcised is like living in a dead body."[86]

Dr. Cornelia Strunz, who works at the Desert Flower Center met Shadia when she came to the center for help, said Shadia needed surgery to help her live with this mutilation.
According to Dr. Strunz, there are many possible problems that result from FGM.

Many women have problems emptying their bladder after FGM. Menstrual blood can't drain properly. For some, sex becomes practically impossible. Women can also develop fistulas — connections between two body parts which should not exist at all in normal circumstances. One example would be a link between the vagina and rectum, leading to them passing stools through the vagina. Obviously, that's not very easy to live with.

As a social norm, FGM conflicts with several social norms of Western civilization. It denies a woman's rights to have control over her own body, as it is a requirement under Shariah. It destroys a woman's ability to enjoy partaking in sexual activity when the woman marries. This makes the act a duty and not a pleasure. The act itself violates the medical Hippocratic Oath "to do no harm." In countries where FGM is banned, parents/guardians who have

---

[86] Grundmann, M. (2020, February 6). *Female genital mutilation feels 'like living in a dead body'*. Retrieved February 11, 2020, from DW.com: https://www.dw.com/en/female-genital-mutilation-feels-like-living-in-a-dead-body/a-52269987.

this done to their own daughters are denying the validity of laws made by men, lifting up Allah's law as superior-Shariah.

Chapter 13

Is it an Islamic social norm that non-Muslim women are sexual prey for any Muslim man?

Since 2015, numerous events have unfolded where Muslim men have been caught sexually assaulting women in Europe, and then expressing shock that what they did is in any way wrong. This has been going on much longer in Europe than once thought. The UK news sources have reported rape gangs; something they call, "grooming gangs." Reports of these gangs being active go back as far back as the 1970s.[87] Denis MacEoin of Gatestone Institute, writes, "Britain's Attorney General stated in the House of Lords that 27 police forces were then investigating no fewer than 54 alleged gangs involved in child sexual grooming."[88] These "rape gangs" were Muslim and the vast majority are migrants or second generation immigrants from Pakistan. In the European news, these men are never identified as Muslim nor are they identified as being

---

[87] Sommerlad, N., & McKelvie, G. (2018, March 12). *Britain's 'worst ever' child grooming scandal exposed: Hundreds of young girls raped, beaten, sold for sex and some even KILLE.* Retrieved March 21, 2020, from The MIrror: https://www.mirror.co.uk/news/uk-news/britains-worst-ever-child-grooming-12165527.

[88] MacEoin, D. (2018, December 20). *Britain's Grooming Gangs: Part 1.* Retrieved March 17, 2020, from Gatestone Institute: https://www.gatestoneinstitute.org/13075/britain-grooming-gangs.

from Pakistan. It is their names that identify them as Muslim. Sources report the vast majority of these villains are from Pakistan. A common feature of these rape gangs is men telling their victims that the Quran justifies their actions.

Despite the truth of the information above, major British news sources like the one by Faima Baka on April 2, 2020 in The Metro titled, "The majority of sexual offenders are white men – there is no 'Muslim problem' with sexual grooming." The title is enough to fool some, but anyone old enough to understand how race is defined, would know that the vast majority of men from Pakistan are classified racially as whites. Ms. Baka goes as far as to make the claim that "There is nothing inherently about Islam that promotes this kind of behavior."[89] Is that true? Ms. Baka never examines if it is true. She just makes the claim. So, what is the truth here?

One of the survivors of one of the Rotherham, UK RAPE gang had this to say:

As a teenager, I was taken to various houses and flats above takeaways in the north of England, to be beaten, tortured and raped over 100 times. I was called a "white slag" and "white c***" as they beat me.

They made it clear that because I was a non-Muslim, and not a virgin, and because I didn't dress "modestly", that they believed I deserved to be "punished". They said I had to "obey" or be beaten.[90]

---

[89] Baka, F. (2020, April 2). *The majority of sexual offenders are white men – there is no 'Muslim problem' with sexual groomin.* Retrieved April 8, 2020, from The Metro: https://metro.co.uk/2020/04/02/majority-sexual-offenders-white-men-no-muslim-problem-sexual-grooming-12451053/.

[90] Hill, E. (2018, March 18). *As a Rotherham grooming gang survivor, I want people to know about the religious extremism which inspired my abusers.* Retrieved March 21, 2020, from The Independent: https://www.independent.co.uk/voices/rotherham-grooming-gang-

Where did this belief come from? Muhammad took sex slaves as part of the "booty" of jihad. The Quran refers to sex slaves by calling them "those whom your right hand possesses." Muhammad had no problem with captive women being raped.

Abu Sirma said to Abu Sa'id al Khadri (Allah he pleased with him):

0 Abu Sa'id, did you hear Allah's Messenger mentioning al-'azl? He said: Yes, and added: We went out with Allah's Messenger on the expedition to the Bi'l-Mustaliq and took captive some excellent Arab women; and we desired them, for we were suffering from the absence of our wives, (but at the same time) we also desired ransom for them. So we decided to have sexual intercourse with them but by observing 'azl (Withdrawing the male sexual organ before emission of semen to avoid-conception). But we said: We are doing an act whereas Allah's Messenger is amongst us; why not ask him? So we asked Allah's Messenger, and he said: It does not matter if you do not do it, for every soul that is to be born up to the Day of Resurrection will be born. (Sahih Muslim Book 8, Hadith 3371)

It must be asked if Muslims in general view themselves as being at war with their non-Muslim "host countries". If the answer is yes, then they feel they have a legitimate right to take slaves and a right to force them to have sex. Keep in mind that Muslims believe the world is divided into Dar al-Islam (Land of Submission to Allah) and Dar al-Harb (Land of Constant Warfare). Only Muslim countries ruled by shariah qualify as Dar al-Islam. If Muslim men believe they are at war with those within the non-Muslim countries that they have come to live in as immigrants, it means that they view their migration as a military exercise of war. This means that they view their travel to the country they are in as

sexual-abuse-muslim-islamist-racism-white-girls-religious-extremism-a8261831.html.

a hijrah before jihad. The Qur'an justifies this position as stated previously in Chapter 1 on the Hijrah:

- Surah 2:218 *"Surely those who believed and those who emigrated and performed jihad."*
- Surah 8:72 *"Surely those who believed and those who emigrated and performed jihad with their money and their lives for the sake of Allah, and those who gave asylum..."*

If this is true for Muslims entering a Non-Muslim country, isn't that reason enough for the country to deport many of them for the safety of the people of that country?

Even if the answer is no, that they do not believe they are at war with those in the non-Muslim countries, we must first ask if they are practicing taqiyya. But for the sake of learning and expanding on that knowledge, it must be asked if there are other Islamic reasons that would justify the sexual abuse of non-Muslim women happening today.

The very same verse that tells Muslim women to dress modestly and wear head coverings such as the hijab, also tells Muslim men that women who do not dress with a hijab are there for the taking. This verse, Qur'an 33:59 was cited earlier in the chapter on hijabs.

> *O Prophet, tell your wives and your daughters and the women of the believers to bring down over themselves [part] of their outer garments. That is more suitable that they will be known and not be abused. And ever is Allah Forgiving and Merciful.*

This verse states that the reason women must wear hijabs is so they will not be sexually assaulted. Under this reasoning, a Muslim man who goes to a non-Muslim country may do so with the belief that he may sexually assault any woman who is not covered. It is in his religious book. It does not matter if he then views his host country as being at war with Islam. He sees the women as provided by Allah to meet his sexual desires.

The concept of Muslim men feeling justified in raping non-Muslim women is not unique to the UK. In 2013, Raymond Ibrahim wrote of a rape of two Egyptian Coptic Christian girls who were videoed being gang raped on a crowded street in broad daylight! No one helped the girls! Not one person!

> *Throughout, the women scream in terror while the men shout "Allahu Akbar," that is, "Allah is Great," as well as chant the shehada, or Islamic profession of faith: la ilaha illa Allah ("There is no god but Allah and Muhammad is the prophet of Allah"). None of the many passersby intervene in any way.*[91]

The fact that Muslim men seem to justify raping non-Muslim women in accordance to their religion is evident in their cries of "Allahu Akbar" (Allah is greater).

January 1, 2016 Cologne, Germany is perhaps the most horrific single night of evidence of this belief amongst Muslim Migrants to Europe. On this night, 1,500+ Muslim migrant men gathered separating German men from their women and daughters, forcing the girls in the center of their circles while the men were kept outside. One thousand two hundred women were sexually assaulted, some were repeatedly raped.[92]

If only this one night were all that existed to prove the point that Muslim men feel justified in sexually assaulting non-Muslim women, the research for this chapter would not have been teeming with examples of Muslims sexually assaulting, or threatening to rape, or raping non-Muslim women. There are far too many

---

[91] Ibrahim, R. (2013, April 11). *Video: Christian Girls Gang Raped to Screams of "Allahu Akbar" in Egypt.* Retrieved March 21, 2020, from RaymondIbrahim.com: https://www.raymondibrahim.com/2013/04/11/video-christian-girls-gang-raped-to-screams-of-allahu-akbar-in-egypt.

[92] BBC News. (2016, January 5). *Germany shocked by Cologne New Year gang assaults on women.* Retrieved March 21, 2020, from BBC News: https://www.bbc.com/news/world-europe-35231046.

examples for me to cite them all in a small chapter. The following are only a few stories.

During the early days of ISIS' conquests in Syria and Iraq, Salafi Sheikh Yasir al-'Ajlawni, a Jordanian of origin who earlier lived in Damascus, Syria for 17 years, posted a YouTube video where he said he was preparing to issue a "legitimate fatwa", making it legal (in the eyes of Islam) for those Muslims fighting to topple secular president Bashar Assad and install Sharia law to "capture and have sex with" all non-Sunni women, specifically naming Assad's own sect, the Alawites, as well as the Druze and several others; in short, all non-Sunnis and non-Muslims.

In Pakistan, in 2016, three Christian girls were walking together on their way home from work. A car with Muslim men who were said to be drunk pulled up. The following is their story:

Kiran (17 years), Shamroza (18 years) and Sumble (20 years) three Christian girls were simply walking home through Defence Colony after a hard day's work as beauticians, on their way to their deprived Christian community in Baowala.

They had set off at 9pm on 13th January, with intention to get home quickly before it got too unsafe so they could get some rest before returning to work the following morning. On this fateful night however, they were accosted by four allegedly drunk Muslims in a maroon car, who started to misbehave with them.

The intoxicated men shouted suggestive and lewd comments at them and were harassing them to get into the car with them for 'a ride and some fun'.

The three girls explained that they were devout Christians and did not practice sex outside of marriage and bravely scolded the young men for their untoward advances. This caused an immediate change in the demeanor of the boys who became more aggressive and started to threaten the girls to enter the car or to be physically forced in.

Terrified of the increasingly dangerous situation they were in, the girls started to run in a fit of panic. This only enraged the young Muslim men further, one of them shouted out at the girls, he said:

"How dare you run away from us, Christian girls are only meant for one thing the pleasure of Muslim men."[93]

These men then ran their car into the girls−, killing one of them and severely injuring the others.

This belief expressed by Muslim males in Pakistan is not new. In February 2013, *Fides*, a Vatican created news agency reported that they had been told that an average of 700 girls are kidnapped and sexually assaulted every year in Pakistan.[94] In this same article, NGO Legal Evangelical Association Development (LEAD) is quoted as having said, "Christian girls are doubly discriminated against and often treated 'as goods.'"

Raymond Ibrahim[95], noted the treatment of women as goods is backed up by Majid Khadduri, who "was internationally recognized as one of the world's leading authorities on Islamic law

---

[93] Chowdhry, J. (2016, January 20). *Christian girl killed for shrugging off advances of wealthy Muslim boys.* Retrieved March 21, 2020, from British Pakistani Christians.org:
https://www.britishpakistanichristians.org/blog/christian-girl-killed-for-shrugging-off-advances-of-rich-muslim-boys.

[94] Agenzia Fides. (2013, February 4). *ASIA/PAKISTAN - Christian minor raped and tortured by Muslims.* Retrieved March 24, 2020, from Fides:
http://www.fides.org/en/news/33195-ASIA_PAKISTAN_Christian_minor_raped_and_tortured_by_Muslims.

[95] Ibrahim, R. (2013, November 8). *The Rape and Murder of Pakistan's Christian Children.* Retrieved March 24, 2020, from RAymond Ibrahim:
https://www.raymondibrahim.com/2012/11/08/the-rape-and-murder-of-pakistans-christian-children-2.

and jurisprudence, Islam, modern Arab and Iraqi history, and politics and personalities of the Middle East."[96] Khadduri wrote in his book War and Peace in the Law of Islam:

> *The term spoil (ghanima) is applied specifically to property acquired by force from non-Muslims. It includes, however, not only property (movable and immovable) but also persons, whether in the capacity of asra (prisoners of war) or sabi (women and children). The element of force ('anwatan) and the imam's permission are essential prerequisites, since property taken by force would be regarded as fay', and if the imam's permission were lacking the possessed property, whether taken by one or a group of jihadists, it would be regarded as theft, not spoil. The imam's permission formalizes fighting as the fulfillment of the jihad duty and invokes the law governing the conduct of fighting as well as the acquisition and the division of the spoil among those who have a right to it...*[97]

> *If the slave were a woman, the master was permitted to have sexual connection with her as a concubine.*[98]

Basically, Muslim males in Pakistan believe they are at war with the non-Muslims in their community and because of that belief, they have a right to take possession of the women and use them as they desire. This belief MUST have been stated in their mosques by their Imams. This is not a new expression of belief! This leads to the question, what are they preaching in mosques in

---

[96] Klubes, F. N. (2007, February 5). *Obituary: Majid Khadduri, Founder of SAIS Middle East Studies Program, Dies.* Retrieved March 24, 2020, from John Hopkins University:
https://pages.jh.edu/~gazette/2007/05feb07/05obit.html.

[97] Khadduri, M. (2006). *War and Peace in the Law of Islam.* Clark, NJ: The Lawbook Exchange, Ltd., p. 119.

[98] Ibid, p. 131.

Europe? Is it any different? The implication here is that Muslims in Europe are being given the same message!

In 2017, six Muslim Migrants from Tunisia kidnapped a woman from Belgian living in Italy.[99] They kept her as a sex slave for two months. Then they decided to turn her into a prostitute and earn money from their sex slave. She only got free because they set her free for some reason.

A Muslim taxi driver in the UK threatened to rape Muslim women who converted to Christianity in December of 2018.[100]

One Muslim migrant Islamic cleric living in Australia put out a video on April 20, 2018 on the topic of a Muslim man's sexual rights and of a woman's obligation to dress modestly. MEMRI caught Nassim Abdi sermons on women dressing immodestly. He did place blame on the husbands, brothers and fathers for allowing their women to dress in a Western manner, not wearing hijabs. He also blamed women who dress immodestly for men committing acts of fornication because they tempt the men.

Due to their lack of wisdom, and knowledge, and perfection in legislation, they allow the woman to dress in a promiscuous manner. We're not justifying anyone to commit any act of sexual assault or sexual harassment or sexual abuse. We're not justifying it. No, if I don't like something, I cover it up. If I don't want you to rob my house, I don't leave my front door open. If I don't want you to go into my bag, I don't open my bag and walk around in the open room with my bag open, as

[99] 7 Sur7. (2019, January 17). *L'horreur pour une Belge en Italie, enlevée par six hommes et violée pendant deux mois.* Retrieved March 21, 2020, from 7Sur7.be: https://www.7sur7.be/monde/l-horreur-pour-une-belge-en-italie-enlevee-par-six-hommes-et-violee-pendant-deux-mois~acc93364.

[100] Baron, O., & Gibbons, B. (2019, September 18). *Taxi driver escapes punishment over vile video threatening to rape Christians who converted from Islam.* Retrieved from Birminham Live: https://www.birminghammail.co.uk/news/midlands-news/taxi-driver-escapes-punishment-over-16939646.

if to say, "Look what's inside." I close my bag and I put it next to me. **If you don't want a person to invade your privacy sexually, you don't put yourself out there.** *Biologically, this is basic science. This is not religion. Basic science, basic make-up of human beings.*[101]

In December of 2018, in Germany, eight Muslim men raped an 18-year-old woman.[102]

In 2019, Oulo, Finland, announced that it would ban migrants from visiting child care facilities and schools because a parent complained about the integration visits made them "feel anxious about their children after the recent attentional wave of rape against young girls."[103]

News articles around the world show Muslim males expressing a right to sexually exploit non-Muslim women. Some have even expressed confusion when told what they have done is wrong. The truly sad element here is that political correctness allows law enforcement and political leaders to ignore this social norm and destroy the safety of women everywhere in the western world.

---

[101] Abdi, N. (2018, April 20). *Australian Cleric Nassim Abdi: Women Shouldn't Put Themselves Out There If They Don't Want Their Privacy Invaded Sexually.* Retrieved March 21, 2020, from MEMRI: https://www.memri.org/tv/australian-cleric-nassim-abdi-women-should-not-put-themselves-out-there.

[102] Kronen Zeitung. (2018, October 26). *Group rape before disco: 8 perpetrators in custody.* Retrieved March 21, 2020, from Kronen Zeitung: https://www.krone.at/1797029.

[103] Kristoffersson, S. (2019, February 6). *Finnish municipality prohibits migrants in kindergartens and schools after rape scales.* Retrieved March 21, 2020, from Samhallsnyt: https://samnytt.se/finsk-kommun-forbjuder-migranter-pa-dagis-och-skolor-efter-valdtaktsvag.

Chapter 14

Is Temporary marriage an Islamic Social norm?

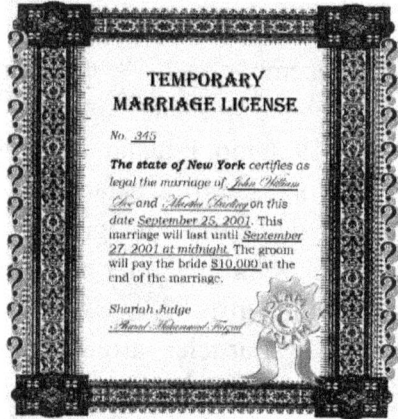

TEMPORARY MARRIAGE LICENSE

No. _345_

The state of New York certifies as legal the marriage of _John Wilson_ _Doe_ and _Martha Smith_ on this date _September 25, 2001_. This marriage will last until _September 27, 2001 at midnight_. The groom will pay the bride $10,000 at the end of the marriage.

Shariah Judge
Harad Mohammad Farzad

This section was originally not going to be included because of the claim that this was not a true social norm for Islam, and that only Shi'ites practiced this belief. After researching the topic more thoroughly, Mut'ah was kept because of the Sunni usage of temporary marriages for jihadis in Iraq and Syria.

The concept of a temporary marriage is something foreign to the Western world. Marriage in the Western civilized world is supposed to be "till death do you part." In Islam, temporary marriage is referred to as Nikah Mut'ah.

Mut'ah or Mutaa marriages were somewhat normal during Muhammad's day. They are marriages that have an end date. Some even have a time. In Shi'a (Shi'ite) Islam, Mut'ah marriages are normal.

The concept of a temporary marriage is based on the Quran 4:24 and 5:27.

And [also prohibited to you are all] married women except those your right hands possess. [This is] the decree of Allah upon you. And lawful to you are [all others] beyond these, [provided] that you seek them [in marriage] with [gifts from] your property, desiring chastity, not unlawful sexual intercourse. So for whatever you enjoy [of marriage] from them, give them their due compensation as an obligation. And there is no blame upon you for what you mutually agree to beyond the obligation. Indeed, Allah is ever Knowing and Wise.

O you who have believed, do not prohibit the good things which Allah has made lawful to you and do not transgress. Indeed, Allah does not like transgressors.

The last verse is further explained in the Hadith Sahih Bukhari, Vol. 1, Book 60, #139:

Narrated Abdullah:
*We used to participate in the holy wars carried on by the Prophet and we had no women (wives) with us. So we said (to the Prophet). "Shall we castrate ourselves?" But the Prophet forbade us to do that, and **thenceforth he allowed us to marry a woman (temporarily) by giving her even a garment,** and then he recited: "O you who believe! Do not make unlawful the good things which Allah has made lawful for you."*

Muhammad and his men were waging jihad. They had been forbidden to have sex outside of marriage and from masturbation. The men were so consumed with lust that Muhammad gave a revelation allowing them to engage in mut'ah.

This revelation of Muhammad for mut'ah was recognized and acknowledged as still current by Sunni scholars during ISIS' beginning conquests. Islamic scholars issued fatwas giving the mujahdeen (fighters/jihadis) the right to rape women. One of these Islamic scholars, "Muhammed al-Arifi issued a fatwa that allows jihadi fighters to rape Syrian women."[104] This fatwa was shared with the world by Lebanon's Al Jadeed TV. Al-Arifi allowed the jihadis to engage in "intercourse marriage" that lasts for a few hours 'in order to give each fighter a turn.'"[105]

What al-Arifi said to the women living there - including the Muslim women - was a little more horrifying. This statement is addressed to all women living in Syria.

It is the women's duty to acquiesce in this arrangement in order to reach paradise because it "boosts the determination of the Mujahideen in Syria" as long they are at least 14 years old, widowed, or divorced.

It is important to recognize that this fatwa recognizes an allowance for temporary marriages, while allowing and ordering the legality of rape.

Both Sunni and Shi'ah Muslims accept the Quran's verses where Muhammad endorsed Mut'ah (temporary marriage).

Mut'ah was something the third Caliph, Umar, was against. He ordered the practice to be stopped. Shi'ites today consider his ruling against the wishes of their prophet, Muhammad.

Most Sunnis today consider Mut'ah marriages unacceptable. A few Sunni Imams like Mufti Abu Layth, make exceptions and allow it under certain circumstances.[106] Mufti Layth would allow it in Western Civilization to allow men and women to date and see if they are "compatible sexually." He would not allow it to equate to prostitution. Regardless of that, he still states that the man needs to pay when the contract is up.

Most non-Muslims, upon hearing of Mut'ah (temporary marriage) and of a payment when done deal, equate mut'ah with

Emerson, S. (2013, January 10). *Fatwa Permits Rape of Syrian Women.* Retrieved March 19, 2020, from Newsmax: https://www.newsmax.com/Emerson/fatwa-rape-Syrian-women/2013/01/10/id/470865.

[105] Ibid

[106] Layth, A. (2019, November 11). *Thoughts on Mutah Marriages.* Retrieved March 12, 2020, from YouTube: https://www.youtube.com/watch?v=NxDu8BU5Mal.

prostitution. When reading the hadiths, this is not far off. Sahih Muslim, Book 16, has passages for and against Mut'ah.

Jabir b. 'Abdullah and Salama b. al-Akwa' said:
There came to us the proclaimer of Allah's Messenger and said: Allah's Messenger has granted you permission to benefit yourselves, i.e., to contract temporary marriage with women. (Sahih Muslim 1405a)

Salama b. al. Akwa' and Jabir b. Abdullah reported:
Allah's Messenger came to us and permitted us to contract temporary marriage. (Sahih Muslim 1405b)

Ibn Uraij reported:
'Ati' reported that jibir b. Abdullah came to perform 'Umra, and we came to his abode, and the people asked him about different things, and then they made a mention of temporary marriage, whereupon he said: Yes, we had been benefiting ourselves by this temporary marriage during the lifetime of the Prophet and during the time of Abu Bakr and 'Umar. (Sahih Muslim 1405c)

Jabir b. 'Abdullah reported:
We contracted temporary marriage, giving a handful of tales or flour as a dower during the lifetime of Allah's Messenger and during the time of Abu Bakr until 'Umar forbade it in the case of 'Amr b. Huraith. (Sahih Muslim 1405d)

Abu Nadra reported:
While I was in the company of Jabir b. Abdullah, a person came to him and said that Ibn 'Abbas and Ibn Zubair differed on the two types of Mut'as (Tamattu' of Hajj 1846 and Tamattu' with women), whereupon Jabir said: We used to do these two during the lifetime of Allah's Messenger. Umar then forbade us to do them, and so we did not revert to them. (Sahih Muslim 1405e)

These verses indicate that Caliphs can abrogate, make haram (forbidden), what their prophet Muhammad allowed. This is contrary to the rules on abrogation though; because abrogation is not a power granted to caliphs. Only Muhammad who had this power through his pronouncements of Allah's words and will that were written into the Qur'an can abrogate. Interestingly, some Sunni scholars understand this and make the claim that Muhammad himself abrogated Mut'ah. Sunnis use Surah 23:1-6 to make this claim.

Certainly will the believers have succeeded: ²They, who are during their prayer humbly submissive ³And they who turn away from ill speech ⁴And they who are observant of zakah ⁵And they who guard their private parts ⁶Except from their wives or those their right hands possess, for indeed, they will not be blamed.

For abrogation to work, verses that come later must negate or change verses that were given earlier. The problem here is that chapter 23 is a Meccan verse given later than chapter 5 but earlier than chapter 4.

While some Sunnis may claim that Mut'ah was abrogated, it is important to acknowledge that the Wahabi sect of Islam, the very sect practiced and promoted by Saudi Arabia and in general, by most of Islam in the Western world, has another form of marriage that is temporary – nikah al-misyar. This is a "traveler's marriage." Arab News published an article on this June 5, 2005. The article makes clear that this is a temporary marriage. It even quotes some men on the topic.

The reasons men gave for favoring misyar most often related to cost, with some asking "why not?" "I get to maintain all my rights, but I don't have to take care of her financially and don't even have to provide a house for her," said 25-year-old Rayan Abdullah, an unmarried medical student at the city university. "It's a great solution — isn't it? It costs less than having a girlfriend — doesn't it?" Or is it a male convenience in a male-dominated culture?

"What are the things most of us married men complain about?" asked Ghazi Ahmad, a 38-year-old husband and father of three children. "Don't all of us constantly complain about the financial burdens, the lack of personal freedom — the routine patterns? Then this is the best marriage ever as far as I'm concerned. Married but not married — perfect."[107]

Therefore, to say that temporary marriage is only a Shi'ite practice is wrong. What does this social norm bring to western culture? If not a belief that women can be used for pleasure as long as you pay them and agree at a price to be paid. Is this a social norm you want brought into your neighborhood? Would you be ok with your daughter being contracted into such a marriage? Would you be ok with a son-in-law contracting a temporary marriage while on a business trip?

---

[107] Jabarti, S. (2005, June 5). *Misyar Marriage -- A Marvel or Misery?* Retrieved March 31, 2020, from Arab News: https://web.archive.org/web/20060526024058/http://www.arabnews.com/?page=9&section=0&article=64891.

Chapter 15

Is there a social norm in Islam that gives a husband the right to beat his wife?

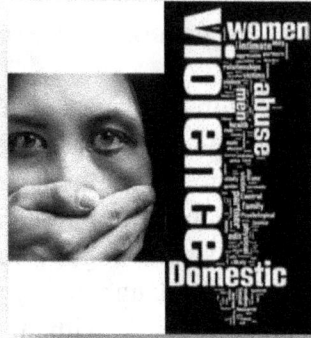

In America and the rest of Western civilization, it is not unusual for women to submit to their husbands. This is part of the Judeo-Christian social norm. It is written into wedding rituals. But there is no expectation that a woman must submit to having her husband beat her. In fact, this abuse is a reason for divorce under the Judeo-Christian social norm. In the USA and many Western countries, such abuse is now cause for criminal complaints and possibly, jail time. Across the United States, law enforcement is now required to make an arrest when they believe they have a person who has been physically abused by a spouse.

Good Muslims have a desire to imitate their prophet Muhammad. What was his stand on wife-beating? In the At-Tafsir Al Kabir, a commentary on the Quran, it states:

"A woman complained to Muhammad that her husband slapped her on the face, (which was still marked by the slap). At first the prophet said to her: "Get even with him", but then added: "Wait until I think about it". Later on, Allah supposedly revealed 4:34 to Muhammad, after which the prophet said:

"We wanted one thing but Allah wanted another, and what Allah wanted is best". [To beat your wife is best.][108]

Quran 4:34 follows:

*Men are in charge of women by [right of] what Allah has given one over the other and what they spend [for maintenance] from their wealth. So, righteous women are devoutly obedient, guarding in [the husband's] absence what Allah would have them guard. But those [wives] from whom you fear arrogance - **[first] advise them; [then if they persist], forsake them in bed; and [finally], strike them.** But if they obey you [once more], seek no means against them. Indeed, Allah is ever Exalted and Grand.*

Muhammad listened to this woman's complaint and then told his men it was permissible to strike your wives if you follow these steps. But was that all Muhammad said on beating your wives?

According to a Hadith given by Muhammad's wife, Aisha, who is considered the "Mother of the believers:"

*Narrated Ikrima: 'Rifaa divorced his wife whereupon Abdur-Rahman married her. **Aisha said that the lady came wearing a green veil and complained to her (Aisha) and showed her a green spot on her skin caused by beating. It was the habit of ladies to support each other, so when Allah's messenger came, Aisha said, "I have not seen any woman suffering as much as the believing women. Look! Her skin is greener than her clothes!** When Abdur-Rahman heard that his wife had gone to the prophet, he came with his two sons from another wife. She said, "By Allah! I have done no wrong to him, but he is impotent and is as useless to me as this," holding and showing the fringe of her garment. Abdur-Rahman said, "By Allah, O Allah's messenger! She has told a lie. I am very strong and can satisfy her, but she is disobedient and wants to go back to Rifaa." Allah's messenger said to her, "If that is*

---

[108] On Sura 4:34.

your intention, then know that it is unlawful for you to remarry Rifaa unless Abdur-Rahman has had sexual intercourse with you." The prophet saw two boys with Abdur-Rahman and asked (him), "Are these your sons?" On that, Abdur-Rahman said, "Yes." The prophet said, "You claim what you claim (that he is impotent)? But by Allah, these boys resemble him as a crow resembles a crow." (Hadith, Bukhari, Vol. 7, # 715)

Muhammad here simply dismissed what his wife said about how beaten the woman was. He simply accepted the husband's word over the woman's. But that is normal in an Islamic court where a woman's word is only worth half that of a man.

Muhammad stood in consolidation with those who beat their wives. According to the hadith in Sunan Abi Dawud:

"The Prophet said: A man will not be asked as to why he beat his wife (Book 11, Hadith 2142)." This should come as no surprise since, since the hadiths record that Muhammad even beat his own wife Aisha.

...I, however, preceded him and I entered (the house), and as I lay down in the bed, he (the Holy Prophet) entered the (house), and said: Why is it, O 'A'isha, that you are out of breath?

I said: There is nothing.

He said: Tell me or the Subtle and the Aware would inform me.

I said: Messenger of Allah, may my father and mother be ransom for you, and then I told him (the whole story).

He said: Was it the darkness (of your shadow) that I saw in front of me?

I said: Yes.

He struck me on the chest which caused me pain, and then said: Did you think that Allah and His Apostle would deal unjustly with you? (Muslim, Book 004, Number 2127)

It is not just in Islamic scriptures, Imams and Muslim leaders publicly talk about the right way to beat your wives. In Detroit, Imam Bassem Al-Sheraa was a class at the Az-Zahraa Islamic Center where he taught "wife-beating serves to remind her that she misbehaved." This video was uploaded to the mosque's YouTube channel on May 19, 2019.

"The Quranic verse that people cite in order to attack Islam, claiming that Islam permits wife-beating... Who says that 'beat them' means that the beating should cause pain? The Prophet Muhammad explained this Quranic verse. He said that 'beat them' means beating them with a sewak. A sewak is a twig one uses to clean one's teeth...That's the sewak. The beating is not meant to cause pain. According to Islamic jurisprudence, if you beat [your wife] and any part of her body becomes red, you have to pay compensation.

"What kind of beating does not cause pain? *[The Prophet] said that the beating is meant to remind her that she has misbehaved in cases when words [of admonishment] do not make her change her ways. First, the husband follows 'forsake them in bed.' He turns his back to her. But what if she says: 'I'm better off [like this]. I don't want to see your face. Turn around'? He can snub her, refuse to talk to her... But what if she says: 'I don't care'? Admonishing her doesn't help either. It is just like when your child reaches to touch the electrical socket or a fire...* ***What do you do? You go like that! It is just like when your child picks up something dangerous and is about to eat it...You hit his hand like that as a reminder. This is a reminder and a means of clarification. This is what the 'beating' means."***

In Morocco, a Muslim country, wife-beating became an unexpected topic. The show received a brief suspension from broadcasting as a result.

"Whoever doesn't beat his wife is not a man," popular singer Adil El Miloudi said in June on a Chada TV show, Kotbi Tonight, drawing laughter from a fellow guest, actor Samy Naceri, and host Imad Kotbi.

"In Morocco, this is normal, anyone can do what he wants with his wife, hit her, kill her," he insisted after Kotbi jokingly said: "It's forbidden to hit one's wife all over the world."[109]

Palestinian Authority TV broadcast a discussion on wife-beating on November 24, 2016 with Cleric Dr. Sameeh Hajaj as the Islamic authority on the matter. Dr. Hajaj discussed an overly abusive case and why it did not comply with Islamic law first, before explaining what is allowed when beating your wife. MEMRI transcribed this discussion into English.

Sameeh Hajaj: *"On the issue of [wife] beating – let me start by relating a story pointing to the Quranic verse: 'As for those women on whose part you fear rebellion – admonish them, refuse to share their beds, and beat them.' A young man's wife was angry with him, so she went to stay with her parents. Various people intervened to get her to return home. Finally, they succeeded. Now, this man wanted to take vengeance upon his wife, so he locked her in the bathroom. She was a woman from a respected family, yet he locked her in the bathroom for 25 days. In the morning, he would bring her a pita bread, a plate of red peppers, and some beatings with a hose. In the evening, he would bring her a plate of red peppers, a pita bread, and some beatings with a hose. This went on for 25 days. On the 25th day, he forgot the bathroom door unlocked,*

---

[109] Tribune.pk. (2019, September 18). *Morocco TV show censured for guest's boast of 'beating wife'*. Retrieved April 13, 2020, from Tribune.pk: https://tribune.com.pk/story/2059551/3-morocco-tv-show-censured-guests-boast-beating-wife.

and the woman fled to her parents' home. 'Why did you do this?' they asked, and he responded: 'Haven't you read the Quran? It is God who said: "As for those women on whose part you fear rebellion-- admonish them, refuse to share their beds, and beat them.'"

Host: *"He took only the part about 'and beat them,' ignoring the beginning of the verse."*

Sameeh Hajaj: *"Well said. It should be a gradual process. Even if he had followed the gradual process, he shouldn't have beaten her like that. With regard to admonishing, let's assume that the husband feels that his wife is lying. At first, he should admonish her, citing verses and hadiths to impress upon her the prohibition against lying. If the admonishing does not help, he should leave the conjugal bed. It means that they should sleep in separate beds, not separate rooms – in order to avoid letting the children sense that there is tension between the man and his wife."*

Host: *"This might affect them psychologically."*

Sameeh Hajaj: *"That's right. The third stage... if admonishing and leaving the bed did not help, we reach the third means, which is beating."*

Host: *"How should this means be used?"*

Sameeh Hajaj: *"Well asked. The Islamic scholars said that the beatings should be carried out either with a miswak dental twig or with a kerchief. There should be no more than 10 blows."*

Host: *"One should not use a rod or a hose."*

Sameeh Hajaj: *"No, and it is forbidden to hit the face. When we use a kerchief or a miswak for the beatings... The Prophet Muhammad said: 'Do not hit her in the face, and do not make* *her ugly.' **If you want to beat her, beat her on the leg, on the back, on places where it doesn't leave a permanent mark.***"*

[...]

"According to our understanding of Islam, the beating is intended solely to convey a message to the wife: 'I'm angry with you. Period! End of story!'"[110]

Note that the Islamic scholars are talking about the use of a toothbrush when beating your wife, but they count the beatings in "blows." This description is a lot harsher than a light tap with a toothbrush.

If you think that most of the Muslims who come to Western countries leave wife-beating behind, you would be surprised at what UK OFSTED school inspectors found on the book shelves in an Islamic school in their country in 2017.

The book Women Who Deserve To Go To Hell, by Mansoor Abdul Hakim, preaches that women should not "show ingratitude to their husbands" or "have tall ambitions".

And those who "grumble," "adorn themselves" or "ape men, get tattoos or cut their hair short" will be punished.

Other books spotted in school libraries insist that in a Muslim marriage, "the wife is not allowed to refuse sex to her husband" or "leave the house where she lives without his permission."

---

[110] Palestinian Authority TV. 2016. "Palestinian Cleric Sameeh Hajaj Explains Wife-Beating in Islam: Not on the Face, No More than 10 Blows, Avoid Permanent Marks." *MEMRI*. November 24. Accessed April 13, 2020. https://www.memri.org/tv/palestinian-cleric-sameeh-hajaj-explains-wife-beating-islam-not-face-no-more-10-blows-avoid.

Kids were taught, "the man by way of correction can also beat her".[111]

This does make one wonder if similar books would be found on the bookshelves of Islamic schools in every non-Muslim country. The UK recorded similar findings in Islamic schools from 2017 to 2019. Several news articles can be found on this in the Telegraph, the Daily Mail and more.

The State University New York Press, the publisher of Al-Tabari's Histories in the USA, printed evidence that agrees with the books found in the UK OFSTED inspection. In Volume 9, Muhammad had some interesting thoughts about women which would explain the very existence of Islamic Gender Apartheid, which go beyond wife-beating.

> *Now then, O people, you have a right over your wives and they have a right over you. You have [the right] that they should not cause any one of whom you dislike to tread your beds, and that they should not commit an open indecency. **If they do, then Allah permits that you shut them in separate rooms, and to beat them, but not severely. If they abstain from [evil] they have a right to their food and clothing, in accordance with custom. Treat women well, for they are [like] domestic animals with and do not possess anything of themselves.*** (9:1754)

The scary truth here is that a Non-Muslim woman who thinks about marrying a Muslim man may not understand beatings are part of being married to a Muslim man. It is how Muhammad treated his wife. Muhammad condoning and explicitly endorsing

---

[111] Taylor, C.-A. (2017, November 28). *HATE SCHOOLS: Inspectors find books in UK Islamic schools that sanction wife-beating and say women can go to hell for cutting their hair.* Retrieved April 13, 2020, from The Sun: https://www.thesun.co.uk/news/5021414/ofsted-finds-books-in-islamic-schools-sanction-wife-beating/.

of spousal abuse ensures that Muslims will not outlaw beating wives. It also ensures that wives of Muslim men continue to suffer beatings in silence. Why silence? In western countries such as the UK where shariah courts exist, it is not unusual for those courts to go against the laws of the land when they learn a woman has been abused, and turn the woman back to her husband instead of recommending a safe haven. Machteld Zee, a Dutch researcher in the UK, had this to say about her interactions with shariah courts:

> *"The judges were very friendly," she says. "We chatted between cases. The problem is not that they were mean, but the foundation of their judice acts in a system of sharia Islamic law, in which the principle focus is making women dependent on their husbands and clerics."*

> *"One judge said: 'Under Islam, we should reconcile marriages even if there is violence'. They don't care. It was shocking: they would have you cling to a marriage."[112]*

An undercover reporter posed as an abused woman before Dr. Hasan of the Leyton Islamic Sharia Council in east London.

> *His first response was to ask if she had done anything to provoke her treatment.*

> *He asked her: "I think that you should be courageous enough to ask this question to him. Just tell me why you are so upset, huh? Is it because of my cooking? Is it because I see my friends, huh? So I can correct myself."*

---

[112] Boztas, S. (2015, December 4). *Sharia in the UK: The courts in the shadow of British law offering rough justice for Muslim women*. Retrieved April 17, 2020, from Independent: https://www.independent.co.uk/news/uk/home-news/sharia-in-the-uk-the-courts-in-the-shadow-of-british-law-offering-rough-justice-for-muslim-women-a6761221.html.

The reporter said she could report the violence to the police, but was warned: "You can involve the police if he hits you, but you must understand this will be the final blow.

"You will have to leave the house. Where will you go then? A refuge? A refuge is a very bad option. Women are not happy in such places."[113]

Understanding that the Islamic social norm of wife-beating is so accepted, that shariah courts stand behind the man as Muhammad would, should it be required by law to inform women not born Muslim that a marriage could involve her being beaten by her husband and that shariah courts will not help her?

---

[113] Fielding, J. (2013, April 7). *Sharia court tells 'abused wife' to stay.* Retrieved April 17, 2020, from Express: https://www.express.co.uk/news/uk/389957/Sharia-court-tells-abused-wife-to-stay.

Chapter 16

Or

What do Islamic social norms say about the Treatment of Dogs?

In Western civilization, dogs are often called "man's best friend." Thousands and thousands of people own and love their dogs. Some treat them like their children. Dogs are also used in Western Civilization in various jobs. Some hold traditional roles such as shepherding, while others work as sighted guides, and others are valued for their noses and serve in multiple roles, from law enforcement to the military.

The United States government uses dogs in the military to sniff out bombs. This enables a quicker rate of response of Explosive Ordinance Disposal (EOD) teams to ensure the safety of those who would be affected. For the handlers of these dogs, a special bond forms that allows them to be highly effective. One of the EOD dogs who received a K-9 Medal of Courage was Coffee. Coffee served three tours of duty. His handler, Army Sgt. 1st Class James Bennett, shared their story.

> "Coffee's purpose originally was IED defeat ... so her job was to clear routes, buildings, paths, looking for explosives, anything that might injure troops. And beyond that, to find caches where they would hide stockpiles of them," said Bennett...

"Overall, her job was literally to lead units, be in front of units and get them from point A to point B safely, so they could effectively do their mission," Bennett said.

"We got every troop home safe, back to base on mission safe, every time we went out. She's never let me down. Not once."[114]

The effectiveness of these dogs was the number one reason it was felt a sign of good friendship to give EOD trained dogs to Islamic countries to aid them in fighting terrorism. This was a great idea, at least it seemed so at first. Then the Islamic social norm about the treatment of dogs prevailed upon our four-footed friends and major news outlets carried the sad stories of neglect in December of 2019.[115]

Kate Ng wrote about this for the Independent. She wrote that, "The US has stopped exporting bomb-sniffing dogs to Egypt and Jordan after a number of animals died from mistreatment and neglect, US authorities said."[116]

Why were dogs trained to sniff out explosives being neglected in Muslim countries? The only commonality in these countries is their belief in Islam. What would Islam have to do with poor treatment of dogs?

Muhammad apparently did not like dogs. We know this from a hadith in Bukhari:

---

[114] Basch, M. (2017, October 11). *5 military dogs honored with K-9 Medal of Courage* . Retrieved April 17, 2020, from WTOP: https://wtop.com/animals-pets/2017/10/5-military-dogs-honored-k-9-medal-courage-photos/.

[115] Ng, K. (2019, December 24). *US suspends export of sniffer dogs to Jordan and Egypt after series of deaths*. Retrieved April 17, 2020, from Inependent:https://www.independent.co.uk/news/world/americas/us-sniffer-dogs-exports-jordan-egypt-deaths-trump-administration-a9259211.html.

[116] Ibid

"Once Gabriel promised the Prophet (that he would visit him, but Gabriel did not come) and later on he said, 'We, angels, do not enter a house which contains a picture or a dog.'" (Sahih Bukhari 4.54.50)

As research on this topic progressed, a question was formed. If Muhammad did not like dogs, would he treat them badly? Would he cause them to be harmed? In the hadiths, Muhammad does exactly this. He orders the killing of dogs with no explanation.

> *"Abdullah (b. Umar) reported: Allah's Messenger ordered the killing of dogs and we would send (men) in Medina and its corners and we did not spare any dog that we did not kill, so much so that we killed the dog that accompanied the wet she-camel belonging to the people of the desert."* — Sahih Muslim 3811

This upset many. Especially those who owned working dogs such as hunting dogs, herding dogs, guard dogs and more. They posed the question about allowing working dogs to live.

"Ibn Mughaffal reported: The Messenger of Allah ordered killing of the dogs, and then said: What about them, i.e. about other dogs? and then granted concession (to keep) the dog for hunting and the dog for (the security) of the herd, and said: When the dog licks the utensil, wash it seven times, and rub it with earth the eighth time."
— Sahih Muslim 551

Does this mean in Islam, that only working dogs are allowed to live? Would Muhammad have all dogs who live as pets killed?

But the real problem today is how dogs are treated by those who feel a need to imitate their prophet Muhammad. Would they want to be near a dog whose very presence negates their prayers? A Muslim who would be responsible for an EOD dog, would not be able to pray, even on break. Simply because, Muhammad claimed their presence negates prayers.

This explains the actions of Muhammad's followers around the globe who work in transportation.

In the UK, a Muslim Uber driver refused to allow a sighted guide dog into his vehicle. The law required him to allow this since the dog was assisting a visually impaired person. Colin Perreira, 24, from Hemel Hempstead said it was his fifth time taking an Uber driver to court for refusing to allow him AND his dog a ride.[117] The commonality of course is left unsaid to protect Muslims.

In Austria, the same issue arises among Muslim cabbies. In August of 2019, Gabriele Jandrasits from Innsbruck attempted to pre-order a taxi to the airport, bringing her beagle in an "airplane friendly transport cage."[118] This proved to be problematic because drivers for the company she called refused to transport a dog even though the animal was in a cage. In this article by Michael Domanig, others had difficulties taking dogs in taxis.

Ms. Jandrasits, who works for the Tyrolean Association for the Blind and Visually Impaired, gives yet another example: A former board member of the association - the lady is completely blind - also ordered a taxi via the radio control center. On the assumption that her companion dog for the blind had to be taken with her anyway, she didn't mention the dog on the phone. The taxi driver then refused to take it with him.[119]

---

[117] Andrews, L. (2020, March 2). *Moment Uber driver refuses to give a ride to a blind man's guide dog before driving off - as he is fined £1,700 for breaching the Equality Act.* Retrieved April 22, 2020, from MailOnline: https://www.dailymail.co.uk/news/article-8066065/Moment-Uber-driver-refuses-ride-blind-mans-guide-dog-driving-off.html.

[118] Domanig, M. (2019, August 8). *Taking dogs in Innsbruck taxis remains an excitement.* Retrieved April 22, 2020, from Tiroler Tageszeitung: https://www.tt.com/artikel/15929619/mitnahme-von-hunden-in-innsbrucker-taxis-bleibt-ein-aufreger?sfns=mo.

[119] Ibid

In this article, they do reference that "around 80 percent of the drivers now have a migration background - and that Muslims traditionally often view dogs as "impure."[120]

This means a social norm does exist that is strong enough to impact the majority of Muslim cabbies in Austria. Is this any different in North America?

On February 2, 2019 CTV news aired an item on a woman being refused a ride with Uber, once again, due to her sighted guide dog. In the video, Shelby Travers a visually impaired woman complains that this has happened at least a dozen times. The last time, the driver drove off with her hand still on the door.[121] According to a follow up article by CTV, the man was charged with a bylaw offense. Travers said she's experienced similar incidents in Calgary and Toronto and added, "I just want this to stop happening."[122]

In the USA, this would be deemed a violation of the Americans with Disabilities Act also known as ADA. It would also be considered a violation of their civil rights. This incurs severe fines, and are grave enough remove drivers from working. However, the same issues are happening in the USA, and no one is talking about why! What is the reason? Why are the news sources hiding the names and the religions of those who won't allow a rider with a dog in their cars?

In 2007, cabs, Ubers etc., had so many refusals by Muslims to take dogs in their vehicles that the Minneapolis-St Paul

---

[120] Ibid

[121] Griff, K. (2019, February 3). *Ont. woman says Uber driver rejected her guide dog.* Retrieved April 22, 2020, from CTV News: https://www.ctvnews.ca/canada/ont-woman-says-uber-driver-rejected-her-guide-dog-1.4280881.

[122] CTV News Ottawa. (2019, February 10). *Uber driver who allegedly refused ride to woman with service dog charged.* Retrieved April 22, 2020, from CTV News: https://www.ctvnews.ca/canada/uber-driver-who-allegedly-refused-ride-to-woman-with-service-dog-charged-1.4290370.

airport took action. At this point, 75% of the drivers were Muslim and primarily from Somalia. Muslim cabbies were not only refusing to transport dogs, they were refusing to transport alcohol, and claiming it was against their religious belief. Patrick Hogan, the spokesman for the Metropolitan Airport Commission said, "There are times where cab after cab will refuse service, and passengers can be waiting for 20 minutes."[123] Mr. Hogan also said that they were seeing about 77 refusals a month!

This problem caused Chuck Samuelson of the American Civil Liberties Union of Minnesota to speak on this issue. He addressed that this was an issue of people used to living under shariah when he said:

This is a public access issue. Bottom line is, we are a secular society, and that's the way it is.[124]

The airport already had a penalty in place for refusing access to people with service dogs. They instituted two penalties. A first offense gets a 30-Day suspension and a second offense earns a two-year revocation. This only removed their ability to pick up at the airport. Refusing service dogs comes with a more severe penalty, including the possibility of being sued for violating the Americans with Disabilities Act.

Muslims tried to fight against taking dogs into their cabs again and took their case to court. In 2008, they lost their appeal.

Perhaps the worst case of cruelty to a dog by a Muslim that went national occurred on October 1, 2019. It resulted in the man pleading guilty. Kyle Hanney, Lead Animal Control Officer said that "the man confessed that he had picked the dog up and then slammed it on the ground multiple times which then caused several compound fractures to the right-rear femur of the

---

[123] Pinto, B. (2007, January 26). *Muslim Cab Drivers Refuse to Transport Alcohol, and Dogs.* Retrieved May 8, 2021, from ABC News: https://abcnews.go.com/International/story?id=2827800.

[124] Ibid.

dog."[125] He was charged with animal torturing in the second degree. There was no reason given for the horrendous crime. Eventually, he did work out a deal that required no jail time.

Was this last news item due to his Islamic beliefs about dogs? The issue here is that the Muslims in non-Islamic countries wish to impose their hatred or at least refusal to transport or be near our four-footed "best friends." The USA protects service animals as workers. This may be a reason there is less news on this topic.

Knowing what you know now, would you invite a Muslim to your house if you have a pet dog? Should you be expected to walk on the other side of the street with your dog when a Muslim passes by to appease a Muslim new to your country?

Further Reading:
https://www.oversight.gov/sites/default/files/oig-reports/ESP-19-06.pdf

---

[125] Ware, A. (2020, February 7). *Dog brutally beaten by Ingham County man gets a second chance*. Retrieved May 8, 2021, from WILX.com: https://www.wilx.com/content/news/Dog-brutally-beaten-by-Ingham-county-man-g-567673011.html.

Islamic Social Norms

vs.

American Constitutional Freedoms

"**What we are taught in our faith is to love the enemy, and freedom and liberty are intertwined with love. That's what the Founders said, when they said "Liberty comes from God" and that it must be at the forefront of everything you do because without it, you can't love your neighbor. Any time there is an encroachment on liberty, there is an encroachment on freedom; it is an encroachment on the God-given liberties that we have, and there is no room for that under the way we were founded.**"

(https://www.youtube.com/watch?v=unVS7y2_-94)

John Guandolo

Chapter 17

Is there an Islamic Social Norm that forbids Freedom of Speech?

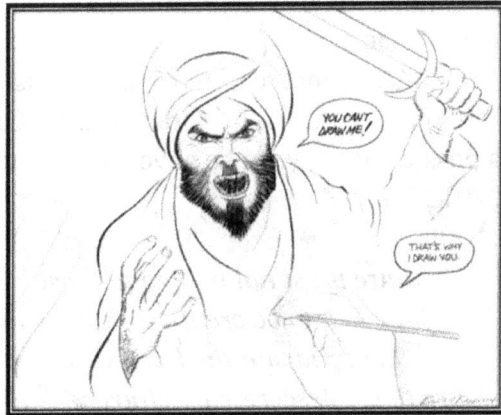

In the United States of America, there are few things held with more reverence than our freedoms guaranteed by the Constitution. Freedom of Speech is in the First Amendment. This Freedom protects what you say and how you express yourself. There are some limits to this freedom, such as the "Clear and Present Danger" test. This is the reason it is against the law to yell "FIRE!" in a crowded movie theater when there is no fire. It is also against the law to lie and slander others. The law stands behind you when you are telling the truth.

In the USA, you are free to critique religions, people; almost everything. You only place yourself at risk of breaking the law regarding this freedom, when you do not share what is true and verifiable. This means that you can critique Jesus, Muhammad, Buddha, the Pope and more. Sticking with what is true is important still. Doing otherwise could get you accused of hate speech. There is no law forbidding hate speech in America. In fact, there is an allowance for it in the law. This makes America very different from the rest of the world.

Canada has laws that cause persons accused of hate speech to be brought before a "tribunal of a Human Right Commission."

Past research on this topic created opportunities to meet some who had gone before this panel, where due process of law seemed to evaporate according to those who were interviewed.

In the United States, it is not against the law to hate someone or to express the hate. UNLESS that hate becomes an action that can cause harm.

The first attempt to outlaw insulting Islam in the United States occurred under President Barak Hussein Obama. He hinted at this as a possible goal when he gave a speech to the UN on September 25, 2012:

The future must not belong to those who slander the prophet of Islam. Yet, to be credible, those who condemn that slander must also condemn the hate we see when the image of Jesus Christ is desecrated, churches are destroyed, or the Holocaust is denied[126]

This is a bit wordy, but President Obama took a world stage and condemned insulting Islam and those who express hate when they see an image of Christ desecrated, a church burned, or the Holocaust denied. So he condemned hatred against actions Muslims may do to Christians and Jews. At no point in this speech did he condemn any hatred a Muslim may hold against a non-Muslim, especially that hatred seen in devout followers of Islam who have committed acts of terror.

But what does Islam and their prophet Muhammad have to do with freedom of speech? How does Muhammad respond to the concept of freedom of speech? Muhammad was the founder/prophet of Islam. How Islam responds to the concept of Freedom of Speech is dependent on how he, responded to the idea of freedom of speech.

[126] Trinko, K. (2012, September 25). *Obama: 'The Future Must Not Belong To Those Who Slander the Prophet of Islam'*. Retrieved April 29, 2020, from National Review:
https://www.nationalreview.com/corner/obama-future-must-not-belong-those-who-slander-prophet-islam-katrina-trinko/.

As a leader of a new faith in Mecca, how did Muhammad respond to being insulted?

Before Muhammad left Mecca, he would worship by kissing the black stone and circling the Ka'aba along with the polytheists that he condemned. Ibn Ishaq relates the following story of how Muhammad dealt with an insult:

> *While they were thus discussing him [Muhammad], the apostle came towards them and kissed the black stone, then he passed them as he walked around the temple. As he passed, they said some injurious things about him. This, I could see from his expression. He went on, and as he passed them the second time, they attacked him similarly. This, I could see from his expression. Then he passed the third time, and they did the same. He stopped and said, "Will you listen to me O Quraysh? By him who holds my life in His hand I bring you slaughter."[127]*

Muhammad returns insults with threats of violence and murder. On the same page of this sirat (biography of Muhammad), the person who narrates this section claims "That is the worst I ever saw the Quraysh do to him." So they did not physically harm him. They only hurled insults at Muhammad, and for that, he threatened to slaughter them.

In the USA children are taught, "Sticks and stones may break my bones but names will never hurt me." While the saying ignores the harm name-calling does, there is no physical action in name-calling. Freedom of Speech is non-existent within Islam. This is more apparent in how Muhammed dealt with the story tellers and poets who insulted him.

---

[127] Ishaq, I. (1982). *The Life of Muhammad.* (A. Guillaume, Trans.) Karachi, Pakistan: Oxford University Press, p. 131.

Now al-Nadr b. al-Harith was one of the satans of <the> Quraysh; he used to insult the apostle and show him enmity. He had been to al-Hira and learned there the tales of the kings of Persia, the tales of Rustum and Isbandiyar. When the apostle had held a meeting in which he reminded them of Allah, and warned his people of what had happened to bygone generations as a result of Allah's vengeance, al-Nadr got up when he sat down, and said, 'I can tell a better story than he, come to me.'

Muhammad was so angry, he had a revelation from Allah and new Quranic scriptures were created (83:13-17).

[13]When Our verses are recited to him, he says, "Legends of the former peoples." [14]No! Rather, the stain has covered their hearts of that which they were earning. [15]No! Indeed, from their Lord, that Day, they will be partitioned. [16]Then indeed, they will [enter and] burn in Hellfire. [17]Then it will be said [to them], "This is what you used to deny."

Al-Nadir joined the Meccan army and was captured at the Battle of Badr along with Uqba bin Abu Maya, by Muhammad and his raiders. Both men had spoken and given poems against Muhammed.

Customarily, at the time, men who were captured were returned for a ransom. But Muhammad ordered him killed for his insults. Uqba pleaded for his life, reminding Muhammed he had children.

When the apostle ordered him to be killed 'Uqba said, 'But who will look after my children, O Muhammad?' 'Hell,' he <Muhammad> said.[128]

Does this sound like Muhammad agrees with the concept of freedom of speech? He even condemned the children of those who spoke against him.

---

[128] Ibid, p. 308.

Muhammad ordered that a few other poets be killed for their words. Abu 'Afak survived the Battle of Badr and wrote a poem against what Muhammad declared Halal (accepted) vs Haram (forbidden). For this, Muhammad asked, "Who will deal with this rascal for me?"[129] His followers quickly dispatched the man whose words endangered Allah.

There is a definite pattern of how Muhammad deals with those who dare to question him or his authority. This pattern is passed on to his followers.

Research on the Islamic scriptures based on supposed death penalty for blasphemy provided eye-opening results. There are NO scriptures from the Quran to support this; the claim that Surah 5:33-34 is unsupported with an actual accurate reading of the verses. This is stated because examples exist where a claim that these two verses support severe penalties for blasphemy, and they're abound on the Internet.

Muslim scholars like Dr. Shehzad Saleem, who wrote an article for Al-Mawrid, titled, "Punishment for Blasphemy against the Prophet," agree that there is NO Quranic or Hadith support for killing someone over Blasphemy. Dr. Saleem himself states:

The law for punishing blasphemy against the Prophet that is invoked in Pakistan has no foundation in the Qur'an or Hadith. Therefore, a pertinent question is: what exactly is the justification for this law?[130]

Dr. Saleem then picks apart the justification provided by Pakistan scholars who claim that Surah 5:33-34 states this and quickly refutes their work through an examination of what was actually stated in Arabic, and reviewing the meaning and intent that are stated.

---

[129] Ibid, p. 675.

[130] Saleem, D. S. (2016, February 6). *Punishment for Blasphemy against the Prophet (sws)*. Retrieved May 18, 2020, from Al-Mawrid: http://www.al-mawrid.org/index.php/articles/view/punishment-for-blasphemy-against-the-prophet-sws.

Did Islam pass on Muhammad's violent hatred of being insulted?

On February 14, 1989 Ayatollah Khomeini wrote a fatwa against Salman Rushdie for his book, *The Satanic Verses*. This fatwa said Salman Rushdie was guilty of blasphemy against Allah. His Fatwa declared:

> "I inform the proud Muslim people of the world that the author of The Satanic Verses book, which is against Islam, the Prophet and the Koran, and all those involved in its publication who are aware of its content are sentenced to death. I ask all the Muslims to execute them wherever they find them."[131]

Many Western democracies during this time rallied in defense of Rushdie, defending his freedom of speech. But Muslims around the world rushed to declare their disgust for Rushdie. In Bradford, UK, Ishtiaq Ahmed led a group to first read the book to see if they agreed with the Ayatollah, and then publicly burned their one and only copy of the book. The BBC record states:

> *The "anger and emotion" within the [Muslim] community at the lack of understanding of their position finally led to calls to "burn the damn thing" in a protest in front of Bradford's key public buildings, he says.*

> "A spot was selected - it had a symbolic meaning... a faith community demonstrating and saying, 'We matter, we exist, we are here, our presence matters'. This police station, town hall, Magistrates' Court - they are ours as much as anyone else's."[132]

---

[131] Bawer, B. (2009, July 24). *Excerpt: 'Surrender'*. Retrieved May 13, 2020, from New York Times:
https://www.nytimes.com/2009/07/26/books/excerpt-surrender.html

Bookstores that carried the books around the world were in danger of being fire-bombed like the ones in Berkeley, California. The Viul bookstore in Oslo, Norway was burned to the ground as a result of bombing.[133] The book's Japanese translator, Hitoshi Igarashi, an assistant professor of comparative culture, at Tsukuba University was murdered and his death credited to the fatwa.[134]Eventually, around 10 countries banned the book, including India, the author's native country.[135]

Norway's Minister of Culture, Åse Kleveland defending the principal of Freedom of Speech, recognizing the horrors and dangers of thought restrictions that were not only being imposed on Muslims, but being enforced on non-Muslims as well, said, "It is our duty to defend freedom of speech. When freedom of speech is so grossly violated as it has been with Khomeini's fatwa, it is our duty to speak out. The Norwegian government and the Norwegian people have always been leaders in these kinds of situations and we will continue to do so in the future."[136]

For about a decade, it seemed quiet. Then, Ayaan Hirsi Ali, a Dutch politician from Somalia contacted Theo Van Gogh in the Netherlands, about a documentary she wished to do on the topic of Islamic Gender Apartheid. Together, they created the short film "Submission." This short film exposed some of the horrors women are subjected to through Islam. These horrors have already been mentioned in previous chapters in this book. Ayaan Hirsi went into great detail in this short film. It was broadcast in prime time on a central Dutch television channel in August 2004.

---

[132] BBC News. (2009, February 13). *What happened to the book burners?* Retrieved May 13, 2020, from BBC News: http://news.bbc.co.uk/2/hi/uk_news/magazine/7883308.stm.

[133] Storhaug, H. (2018). *Islam: Europe Invaded America Warned.* Kolofon, p. 79

[134] Weisman, S. R. (1991, July 13). *Japanese Translator of Rushdie Book Found Slain.* Retrieved May 13, 2020, from New York Times: https://archive.nytimes.com/www.nytimes.com/books/99/04/18/specials/rushdie-translator.html.

[135] Op Cit, p. 79.

[136] Ibid, p. 81.

Three months later on November 2ⁿᵈ, Theo Van Gogh was riding his bicycle on his regular route through Amsterdam. Mohammed Bouyeri, a second generation Muslim migrant from Morocco, fired his gun eight times, striking Theo. Theo, still barely alive, was begging for mercy according to eyewitnesses, when Bouyeri slit his throat in attempt to decapitate him. Then Bouyeri attached a note to his victim, with a smaller knife than the one used to kill Van Gogh. The letter was meant for Ayaan Hirsi Ali.

With your Apostasy [leaving Islam], you have not only turned away from the truth, but you are marching with evil soldiers. You spew untruths against Islam and Muhammad, the Messenger of Allah. With this letter, I will try to stop you forever.... Peace be upon the Emir of the Holy Warriors, the laughing killer Muhammad, the Messenger of Allah, his family and those who follow him faithfully.[137]

Theo Van Gogh's death shocked the world; the concept that someone who had no fear of Islam and felt safe in his home could be attacked and murdered in such a savage way, for just exercising his rights to freedom of speech. His death, more than many others, awakened the media to the censorious nature of Islam. The Islamic proclamation to be careful what you say and to make sure you do not insult Islam were very clear.

Writers such as Ayaan Hirsi Ali, felt the very real dagger at their daringness to share what is true because the god of Islam may get angry and send people to kill who ever offends Islam.

On September 30, 2005 Jyllands Posten, a newspaper in the Netherlands, published 12 cartoons of Muhammad. Kurt Westergaard's biographer, John Lykkegaard, wanted us to reflect on what was happening before the cartoons were published.[138] He believed it was important to understand what was happening in the world at that point! He reminded us that the attack on the United

---

[137] Ibid, p. 84.

[138] Lykkegaard, J. (2012). Kurt Westergaard: The Man Behind the Muhammad Cartoon. Copenhagen, Denmark, Location 82.

States on September 11, 2001 horrified many around the world. Next came the 2002 attack on a nightclub in Bali, and then the 2004 bombing at the Atocha Station in Madrid, Spain. In addition, the Islamic terror attack of the London underground in July 2005. These attacks awakened the world to Islam and its violence upon non-Muslims. Westergaard created the cartoons as a "protest against <Islamic> fundamentalist violence"[139] that seemed to be in the news all too often.

John Lykkegaard, also had information on how Kurt Westergaard's cartoons caused a worldwide uproar amongst Muslims. He stated:

One of the "most important reasons for the cartoon-related unrest in the Middle East in 2006, was that imam Raed Hlayhel from Brabrand, an Aarhus suburb, and Abu Laban from Copenhagen, among others went on a tour in the Middle East to draw attention to the cartoons.

To ensure a successful result, they brought along other drawings and images. The image which at first was perceived as the greatest insult against Mohammad was a photo from a pig squealing competition in France, depicting an innocent mechanic wearing a pig mask. The reverend muftis and imams were properly deceived, but the tour was a success in the sense that it led to a boycott of Danish goods..."[140]

The publisher and this cartoonist had their lives and businesses threatened because Shariah forbids pictures of Muhammad. People forget that Islam teaches that Shariah rules the lives of Muslims and Non-Muslims.

Middle East Media Research Institute took note of how the Muslim community around the world had become informed about a few cartoons in a Netherland's newspaper. They captured some of what was being said. Muhammad Foda, who wrote in the evening supplement of the Egyptian government daily *Al-Gumhouriyya*, wrote "The Muslims worldwide - some billion and

---

[139] Ibid, Location 225.
[140] Ibid, Location 93-103.

a half... are facing a new kind of Crusader war, whose weapon is the pen, not the rifle." [141] MEMRI also noted in the report that a lot more people got involved because a well-known Egyptian singer Sha'aban Abd Al-Rahim wrote a song about the cartoons in the Netherlands. [142]

MEMRI documented leaders of Al Qaeda stating their thoughts on the issue. Bin Laden released a tape on April 23, 2006 where he "demanded that the Western governments hand the cartoonists who had defamed the Prophet over to the Muslims, so that they could be tried according to shari'a law. He stressed that anyone who mocked the Prophet or Islam should be killed." [143] On May 15, 2006 Sheikh Aby Yahya Al-Libi, another leader of the terror group said that "the Muslims should talk less and do more: They should fight Denmark and Norway, and not be content with demonstrations and other forms of protest." [144]

The threats to Mr. Westergaard and Jyllands Posten reached into the United States and Canada. In October of 2009, the FBI arrested two men in connection with a "conspiracy to provide material support and/or to commit terrorist acts" against "the facilities and employees of a Danish newspaper that published cartoons of the Prophet Mohammed in 2005." [145]

David Coleman Headley, formerly known as Daood Gilani, and Tahawwur Hussain Rana, also known as Tahawar Rana had Canadian citizenship. Both men resided in Chicago, Illinois and

---

[141] MEMRI. (January 4, 2007). *A Retrospective Study of the Unfolding of the Muhammad Cartoons Crisis and its Implications.* Middle East Media Research Institute. Retrieved May 15, 2020, from MEMRI:https://www.memri.org/reports/retrospective-study-unfolding-muhammad-cartoons-crisis-and-its-implications.

[142] Ibid.

[143] Ibid.

[144] Ibid.

[145] US Department of Justice. (2009, October 27). *Two Chicago Men Charged in Connection with Alleged Roles in Foreign Terror Plot That Focused on Targets in Denmark.* Retrieved May 15, 2020, from USA Department of Justice: https://www.justice.gov/opa/pr/two-chicago-men-charged-connection-alleged-roles-foreign-terror-plot-focused-targets-denmark.

were caught with murderous intentions. Headley had gone to Denmark previously, even going so far as to visit Jyllands Posten, to scout the location for an attack.

A few months later, on January 1, 2010, New Year's Day in the Netherlands, Kurt Westergaard, the cartoonist, and his family woke to a Muslim migrant from Somalia, breaking into his house with an axe.[146] Due to the intelligent preparation of the Danish Security and Intelligence Service of a safe room, Kurt and his family lived to tell the story.

South Park, an adult-themed cartoon on prime time television had done caricatures of Jesus and other religious persons, mocking them. They decided to add the prophet Muhammad disguised in a bear suit to a cartoon which they broadcast in 2010. In response, RevolutionMuslim.com posted the following note on their site with a screen capture of the episode. Next to it was a scene of the bloody murder of Theo Van Gogh.

We have to warn Matt and Trey that what they are doing is stupid and they will probably wind up like Theo Van Gogh for airing this show," the posting reads. "This is not a threat, but a warning of the reality of what will likely happen to them."[147]

As a result, Comedy Central who broadcast the show censored every depiction of Muhammad with a blob stamped CENSORED.

Proponents of Freedom of Speech in the Western world once again woke up to this attempt of Muslims to force censorship – a violation of what America and many western nations teach in their schools as a belief that people have a God-given right to express themselves as they wish.

Molly Norris from Seattle, Washington, answered the call to stand up this time. She put out the images of things like a tea cup, a domino, a spool of thread and more, claiming to be the likeness

---

[146] Lykkegaard, J. (2012). Kurt Westergaard: The Man Behind the Muhammad Cartoon. Copenhagen, Denmark, Location 168.

[147] Miller, J. R. (2010, April 22). *Comedy Central Censors 'South Park' Episode After Muslim Site's Threats.* Retrieved May 15, 2020, from FOX News: https://www.foxnews.com/entertainment/comedy-central-censors-south-park-episode-after-muslim-sites-threats.

of Muhammad. Also, she called for the *Everybody Draw Muhammad day*. The date was set one month from the day of publication. May 20th was to be the date. Molly and an associate set up a Facebook group where people joined by the thousands. By May 20th, there were 101,870 members.[148] An oppositional group was also created, garnering just a little more in number. But then, as we know, Facebook engages in censorship. It is possible that FB was limiting who could see the group.

---

[148] Yuen, J. (2015, May 20). *Draw Mohammed drawing in fans, foes.* Retrieved May 21, 2020, from Toronto Sun: https://web.archive.org/web/20100524091256/http://www.torontosun.com/news/torontoandgta/2010/05/20/14026241.html.

Sadly, Molly and the Facebook organizer ended up running from the group. Their lives were threatened. Imam Dr. Zijad Delic of the Canadian Islamic Congress, said "Those who are creating these (pro Draw Mohammed) Facebook groups with intention to create more controversy are doing a disservice to this great country."[149] This was a claim that drawing Muhammad would make him and other Muslims victims.

Five years later, in the United States, the opposition to Freedom of Speech events like "Everybody Draw Muhammad" led to the creation of a "Stand with the Prophet" event planned for January 15, 2015 in Garland, Texas. Informed media, who worked for The United West and Jesse Watters purchased tickets online to be able to see the event.

One week before this event, *Charlie Hebdo,* a French satirical magazine was attacked for publishing cartoons of Muhammad. January 7, 2015, brothers, Cherif and Said Kouachi got out of their car armed with Kalashnikov assault rifles and entered the building. They went to the second floor and killed 10 people. In the pursuit, they murdered two police officers.

Witnesses to the event claimed they heard them shout, "We have avenged the Prophet Muhammad" and "Allah Akbar,"[150] which means "Allah is greater." It was not until three days later that the two attackers were caught. They came out, shooting, and were quickly put down like dispatched rabid dogs.

This attack horrified the world. *Charlie Hebdo* was known for its irreverence of all things religious. It had been a bastion of declaration of the belief in Freedom of Speech. While many may not have agreed with its views, it rode the edge of what was protected speech.

Some thought this horrifying event may cancel the "Stand with Muhammad" event. But it went on as planned. Adam Kredo wrote about the upcoming event at the Washington Free Beacon on

---

[149] Ibid.

[150] BBC News. (2015, January 15). *Charlie Hebdo attack: Three days of terror.* Retrieved May 21, 2020, from BBC News: https://www.bbc.com/news/world-europe-30708237.

January 12, 2015 "being billed as a 'movement to defend Prophet Muhammad, his person, and his message,"[151] citing event brochures. Adam continued his description of the upcoming event, as seeking "to combat 'Islamophobes in America' who have turned the Islamic Prophet Muhammad 'into an object of hate,' according to organizers."[152] Adam Kredo's decription and the anti-Jihadi contingent that were concerned about Freedom of Speech in America as a result of the gathering of Islamists under a banner of shariah, combined with the horrific attack on Charlie Hebdo in France, led to over 2000 protestors showing up. Pamela Geller went live as part of the protest at the event, on January 15, 2015 thanks to The United West, and said;

We are standing in defense of free speech. People need to understand that, not a week after the slaughter of the editorial staff of the Charlies Hebdo, the Islamic leadership in this country [the USA] is holding a conference to restrict our Freedom of Speech. It's the same exact premise. The same ideology. It's the same system of governance — Shariah. That was behind those murders. They seek to impose the same type of draconian restrictions of free speech, and we are saying 'NO! Absolutely not![153]

Robert Spencer, of Jihad Watch was also present at this event. He said,

This event is dedicated to eradicating Islamophobia. Which really means dedicated to eradicating any honest discussion on how Islamic jihadists use the texts and the teachings of

---

[151] Kredo, A. (2015, January 12). *Muslim Leaders to Hold 'Stand With the Prophet' Rally in Texas.* Retrieved May 24, 2020, from Washington Free Beacon: https://freebeacon.com/issues/muslim-leaders-to-hold-stand-with-the-prophet-rally-in-texas.

[152] Ibid.

[153] The United West. (2015, January 17). *Over 2,000 Protest Stand with Mohammad event in TX.* Retrieved May 21, 2020, from YouTube: https://www.youtube.com/watch?time_continue=65&v=VQMtNvx_g nw&feature=emb_logo.

Islam to justify violence and hatred, and they have too long controlled the discourse and shut down any honest examination of the motives and goals of terrorists by crying Islamophobia. The American people out here are saying enough! Enough is enough! We are not going to stand for this anymore. We demand the truth from our leaders, and we are mobilizing to fight for freedom.[154]

Islamic leaders who ran the conference made the claim that the conference was about inclusion. What they meant was inclusion of Muslim perspective ONLY. This became apparent when two Jewish men were denied access as members of the press even though they had purchased tickets ahead of time. Damon Rosen and Alan Kornman, two Jewish men who work for The United West were denied access under the claim that they had oversold the conference.[155] Jesse Watters of FOX News was also denied access. On video, Alia Salem, a CAIR Director lied to Jesse, claiming he never filled out a press pass, while he had already shown his email of the denial of his ticket and press pass which came to him when he landed in Texas. She also talked to Adam Kredo of the Washington Free Beacon and Alan Kornman, but again, stated a line of disbelief that they filled out the press passes, etc.[156]

Siraj Wahaj was to speak at this event. Siraj Wahaj served as a character witness for the Blind Sheikh in the first bombing of the World Trade Center, and was later listed as an unindicted co-conspirator in the USA vs. Holy Land Foundation trial; the biggest terrorism finance trial ever in the USA. His presence convinced many that this event was to promote Shariah over Freedom of Speech.

---

[154] Ibid.

[155] The United West. 2015. "Islamists Deny Media Access at At Muslim Free Speech Conference." *YouTube*. January 20. Accessed May 21, 2020. https://www.youtube.com/watch?v=FoOCMjc-n_o.

[156] Ibid.

The media was only allowed in for the first 20 minutes. This event that invited people to get press passes closed to the media after the first 20 minutes!![157]

It was this last event in Garland, Texas and the Charlie Hebdo attack that convinced Pamella Geller and Robert Spencer to organize an event that would become the climax of the fight to maintain Freedom of Speech in America. They picked the exact location as "Stand with the Prophet" chose – Garland, Texas.

Randy Potts of the Daily Beast provided us with a description of what happened at the event:

When Geller stepped up to the podium, the room fell silent. Closing my eyes for a moment, I recognized the rhythm immediately: the singsong cadence of a preacher, New York accent, notwithstanding. I had expected the often shrill persona I had heard online, but this Geller was mesmerizing: gentle, encouraging, motherly even. Now and then, "amen" echoed through the room, often after references to the Bible. Geller was quick; 8 to 10 minutes, and she was done, introducing the controversial Dutch politician Geert Wilders, who was flanked by several security guards, and didn't enter the room until Geller called his name.

Wilders spoke for 15 minutes, didactic, explaining why, he said Islam was an ideology not a religion. The crowd gave him several standing ovations, not because his speech was rousing, but because of what his presence represented: how long he had been fighting Islam, how much security he needed, how two U.S. Muslim congressmen tried to keep him out of the country.

It was left to Geller and Freedom Defense Initiative co-founder Robert Spencer to announce the contest winner, Bosch Fawstin, who was raised Muslim but now says he worships at the church of Ayn Rand. The platinum-blond Fawstin talked about growing up Muslim, and his realization

---

[157] Ibid.

that it wasn't for him. He talked about the new comic he was working on—a superhero dressed in pigskin, practicing "pigotry". Muslim mistreatment of gays, he said, is another reason he draws Muhammad. "You tell me I cannot draw Muhammad," he said. "I will draw Muhammad!"[158]

During Geller's closing speech, two men drove up in a dark sedan to the event. Elton Simpson and Nadir Soofi quickly jumped out of the car, wearing body armor and carrying assault rifles. They approached a police car that had stopped and had two men exiting, one of whom was an unarmed school security officer (SSO); the other was an off-duty Garland traffic police officer with a service pistol.[159] One of the jihadis opened fire, hitting the SSO in the leg. The highly trained police officer returned fire, killing both jihadis. No one died at the hands of jihadis at this event. No one inside the event was aware of what was happening outside, except for those on the security team until after the death of the jihadis. The excellent planning and security that Geller and Spencer hired saved the lives of everyone present. After the failed attack, the area was checked for bombs and other possible dangers but none were found.

ISIS claimed the attack was theirs the following day, marking the first ISIS terror attack on US soil. It was later learned that the FBI had followed the two jihadis on their trip to Garland and did not attempt to stop the attack.

This event like 9/11 had a huge impact in America. Colleges and universities felt the impact. One such example is the University of Minnesota's reaction to a poster from a university group that featured a Charlie Hebdo cartoon of Muhammad as shown below.

---

[158] Potts, R. R. (2015, May 4). *Exclusive: Inside the Texas 'Draw Muhammad' Event as Shots Rang Out.* Retrieved June 11, 2020, from The Daily Beast: https://www.thedailybeast.com/exclusive-inside-the-texas-draw-muhammad-event-as-shots-rang-out.

[159] Glenza, J. (2015, May 4). *Texas police widen search but admit: 'This is not going to be a fast investigation'.* Retrieved June 16, 2020, from Guardian: https://www.theguardian.com/us-news/2015/may/04/garland-texas-attack-investigation-gunmen-details.

Can One Laugh At Everything?
Satire and Free Speech After Charlie

January 29, 2015
4pm

Anderson Hall 230
West Bank
University of Minnesota

Free Speech Laws: A Comparative Study
Anthony S. Winer
Professor of Law, William Mitchell College of Law

Figurative Representation in the Islamic Tradition
William Beeman
Professor and Chair of Anthropology, University of
Minnesota

"As Welcome as a Bee Sting": Why We Must Protect
"Outrageous" Speech
Jane E. Kirtley
Silha Professor of Media Ethics and Law | School of
Journalism and Mass Communication
Director, Silha Center for the Study of Media Ethics and
Law, University of Minnesota

Antisemitism and Islamophobia: A Double Standard?
Bruno Chaouat
Professor and Chair, French and Italian, University of
Minnesota

Brief Reflections on Editorial Cartoons
Steven Sack
Editorial Cartoonist, Minneapolis Star Tribune

In the United States where Freedom of Speech has been so revered that libraries have had Banned Book weeks, typically on the last week in September, a banned cartoon on a poster sounds almost ridiculous in comparison. But this depiction of Muhammad was enough to make eight Muslim students file complaints. About 260 Muslims filed a petition against the poster. The university claimed that 40 non-Muslims also signed in support of the Muslims' desire to remove Freedom of Speech from students and professors on the basis that they claimed to be offended.

Amusingly, their very claim was scheduled to be addressed at the event! The University originally demanded the poster be taken down. "Then the Office of Equal Opportunity and Affirmative Action investigated and advised the dean of liberal arts to disavow the use of the offending image and in their own words, they added, 'use your leadership role to repair the damage' it caused in the

Muslim community."[160] This made the local news on April 29, 2015 and became national news after the failed Garland ISIS attack.

The Star Tribune was able to get the perspective of two of the professors slated to speak at the event on the poster. Professor Jane Kirtley's response to the University was strong and critical. Kirtley at the time, was the Silha Professor of Media Ethics and Law at the Hubbard School of Journalism and Mass Communication. She said, "There is no question in my mind that this [poster] was protected speech."[161] Dr. Bruno Chaouat, one of the organizers of the event, said it "was designed as 'an opportunity' to educate about free speech." He called the university's reaction — deciding to launch an investigation — part of a worrisome trend.[162]

Perhaps the most important quote from the Star Tribune on this issue came from the University's liberal-arts Dean, John Coleman; "I really think the important thing here is to affirm and reaffirm the importance of open debate." That freedom, he noted, applies to everyone, including "Muslim students, Christian students, and Jewish students. We want everybody to feel that they are able to express their views, and either agree or disagree."[163]

But it was Dr. Bruno Chaouat's words on this event that became prophetic.

> Chaouat said that the planners had no intent to offend anyone when they chose the poster, and that he saw the outcry as an attempt to silence debate. "It was an operation of intimidation," he said. And he argued that it was especially effective in the wake of January's bloody attack on the French magazine.

---

[160] Lerner, L. (2015, May 5). *Poster for free-speech forum sets off debate at University of Minnesota.* Retrieved July 1, 2020, from Star Tribune: https://www.startribune.com/poster-for-free-speech-forum-sets-off-debate-at-university-of-minnesota/302689691/?refresh=true.

[161] Ibid.

[162] Ibid.

[163] Ibid.

"This is my main concern, that we're going to make excuses," he said. "We're going to pretend it's out of compassion, when it's out of fear that we're censoring ourselves."[164]

Fast forward five years after numerous clashes on freedom of speech by Muslims on college campuses, fighting the right of clubs to choose their speakers that do not meet Islamic approval, they are now intending to censor what is taught in College classes! The cry of Islamophobia is reaching into colleges, causing speakers who take public stands against jihad to be forcibly uninvited and to cause censorship of course material that could be deemed offensive to Muslims regardless of its factual content displayed by several citations. One such case occurred in May 2020, when one of Dr. Nicholas Damask's Muslim students at Scottsdale Community College complained to the president of the college and then to the community about questions related to Islamic terrorism on a test. Dr. Damask had been teaching this class for 24 years without a complaint. The questions objected to include;

- Who do terrorists strive to emulate? A. Mohammed.
- Where is terrorism encouraged in Islamic doctrine and law? A. The Medina verses [i.e., the portion of the Qur'an traditionally understood as having been revealed later in Muhammad's prophetic career].
- Terrorism is _____ in Islam. A. justified within the context of jihad.

Dr. Nicholas Damask has an MA in International Relations from American University in Washington, D.C., and a Ph.D. in Political Science from the University of Cincinnati. Dr. Damask stated, "to my knowledge, the only tenured political science

---

[164] Ibid.

faculty currently teaching in Arizona to write a doctoral dissertation on terrorism."[165]

Dr. Damask had taught a series of lessons on terrorism previously; one section of the series involved Islamic terrorism. No one complained about the material or questioned its accuracy when it was being taught. Each of the items taught had a source cited. This test was specifically on Islamic terrorism, as other forms of terrorism had previously been tested. As a result of these students' complaints being made public, death threats were made against the professor and his family. Threats were made against the college also.

His classroom material on terrorism was impressive. Dr. Andrew Harrod, a highly published expert on the topic of jihad and Islamic terrorism had a chance to review the material and called it, "a very impressive PowerPoint...The scholarship <Dr. Damask> had behind this - I am going to say from my own observation - is excellent. I have written about these jihadist doctrines for quite a bit now in this past decade or so, and just by looking at your presentation, I found details I was not specifically aware of."[166]

The college told Professor Damask to write an apology to the student. BUT, there was no formal complaint filed. The student did not follow the process for filing a complaint. One month after the student complained to the college president, there was still no formal complaint filed. The college had not responded to ensure the safety of their college professor and his family.

In fact, Prof. Damask was told by Scottsdale Community College's President, Kristina Hayes, that his "coursework was a contradiction to the college's community values."[167] Privately, Prof. Damask was told that his material had to be reviewed by Muslims before it could be taught, and that he needed to take

---

[165] Harrod, A. (2020, May 8). *Islam in Focus--Arizona's Scottsdale Community College Sharia Censorship*. Retrieved June 16, 2020, from Blog Talk Radio.com: https://www.blogtalkradio.com/global-patriot-radio/2020/05/08/islam-in-focus-arizonas-scottsdale-community-college-sharia-censorship.

[166] ibid

[167] Ibid.

classes on Islam. This was all before the college even saw the content that he had been teaching for over 20 years!

In the United States, college professors have academic freedom to prepare and present material to students relevant to the course they teach. In this case, Professor Damask's freedom of speech and his obligation to teach course material relating to terrorism was being violated so that Muslims could be appeased. Dr. Damask and men like Steven Kirby pointed out that this appeasement to feelings of being offended forces truth to no longer be taught.

Canada

In Canada, they do not have Freedom of Speech, they have Freedom of Expression. But Muslims pushed the concept of Islamophobia as a form of hatred and as a cause of danger to Canadian Muslims in 2017. Iqra Khalid, a member of parliament proposed Motion-103, to make criticizing or making derogatory or insulting remarks about Islam illegal. They were trying to outlaw any kind of criticism of Islam, or commentary on Islamic terrorism. The definition of Islamophobia was up for discussion with respect to the fact that it should be outlawed according to Iqra Khalid and other Muslims pushing the Motion.

Scott Reid, a Member of Canada's Parliament was against M-103 and shared out the differing understandings of Islamophobia:

1. "Islamophobia, to me, means **uttering death threats, assaulting, hatred, threats of violence towards people, and vandalism of their places of worship**." —Mr. Arif Virani, MP.

2. "The definition of Islamophobia I subscribe to is **an irrational fear or hatred of Muslims or Islam that leads to discrimination**." —Iqra Khalid, MP.

3. **"Expressions of fear and negative stereotypes, bias, or acts of hostility towards the religion of Islam and individual Muslims."** —Definition used by the Canadian Race Relations Foundation, as reported to the committee by Dan Vandal, MP.

4. **"A widespread mindset and fear-laden discourse in which people make blanket judgments of Islam as the enemy as the 'other', and as a dangerous and unchanged, monolithic bloc that is the natural subject of well-deserved hostility from Westerners."** — Definition of Islamophobia proposed in 2008 by J.P. `, as reported to the committee by Samer Majzoub (President, Canadian Muslim Forum).

5. **"A rejection of Islam, Muslim groups, and Muslim individuals on the basis of prejudice and stereotypes. It may have emotional, cognitive, evaluative as well as action-oriented elements like discrimination and violence."** —Definition of Islamophobia proposed in 2005 by J. Stolz, as reported to the committee by Samer Majzoub (President, Canadian Muslim Forum).

6. "The term "Islamophobia" is often falsely equated with the term "anti-Semitism". MP Khalid has also alluded to an equivalence between the two, yet the two are vastly different...**A common dictionary meaning of anti-Semitism is 'hostility to or prejudice against Jews'. Islamophobia, on the other hand, also includes criticism of Islam as a religion.** The common dictionary meaning is 'intense dislike or fear of Islam, especially as a political force; hostility or prejudice towards Muslims'." —Farzana Hassan (Author/Columnist, Individual). The dictionary definition she cites is from the *Oxford English Dictionary.*[168]

Definition 6 here is the largest concern. If the Canadian Parliament made Motion 103 law, no Canadian would be allowed

---

[168] Reid, S. (2017, November 14). *Here are 26 reasons why the M-103 committee's report should condemn anti-Muslim discrimination rather than the undefined term, 'Islamophobia.'*. Retrieved June 11, 2020, from Scott reid, MP: https://scottreid.ca/here-are-26-reasons-why-the-m-103-committees-report-should-condemn-anti-muslim-discrimination-rather-than-the-undefined-term-islamophobia.

to enjoy their Freedom of Expression with respect to Islam. It would in effect have placed a restraint on any college classes on Islam that function critically. But at the same time, would allow criticism of any other religion. This would in effect give Muslims a special higher status than any other citizen in Canada.

Dhimmis and Censorship

Dhimmis are persons who are subservient to their Muslim masters and mistresses. These people will impose sharia, censorship and more to protect the religion of Islam, whether they do this under threat or coercion, with no concern, as they are acting to remove freedoms given by God, such as the Freedom of Speech.

In Europe, dhimmitude has removed any mention of the terminology of 'Islamic terrorism," or "jihad" from the news. When a terrorist attack using a truck to mow people down is referred to in the head headlines today, it reads like this headline in Reuters on December 23, 2016: "Berlin truck attack suspect shot dead by police in Italy."

Today

It is impossible today, to make the claim that Islam does not have an effect on what you say and how you say things. People fear being labeled an "Islamophobe." They fear being called "racist" even though Islam is not a race. They fear being harmed for stating something even if it is true!

This task is harder for teachers; teachers who are required to teach Civics or what we call in the USA, Social Studies. Why is this? That is because even though these teachers are required to teach cause and effect, they fear doing this when Islam is involved.

When the Armenian Genocide became required to teach about the Armenian genocide, teachers feared presenting the primary document that was the cause of it – The 1915 Fatwa, a document kept under lock and key by the United States State Department for 50 years for fear it could start a war here. That document is included in the Appendix of this book.

In France, Samuel Paty, simply taught his class, as required, about Freedom of Expression, and talked about the Charlie Hebdo cartoons. He offered his Muslim students the opportunity not to see the cartoons if they did not want to see them. As a result,

Samuel Paty was disciplined; not for showing the cartoons, but for not showing them to all of his students. He was murdered over this lesson on October 16, 2019.

Chapter 18

Are there Islamic Social Norms that Forbid Freedom of Expression through Music?

Music is performed with and without instruments. Music has been created for worship of a god, or as an expression of how the present world is to the composer. Often, it's just for entertainment. The more educated and trained a composer is, the possibilities for a wider range of instrumentation and vocals come into play. Music is a form of communication that makes people feel the emotion of the composer.

An individual's taste in music can be broad or narrow. There are several kinds of music today: classical, jazz, blues, rock, R&B, and much more. Many famous sayings have been made about the importance of music also, such as:

- "Where words fail, music speaks." – Hans Christian Andersen.
- "Life seems to go on without effort when I am filled with music." – George Eliot.

164

- "Music is to the soul what words are to the mind."
  — Modest Mouse.
- "Music gives a soul to the universe, wings to the mind, flight to the imagination and life to everything." – Plato.
- "Music is the language of the spirit. It opens the secret of life bringing peace, abolishing strife." — Kahlil Gibran.
- "Without music, life would be a mistake." — Friedrich Nietzsche.
- "Music is powerful. As people listen to it, they can be affected. They respond." – Ray Charles.
- "Music is … A higher revelation than all Wisdom & Philosophy" — Ludwig van Beethoven.

Nietzsche called life without music a mistake. Only one culture in the world forbids most music today. That is Islam. Islamic scholars of all 4 Sunni schools on sharia, Islamic jurisprudence, agree that music with instruments is forbidden. These schools only allow a tambourine as shariah requires. 'Umdat al-Salik aka Reliance of the Traveller, a book of shariah translated into English states:

r40.1 (Ibn Hajar Haytami:) As for the condemnation of musical instruments, flutes, strings, and the like by the Truthful and Trustworthy, who:

"Does not speak from personal caprice: it is nothing besides a revelation inspired" (Koran 53:3-4),

Let those who refuse to obey him beware, lest calamity strike them, or a painful torment. The Prophet said:

(1) "Allah Mighty and Majestic sent me as a guidance and mercy to believers, and **commanded me to do away with musical instruments, flutes, strings,** crucifixes, and the affair of the pre-Islamic period of ignorance."

(2) "On the Day of Resurrection, **Allah will pour molten lead into the ears of whoever sits listening to a songstress."**

(3) "Song makes hypocrisy grow in the heart as water does herbage."

(4) "This Community will experience the swallowing up of some people by the earth, metamorphosis of some into animals, and being rained upon with stones." Someone asked, "When will this be, O Messenger of Allah?" and he said, "When songstresses and musical instruments appear, and wine is held to be lawful."

(5) "There will be peoples of my Community who will hold fornication, silk, wine, and musical instruments to be lawful ...."

All of this is explicit and compelling textual evidence that musical instruments of all types are unlawful (Kaff al-ra'a' 'an muharramat al-lahw wa al-sama' (y49), 2.269-70).

r40.2 (Nawawi:) **It is unlawful to use musical instruments** — such as those which drinkers are known for, like the mandolin, lute, cymbals, and flute — or to listen to them. It is permissible to play the tambourine at weddings, circumcisions, and other times, even if it has bells on its sides. Beating the kuba, a long drum with a narrow middle, is unlawful (Mughni al-muhtaj ila ma'rifa ma'ani alfaz al-Minhaj (y73), 4.429-30).

SINGING UNACCOMPANIED BY MUSICAL INSTRUMENTS
r40.3 (Ibn Hajar Haytami:) As for listening to singing that is not accompanied by instruments, one should know that singing or listening to singing is offensive except under the circumstances to mentioned in what follows: Some scholars hold that singing is sunna at weddings and the like, and our Imams, Ghazali and 'Izz ibn 'Abd Al Salam say that it is sunna if it moves one to a noble state of mind that makes one remember the hereafter. It is clear from this that all poetry which encourages good deeds, wisdom, noble qualities, abstinence from this-worldly things, or similar pious traits

such as urging one to obey Allah, follow the sunna, or shun disobedience, is sunna to write, sing, or listen to, as more than one of our Imams have stated is obvious, since using a means to do good is itself doing good.

Now it is important to understand that shariah forbids most forms of music. In fact as seen in shariah r1-r3, it eliminates all music that is instrumental. Thus, all classical music is now viewed as haram (forbidden); smooth Jazz, and any other music that has instruments. That means, no Blues, no rock and roll, no country music, and no music at all unless, it is for Allah, and then, only with vocals and a tambourine. This even eliminates all acapella music, vocal music without instrumental accompaniment unless it is directed in acceptance of shariah's very narrow window.

Islamic Teachings, a Sunni Islamic site that answers proposed questions tackled the topic of the legality of acapella music that is not sung by women, and is not about nor encouraging of immoral acts.[169] They began by referring to Surah 31:7:

And of the people is he who buys the amusement of speech to mislead [others] from the way of Allah without knowledge and who takes it in ridicule. Those will have a humiliating punishment.

The site refers to Ibn Mas'ūd (Radiyallāhu 'Anhu) who "was asked regarding this verse and he replied, 'It is music, by the oath of that being, there is no deity except Him.'" – (Al-Musannaf of Ibn Abi Shayba 11/101 Majlis al-'Ilmi)

This site also quoted a Hadith from Sunan Ibn Mājah:

---

[169] Ummtaalib. (2015, January 29). *Instrument Free Music*. Retrieved July 8, 2020, from Islamic Teachings.com: https://www.islamicteachings.org/forum/topic/22387-instument-free-music.

Abu Mālik al-Ash'ari (Radiyallāhu 'Anhu) narrates that the Prophet of Allāh (SAW) said: "Soon, people from my Umma will consume alcohol and call it with another name. On their heads will be instruments of music and singing women. Allāh will make the ground swallow them up, and turn them into monkeys and swine."

This non-allowance of vocal music could be quickly thought of as hypocritical, given how the Adnan, "Call to Prayer" is done in a "melodious sing song manner." Many who learn to memorize the Quran also use a similar manner of recitation to assist in memorization. This is actually allowable in Islam. There is a hadith that promotes this:

Abu Huraira (ra) reported that the Messenger of Allah said; "The one who does not recite the Qur'ān in a melodious manner is not from us." (Sahih Bukhari no. 7527)

This becomes almost a ban on music as a whole, unless it is acapella and is a promotion of Islam. It would ban the acapella music of Muslim singer and composer, Hisham Fageeh whose acapella work "No woman No drive" was accepted in America for entertainment, but was actually both humorous and a political statement about Saudi Arabia, against women not driving. Not long after his music was released, women were given some allowance to drive.

Kamal el-Mekki is a favorite cited by American Muslims on the topic of music; he gave a sermon titled "The End of Music" around June 2008. He states in the sermon that "it <music> can do what alcohol can do to people." El-Mekki says you should keep music away from women. He stated, "Do not let them hear it." He says "singing is one of the callers to fornication." He talks about the <sexual> "effect" male singers can have on women. He does this by talking about horses, camels, and sheep whose males make a sound and "then their females prepare themselves" for sex. He compares the influence of music similar to a camel's acceptance of melodious men reading poetry rhythmically and how it soothes the beasts of the desert.

El-Mekki goes on and talks about a man who would attack people with his poetry; the day he could not find someone, he attacked his own mother with his poetry. When there was no one left to attack, he attacked himself. El-Mekki also talks about Ozzy Osburne being sued because it was believed his music was the cause of a teen committing suicide. Further on El-Mekki's sermon, he talks of a letter written by a wealthy Muslim to the tutor of his sons.

"He wrote to the tutors of his sons…who would teach poetry and refined manners and things to that sort. So he wrote to him, saying, let your first lesson to them be the hatred of musical instruments that begin with the Satan and end with the wrath of Allah. It grieves me that people with knowledge from listening to music and songs grow hypocrisy in their hearts the same way water causes plants to grow. So with that, we say to the one who listens to music, Oh Muslim, lawful things have good attributes.

Where is the good in singing, and dancing
    and listening to flutes?
Can we compare the wisdom and songs of musicians
    to the glorious Quran, its wisdom and admonitions?
 How many singers do you know and give admiration?
 And how many do you know of the companions
    and the following generation?
How much do you spend on singers from your dollars
    compared to what you know of Islamic scholars?
Do you see how much is memorized of music and songs,
    while you ignore the book to which memorization belongs.
How much do you memorize of these incantations
    and sway back and forth in intoxication?
Have you not seen those who follow the misguided
    and increase the loudness of the music
    when they should hide it? …"[170]

---

[170] El-Mekki, K. (2008, June 9). *The End of Music*. Retrieved July 9, 2020, from YouTube:

169

Shi'ites also do not accept musical instruments. On Shia Chat.com, a question was asked if music (in general) was forbidden. Syed Rizvi answered the question by citing Shi'ite traditions:

Hazrat Imam Ali ar-Reza (a.s.) remarks, "A person invites Divine wrath when in his house, instruments like flute, drum and chess are played for forty days. If this man dies within these forty days, his death would be of a sinner and a transgressor. His place shall be in Hell. And what a dreadful place it is!" (Mustanad al Taraqi)

The Holy Prophet (s.a.w.) has stated, "A person who possesses a sitar, on the day of Qiyamat will be raised with a **black face**. His hands will be holding a sitar of fire. Seventy thousand angels with maces of fire will be **hitting him on the face and the head**. The singer will arise from his grave, blind, deaf and dumb. The adulterer will be similarly raised. The player of flute will also be made to rise in this way as will be the drum player." (Mustadrakul Wasael)

Hazrat Imam Ali ar-Reza (a.s.) has said, "To listen to a musical instrument is one of the Greater Sins." (Mustadrakul Wasael)

Amirul Momineen Ali (a.s.) says, "Angels do not even enter a house that has wine, drum, tambourine or a flute. Even the prayers of the inhabitants of this house are unacceptable. They are deprived of barakat." (Wasaelush Shia)[171]

---

https://www.youtube.com/watch?time_continue=92&v=RthlUOYkl7M&feature=emb_logo.

[171] Rizvi, S. (2007, June 28). *Is Music forbidden in Shia Islam?* Retrieved July 9, 2020, from ShiaChat.com: https://www.shiachat.com/forum/topic/234928794-is-music-forbidden-in-shia-islam.

The Shi'ites do not even make allowances for tambourines.

Interestingly, many Muslims living in Western civilization hold opposing views about music. Some claim that there is no prohibition against music. Some only prohibit instrumental music. But the problem with an individual Muslim disagreeing with this is that Shariah as a whole forbids them from having an opposing view.

a4.5 It is obligatory for one to know what is permissible and what is unlawful of food, drink, clothing, and so forth, of things one is unlikely to be able to do without. And likewise for the rulings on treatment of women if one has a wife.

Muslims are not allowed to disagree with the scholarly consensus that creates Shariah. They must accept it. So those Muslims who argue for the acceptance of music in any way other than is defined by shariah as acceptable are in essence, apostates.

How does this affect Muslims? How does this effect all the non-Muslims? Muslims believe shariah should be the law of the land. They want all non-Muslims to comply with shariah.

In September of 2015, in the country of France, a Muslim was seen on camera, teaching Muslim children about music. The children in the video were between 8 and 12 years of age.

"When Allah speaks of music in the Quran, he reminds us that <music> is Satan's language. When did he remind us of this? So those who love music, and listen to music, who are they listening to?"

<The children and the Imam respond,> "Satan."

<The preacher continues,> "They listen to the devil. There are people who have disobeyed Allah and listen to the devil. What did the Prophet say about these people? He said: 'They will be swallowed up by the earth.'"

<A child responds surprised,> "Really?"

171

<The imam lets the child see he heard him and says,> "…and they will be transformed into apes and into pigs. So he risks being swallowed up by the earth. Second point, Allah will transform them into apes and pigs. Those who love music would love to be transformed into apes and pigs. You agree! No matter what language the music, Arabic, French, Turkish … never mind. If there is a song and there are musical instruments, when you hear a violin, a drum or a synthesizer, it is?"

The children respond, "HARAM."

<The preacher adds,> "And the one who likes haram will be with the devil. And he who like the music, is liked by Satan or Allah?"

The children quickly answer, "Satan."

"So you must choose your side. Empty your mp3, transform it and replace it with the best words that exist - the Quran. Musical instruments are haram, and music is haram. Those who love music or listen to music risk being transformed into a pig or who will look like who?"

The children and the Imam answer, "Satan."[172]

In Muslim countries, they do more than condemn music with words, they arrest people for creating music! Mehdi Rajabian was arrested three times for making music. The first time, he was kept in solitary confinement for three months. The second time, he was sentenced to six years in prison and was forbidden from engaging

---

[172] *Muslim Music Lessons for Children in France (Sept 2015).* (2020, January 1). Retrieved July 13, 2020, from VladTepesBlog at 3Speak: https://3speak.online/watch?v=vladtepesblog/zopmwglx&utm_sourc e=studio.

in musical activities forever.[173] There was an appeal due to international pressure, and Mehdi was released after having served three years and was on probation for an additional three years. Mehdi was arrested for the third time in January 2020. Mehdi has a love for music. He said, "In the Middle East, an instrument can be as powerful as a gun."[174]

The Washington Report on Middle East Affairs ran an article titled, "The Suppression of Musical Culture in Gaza" in their June/July 2019 issue by Salsabeel H. Hamdan. The article begins with a quote from Naem Nasir, "WHEN MUSIC IS SUPPRESSED within a society, there is something wrong within its history, ideology, mind and—of course—spirit." Naem Nasir, is a former music teacher and now a well-known director of plays produced in both Gaza and the West Bank. Islam suppresses music so much in the Middle East, that "there are no music majors in secondary school or university, for example, and most (if not all) of few private teachers have left the Strip. The only music funded or otherwise supported to any significant degree is that which exalts Islam or adheres to a narrow definition of Palestinian heritage."[175]

Saudi Arabia ordered the arrest of a young woman for rapping in a video in February 2020 that went viral on YouTube. Because the video was about women and culture, and was not particularly about Islam, its content was judged "un-Islamic".[176]

Daniel Pipes, founder of the Middle East Forum, has written several articles on music and Islam; some of these articles, he

[173] Savage, M. (2020, January 1). *Mehdi Rajabian was sent to prison for making music - but he says that won't stop him.* Retrieved July 13, 2020, from BBC: https://www.bbc.com/news/entertainment-arts-51188865.

[174] Ibid.

[175] Hamdan, S. H. (2019, June/July). *The Suppression of Musical Culture in Gaza.* Retrieved July 13, 2020, from The Washington Report on Middle East Affairs: https://www.wrmea.org/2019-june-july/the-suppression-of-musical-culture-in-gaza.html.

[176] BBC News. (2020, February 22). *Saudi rapper faces arrest for Mecca Girl music video.* Retrieved July 13, 2020, from BBC News: https://www.bbc.com/news/world-middle-east-51597561.

updates whenever possible. He documented, "Mahmoud Ahmadinejad, seemingly addicted to making inflammatory statements, <on December 19, 2005> announced the banning of Western music from Iran's radio and television stations. 'Blocking indecent and Western music from the Islamic Republic of Iran Broadcasting is required,' came a laconic statement from on the Supreme Cultural Revolutionary Council which he heads."[177]

Pipes knows the difficulty that Islam has with music. He knows the difficulty Iran has had with banning music. He also understands that a refusal to accept music disables Iran's and even Islam as a whole in their ability to understand Western culture. This can be seen in statement:

"Various forms of Western music - from classical to rap - have appeared in Iran in recent years, so – should it be implemented – this will come as a wrenching cultural change. (And will it, I wonder, prohibit the sugary-sweet Western-music *nasheed*s such as "Gives Thanks to Allah" or those sung by Cat Stevens – previously, a favorite in Iran?) Not only does the decree hark back to the early days of Ayatollah Khomeini's Islamic revolution, but it also touches a deep chord within Muslims, something I wrestled with in some detail in a 1998 article, "You Need Beethoven to Modernize," where I made two points: to many Muslims, Western music symbolizes the whole of Western culture; and therefore, mastery of Western music serves as a proxy in for mastery of Western - i.e., modern - culture as a whole."[178]

Pipes is exactly right about music and western civilization. An inability to grasp music is an inability to grasp or understand the beliefs Western culture has about freedom and civilization as a whole. Daniel Pipes also provides one of the best resources, documenting Islam's inconsistency on Islam and music in his blog

---

[177] Pipes, D. (2005, December 29). *The Erratic Career of Western Music in Iran.* Retrieved July 16, 2020, from DanielPipes.org: http://www.danielpipes.org/blog/2005/12/ahmadinejad-bans-western-music-in-iran.

[178] Ibid.

posting "Islamists and Music."[179] One of the articles he references in the blog comes from May 2009. A French embassy in Riyadah sponsored operatic soprano Isabelle Poulenard and a female accompanist. Two days before the event was to take place, the event was forbidden. The reason the concert was granted permission was because of an "apparent high-level skirmish between religious and other officials."[180] Later in July of 2009, a concert billed as "Midnight Acoustic" was scheduled to take place inside a Riyadah housing compound for foreigners. A place "normally insulated from the Saudi cultural rules was shut down halfway through the performance! The religious police's arrival at the compound's gates ended the concert. This may have been because a concert slated as being for foreigners was half-filled with Saudis.[181]

Even as Daniel Pipes correctly documents that enforcement and bans on music seem inconsistent, the questions remain the same. If Islam as a whole thinks that music is evil, what will they do when given a chance to write law on a federal level? Will they impose a ban on music to be enforced on Muslims and non-Muslims? Will Muslims attempt to ban non-Muslims from making music or listening to if it they have control of a village, town or, city? Is this something you are willing to risk?

---

[179] Pipes, D. (2007, August 3). *Islamists and Music.* Retrieved July 16, 2020, from DanielPipes.org:
http://www.danielpipes.org/blog/2007/08/music-and-islamists.

[180] Daily NewsEgypt . (2009, July 21). *Saudis reel as clerics say movie show must not go on.* Retrieved July 16, 2020, from The Free Library.com:
https://www.thefreelibrary.com/Saudis%20reel%20as%20clerics%20say%20movie%20show%20must%20not%20go%20on.-a0204139040.

[181] Ibid.

Chapter 19

Is there an Islamic social norm of Hatred Against all that is non-Muslim?

The United States of America was founded on the belief that people should be able to worship God as they pleased. The Brownists in England were being persecuted by the Church of England for expressing a disgust towards the church and her leaders for compromising on Christian doctrines. After a period of strife and persecution, they were encouraged to find their way to America on the Mayflower.

The USA has had many arguments on religion since its colonial days. Even an argument about a claim that there exists "separation of Church and state" in the Constitution; it must be noted that that phrase is not in the Constitution, but can be found in the Communist Manifesto.

In Europe, after the period of the Inquisition, countries were tired of persecution because of religion and fought for freedom of religion. The belief that people should be able to worship as they desire became very important.

Unlike citizens in America, Canada, and most of Europe, freedom to worship God in the way you choose is forbidden in most Islamic countries. Worshipping a God other than Allah is often considered illegal. Christians can be charged with shirk, the worst of all crimes under Shariah; the crime of polytheism. This is because Muslims are taught that Christians believe in three gods.

The Islamic social norm against freedom of religion was established in the Quran.

"If anyone desires a religion other than Islam (sub-mission to Allah), never will it be accepted of him; and in the Hereafter, He will be in the ranks of those who have lost (All spiritual good)." (Quran 3:85)

"...The only religion in the sight of God is Islam..." (Quran 3:19)

Islam is an exclusive faith. It not only excludes those of other faiths, it allows for physical attacks, fights, wars, and more as a method of spreading Islam. Islam allows Muslims to unite to stand against unbelievers.

"Muhammad is the messenger of Allah; and those who are with him are strong against Unbelievers, (but) compassionate amongst each other." (Quran 48:29)

"O Prophet! Strive hard against the unbelievers and the Hypocrites, and be firm against them. Their abode is Hell - an evil refuge indeed." (Quran 9:73)

"We will cast terror into the hearts of those who disbelieve, because they set up with Allah that for which He has sent down no authority, and their abode is the fire, and evil is the abode of the unjust." (Quran 3:151)

"And if any believe not in Allah and His Messenger, We have prepared, for those who reject Allah, a Blazing Fire!" (Quran 48:13)

You would think from reading these verses that Islam is engaging in a war against all who are not Muslims. But that is only part of where hatred against others is placed. There is also a hatred against those who call themselves Muslims and are deemed hypocrites. This is why the "Great Apostacy" (Riddah) War happened before Islamic expansion. Surah 9:73 tells us that

177

Muslims have no problem killing other Muslims who they deem not Muslim enough.

Hatred and violence against hypocrites is historically deemed as preferable by Muslims, versus engaging in jihad. This is because the acts of hatred against hypocrites are seen as an act of purification of Islam.

Why is this possible? How could a religion permit attacking their own? Their Quran has the answer:

*They wish you would disbelieve as they disbelieved so you would be alike. So, do not take from among them allies until they emigrate for the cause of Allah. **But if they turn away, then seize them and kill them wherever you find them** and take not from among them any ally or helper. Except for those who take refuge with a people between yourselves and whom is a treaty or those who come to you, their hearts strained at [the prospect of] fighting you or fighting their own people. And if Allah had willed, He could have given them power over you, and they would have fought you. So if they remove themselves from you and do not fight you and offer you peace, then Allah has not made for you a cause [for fighting] against them. You will find others who wish to obtain security from you and [to] obtain security from their people. Every time they are returned to [the influence of] disbelief, they fall back into it. So if they do not withdraw from you or offer you peace or restrain their hands, **then seize them and kill them** wherever you overtake them. And those - We have made for you against them a clear authorization. (Surah 4:89)*

But if they repent, establish prayer, and give zakah, then they are your brothers in religion; and We detail the verses for a people who know. And if they break their oaths after their treaty and defame your religion, then fight the leaders of disbelief, for indeed, there are no oaths [sacred] to them; [fight them that] they might cease. (Surah 9:11-12)

Even Hadiths justify killing those who leave Islam if one simply does not agree with one little thing. Bukhari is one of the most respected collections of hadiths.

Narrated Ikrima:

Ali burnt some people and this news reached Ibn 'Abbas, who said, "Had I been in his place I would not have burnt them, as the Prophet said, 'Don't punish (anybody) with Allah's Punishment.' No doubt, I would have killed them, for the Prophet said, 'If somebody (a Muslim) discards his religion, kill him.'" (Sahih Bukhari 52:260)

Narrated Abu Burda:

*Abu Musa said, "I came to the Prophet along with two men (from the tribe) of Ash'ariyin; one on my right, and the other on my left, while Allah's Apostle was brushing his teeth (with a Siwak), and both men asked him for some employment. The Prophet said, 'O Abu Musa (O 'Abdullah bin Qais!).' I said, 'By Him Who sent you with the Truth, these two men did not tell me what was in their hearts and I did not feel (realize) that they were seeking employment.' As if I were looking now at his Siwak being drawn to a corner under his lips, and he said, 'We never (or, we do not) appoint for our affairs anyone who seeks to be employed. But O Abu Musa! (or 'Abdullah bin Qais!) Go to Yemen.'" The Prophet then sent Mu'adh bin Jabal after him and when Mu'adh reached him, he spread out a cushion for him and requested him to get down (and sit on the cushion). Behold: There was a fettered man beside Abu Muisa. Mu'adh asked, "Who is this (man)?" Abu Muisa said, "He was a Jew and became a Muslim and then reverted back to Judaism." Then Abu Muisa requested Mu'adh to sit down but **Mu'adh said, "I will not sit down till he has been killed. This is the judgment of Allah and His Apostle (for such cases) and repeated it thrice. Then Abu Musa ordered that the man be killed, and he was killed.** Abu Musa added, "Then we discussed the night prayers and one of us said, 'I* *pray and sleep, and I hope that Allah will reward me for my sleep as well as for my prayers.'"* (Sahih Bukhari 6923)

The apostate was put to death without a second thought. It was so easy for them to perform the act that they talk about Allah rewarding them! If it is easy to kill those who leave Islam, how easy it is to demand such a thing for other religions? Under the first Caliph Abu Bakr, those who did not want to pray at a certain time were attacked! These acts of violence are seen as uniting Islam.

Narrated Abu Huraira:

*The Prophet said, "No prayer is harder for the hypocrites than the Fajr and the 'Isha' prayers, and if they knew the reward for these prayers at their respective times, they would certainly present themselves (in the mosques) even if they had to crawl." The Prophet added, "Certainly, I decided to order the Mu'adh-dhin (call-maker) to pronounce Iqama and order a man to lead the prayer and **then take a fire flame to burn all those who had not left their houses so far for the prayer along with their houses.**"* (Sahih al-Bukhari 657)

Are these things happening today? Is Islam killing off those who leave it or disagree with Islam in one slight way?

If so, they must be teaching hatred of all that is not Islam. That would mean that anyone and anything not Islamic should receive no respect. Could this be why presidential candidate Donald Trump stated, "I think Islam hates us."[182] Was Donald Trump right about Islam in 2016?

There are hadiths that discuss this refusal to allow others to believe differently about God.

---

[182] Schleifer, T. (2016, March 10). *Donald Trump: 'I think Islam hates us'.* Retrieved July 28, 2020, from CNN: https://www.cnn.com/2016/03/09/politics/donald-trump-islam-hates-us/index.html.

"It has been narrated by 'Umar b. al-Khattib that he heard the Messenger of Allah (say: "It has been narrated by 'Umar b. al-Khattib that he heard the Messenger of Allah ((say: I will expel the Jews and Christians from the Arabian Peninsula and will not leave any but Muslim." (Sahih Muslim, Hadith 1767)

This can be viewed in a simpler manner. Does Islam teach hatred of other religions? Does it teach disrespect towards any who hold another belief other than a belief in Muhammad and his god Allah? Reread the Hadith, what do you think?

If it teaches hatred of other religions, would it then teach hatred of those who leave Islam? Islam requires those who leave it to be labeled Apostates. Apostates can be killed under sharia.

The Islamic doctrine of *al-wala' wa'l-bara'* mentioned in Chapter 3 can also be translated as 'loving and hating' according to Raymond Ibrahim.[183] In January 2020, the two jihadis that stabbed and killed two police officers in Russia released a picture of themselves holding their knives before going on jihad. Underneath they wrote, "Love and hatred <is> based on Tawhid <oneness of Allah>!"[184] This oneness is both loving and hating according to this teaching.

This claim that hatred is based on their god Allah is something often overlooked as impossible to accept by the rest of the world. Even though the Quran has been around for over a thousand years, very few have looked at it and examined it for how much it teaches and embraces a culture of hatred of those outside the faith and a love for those inside.

---

[183] Ibrahim, R. (2020, January 18). *"Hating and Loving" for Islam.* Retrieved July 28, 2020, from Yonkers Tribune.com: https://www.yonkerstribune.com/2020/01/hating-and-loving-for-islam-by-raymond-ibrahim.

[184] Stewart, W. (2020, January 1). *Horrifying moment two 'Islamic terrorists' - including an arm-wrestling champion - kill two cops in a knife frenzy after mowing one down in a car in a Russian city.* Retrieved July 28, 2020, from Daily Mail: https://www.dailymail.co.uk/news/article-7842643/Horrifying-moment-two-Islamic-terrorists-kill-two-cops-knife-frenzy-Russia.html.

Usama Dakdok points out that daily prayers are immersed in teaching this hatred through rote memorization and repetition of Surah 1, which "Muslim children learn at an early age, and which all Muslims repeat up to 17 times in their 5 daily prayers."

1   In the name of Allah, the Entirely Merciful, the Especially Merciful.
2   [All] praise is [due] to Allah, Lord of the worlds.
3   The Entirely Merciful, the Especially Merciful.
4   Sovereign of the Day of Recompense.
5   It is You we worship and You we ask for help.
6   Guide us to the straight path –
7   The path of those upon whom You have bestowed favor, not of those who have evoked [Your] anger or of those who are astray.

Verse 7 refers to "those who have evoked your anger or those who are astray." Who are these two groups? The answer is in another English translation of the Quran. Mohsin Khan's translation of verse 7 reads:

The Way of those on whom You have bestowed Your Grace, not (the way) of **those who earned Your Anger (such as the Jews),** nor of **those who went astray (such as the Christians).**

Teachers understand the importance of repetition when teaching new concepts. Zig Ziglar said, "Repetition is the mother of learning, the father of action, which makes it the architect of accomplishment." 17 repetitions each day about those who have earned hatred and those who have gone astray is only touching on the teaching and training of hatred in Islamic culture. Anthony Robbins said, "Repetition is the mother of skill." Those involved in law enforcement and the military understand the importance of this phrase. They practice something 2,500 times to make their reactions instinctive, not reactive.

17 prayers x 7 days =   119 prayers a week.
119 prayers x 4 weeks = 476 prayers a month.
476 prayers x 12 months = 5,712 prayers a year.

These are prayers that teach Muslims that God hates Jews and that Christians have abandoned their Allah. But it is only of one chapter in the Quran.

Mohsin Khan's translation of Surah 2:8-9, 14 is also of interest;

And of mankind, there are some (hypocrites) who say: "We believe in Allah and the Last Day" while in fact they believe not. They (think to) deceive Allah and those who believe, while they only deceive themselves, and perceive (it) not! ... And when they meet those who believe, they say: "We believe," but when they are alone with their Shayatin (devils - polytheists, hypocrites, etc.), they say: "Truly, we are with you; verily, we were but mocking.

This passage allows for distrust, even of other Muslims. Not only distrust, but a reason for anger. Sadly, this creates a paranoia, wondering who amongst the followers of Allah should not be trusted and must be excluded, from amongst not only Islam itself but each and every gathering of Muslims.

Hatred against those who are not Muslim is idealized in Surah 58:22 according to Mohsin Khan's translation. It reads:

*You (O Muhammad) will not find any people who believe in Allah and the Last Day, making friendship with those who oppose Allah and His Messenger (Muhammad), **even though they were their fathers, or their sons, or their brothers, or their kindred (people)**. For such, He has written Faith in their hearts, and strengthened them with Ruh (proofs, light and true guidance) from Himself. And We will admit them to Gardens (Paradise) under which rivers flow, to dwell therein (forever). Allah is pleased with them, and they, with Him. They are the Party of Allah. Verily, it is the Party of Allah that will be the successful.*

Ibn Kathir, a commentator on the Quran said that this verse has a secret meaning; "(Allah is well pleased with them, and they are well pleased with Him) contains a **beautiful secret. When the believers became enraged against their relatives and kindred in Allah's cause, He compensated them by being pleased with them** and making them pleased with Him from what He has granted them of eternal delight, ultimate victory and encompassing favor. Allah's statement."[185] This favors the concept of honor killing!

Hatred seems embedded in this faith. When they teach children about Islam, they teach concepts like "Who is a real Muslim?" and "Who is a Kaffir?" before going beyond and defining Islam. This can be found in a textbook for 7th grade students in Islamic Schools in America titled <u>What Islam Is All About</u> by Yahiya Emerick. This book states:

A person who rejects the message of the Shahadah is called a **Kafir**. The word comes from the Arabic term *Kafara* which means to cover up or hide something. A kafir is a person who covers up the truth and tries to hide it (i.e., a Truth Hider). Whether it's through laziness, outright rebellion or simple ignorance, a person who does not even make the effort to obey what Allah has ordained can never be counted among the believers. They are the ones who will be unhappy in this life and punished in the next because they are false to their inner nature. (7:182-183)[186]

Verse 182-183 cited here are significant. The Standard English translation states:

But those who deny Our signs - We will progressively lead them [to destruction] from where they do not know. And I will give them time. Indeed, my plan is firm.

---

[185] Kathir, I. (n.d.). *Tafsir Ibn Kathir- Surah 58. Al-Mujadila , Introduction.* Retrieved July 29, 2020, from Alim.org: http://www.alim.org/library/quran/AlQuran-tafsir/TIK/58.

[186] Emerick, Y. (1997). *What Islam Is All About.* Long Island City, NY: International Books and Tapes Supply, p. 56.

Moshin Khan's translation is even harder against the kafir:

Those who reject Our Ayat (proofs, evidences, verses, lessons, signs, revelations, etc.), We shall gradually seize them with punishment in ways they perceive not. And I respite them; certainly My Plan is strong.

This means that Allah does not love the person who does not believe. In fact, he seems to do the opposite and hate. So, what about Muslims? Are all those who consider themselves Muslim safe from being in trouble and called a kafir? Yahiya Emerick tells 7th grade American Muslims, "If a person thinks that they are a Muslim, but they have no faith in Islamic teachings and make no effort to make Islamic learning and practices part of their life, then they are no Muslim at all!"[187] While the section continues and tells children not to call non-Muslims kafirs and tells them to reason unbelievers in a "superior manner," it has taught them to disrespect and despise the non-Muslim; even a Muslim who is not Islamic enough should be thought of as not Muslim.

This again sets the stage for honor killings. When children or relatives decide not to obey the shariah, there is a penalty that can be paid – DEATH! In American law, Murder is a crime punishable by death in some states. The laws have some exceptions, one of them being self-defense. In sharia, murder is a capital crime, for which there are also allowances. Here are four of them.

(1) A child or insane person, under any circumstances.
(2) A Muslim for killing a non-Muslim.
(3) A Jewish or Christian subject of the Islamic State for killing an apostate from Islam because a subject of the state is under its protection, while killing an apostate from Islam without consequences.

---

[187] Ibid.

(4) A father or mother (or their fathers or mothers)
for killing their offspring, or offspring's
offspring.[188]

One such honor killing occurred in India a few days before
this part was written. On August 5, 2020 in Karcha village in
Mataundh, not far from Utter Pradesh, India, a 19-year-old
woman and her alleged boyfriend were caught in
"compromising position." The family members locked them in
the hut and set it on fire.[189]

In Islam, a compromising position can be simply being with
a member of the opposite sex who is not a family member,
without supervision. It could be that they were caught kissing.
That is why the news article does not define the term. The
moment these two were caught not being an example of Islam,
they were condemned as not being Islamic enough and
executed. Hatred is sown and cultivated in Islam against all that
is not Islamic to such an extent that even family members must
die if they are not Islamic enough. This is a judgement that they
have left Islam, thus, they are guilty of apostasy.

o8.0 APOSTASY FROM ISLAM (RIDDA) (O: Leaving
Islam is the ugliest form of unbelief (kufr) and the worst. It
may come about through sarcasm, as when someone is told,
"trim your nails, it is sunna," and he replies, "I would not
do it even if it were," as opposed to when some
circumstances exist which exonerates him of having
committed apostasy, such as when his tongue runs away
with him, or when he is quoting someone, or says it out of
fear.)

---

[188] Reliance of the Traveller, o1.2, p. 582.

[189] India TV News. 2020. "Couple burnt alive in suspected honour killing in
Uttar Pradesh." *India TV News.* August 6. Accessed August 7, 2020.
https://www.indiatvnews.com/crime/couple-burnt-alive-in-suspected-
honour-killing-in-uttar-pradesh-639962.

o8.1 When a person who has reached the age of puberty and is sane voluntarily apostatizes from Islam, he deserves to be killed.

The wording in shariah here allows accusations to quickly give rise to condemnation and a death sentence. Such is the excuse given for many an honor killing. A wife, daughter or son has disobeyed Allah by not obeying shariah and thus the parent is justified by killing them.

In Germany, honor killings have gone from something you read in the news from Pakistan, to something you can now see while riding the bus to work. On July 6, 2020 in Obergünzburg (Ostallgäu district),[190] what was known as a quiet town, a 37-year-old Afghan migrant killed his wife with a knife right on the bus in front of everyone before running off. Under shariah, she had no right to leave him, but she had, legally, under German law. That was all he needed to take her life, a violation of shariah.

On September 5, 2019 in King's Crossing, a sub-division in Corpus Christi's southside, 72-year-old Mohammad Sahi, killed his daughter and grandson, and brutally beat to the edge of death his other grandson.[191] He quickly confessed to the crime after the brutal murder. It is thought that he viewed this as an honor killing.

---

[190] Welt. (2020, July 6). *Man kills his wife - in the middle of a bus.* Retrieved August 12, 2020, from Welt.de: https://www.welt.de/vermischtes/article211129199/Bayern-Mann-toetet-seine-Ehefrau-mitten-in-einem-Linienbus.html,

[191] Churchwell, B., & Munson, J. (2019, September 13). *'Yes that's fine. I did it,': Mohammad Sahi makes first court appearance since chilling double homicide.* Retrieved August 12, 2020, from WTSP.com: https://www.wtsp.com/article/news/crime/yes-thats-fine-i-did-it-mohammad-sahi-makes-first-court-appearance-since-chilling-double-homicide/503-b23e1ff3-9a19-4f9a-834b-b0b24018b088.

This horrible crime of "honor killing" is thought to now occur in the United Kingdom 12 times a year.[192] Soren Kern tracked 30 honor killings in Germany in the first five months of 2017.[193] A 2014 study done by the Department of Justice in the United States of America, before the massive hijra into Europe and North America in 2015, had some surprising estimates.

On August 21, 2020 *Le Parisien* posted an article about a 17-year-old Muslim girl who fell in love with a 20-year-old man they call a Christian, and moved in with him.[194] They went to visit her parents, because she missed them. They assaulted her, shaving her head, breaking her ribs and could have continued further and killed her. But the young man who came with her broke free and grabbed local law enforcement. The numerous bruises around her ears say everything about the murderous intentions of her parent's actions of hatred against their daughter who was not Islamic enough. The parents were charged with "violence against a minor" in France. Under shariah, this would not be a crime. The parents did not see what they did as something wrong.

On August 26, 2020 Yaser Abdel Said, was captured after 12 years on the run because, murder of your children is a crime

---

[192] Lake, E. (2018, September 17). *HONOUR CRIMES What is an honour killing and how common are the horrific crimes in the UK?* Retrieved August 12, 2020, from The Sun:
https://www.thesun.co.uk/news/4091357/what-is-honour-killing-murder-uk/#:~:text=Data%20from%20the%20HBVAN%20estimates,can%20include%20abductions%20and%20beatings.

[193] Kern, S. (2017, May 30). *Germany: Wave of Muslim Honor Killings.* Retrieved August 12, 2020, from Gatestone Institute:
https://www.gatestoneinstitute.org/10441/germany-muslim-honor-killings.

[194] Le Parisien. (2020, August 21). *Besancon: shaved and beaten by her family because she is seeing a Christian.* Retrieved August 22, 2020, from Le Parisien: https://www.leparisien.fr/faits-divers/besancon-tondue-et-frappee-par-sa-famille-parce-qu-elle-frequente-un-chretien-21-08-2020-8370981.php.

in America.[195] This heinous murder and his eluding the police put him on the Top 10 Wanted list of the FBI in December of 2014.[196] Yaser Said, shot and killed his teenage daughters, Amina (18) and Sarah (17), while taking them for a ride in his taxi under the pretense of getting something to eat.

This act of violence was not the first one they had received at the hand of their father. Allegations of physical and sexual abuse were made by Amina and Sarah against their father to the police before their mother made the choice to flee with the girls in 2007. [197] Amina even told others her Dad would kill her if he could.[198]

Their mother "Tissie" returned to their father after not even a year apart. Dr. Phyllis Chesler, noted scholar and warrior for the rights of those suffering from Islamic Gender Apartheid, along with the girl's aunt, believes that Tissie took part in an elaborate ruse to trick the girls into seeing their father, knowing full well he would kill them if given the chance.[199]

What had they done to warrant such hatred and evil from their father and mother? Part of this begins from birth with the devaluing of Islamic females from birth, as shown in Chapter

---

[195] Heinz, F. (2020, August 26). *Yaser Said, Taxi Driver Accused of Killing His Teen Daughters in 2008, Caught in North Texas.* Retrieved August 27, 2020, from NBC - Dallas Fort Worth: https://www.nbcdfw.com/news/local/yaser-said-taxi-driver-accused-of-killing-his-teen-daughters-in-2008-caught-in-north-texas/2433246/.

[196] Newsome, J. (2014, December 4). *Capital Murder Suspect Added to FBI's Ten Most Wanted Fugitives List.* Retrieved August 27, 2020, from FBI.gov: https://www.fbi.gov/contact-us/field-offices/dallas/news/press-releases/capital-murder-suspect-added-to-fbis-ten-most-wanted-fugitives-list.

[197] Chesler, P. (2012, May 12). *Arrest mother as accomplice in Texas honor killing.* Retrieved August 27, 2020, from Fox News: https://www.foxnews.com/opinion/arrest-mother-as-accomplice-in-texas-honor-killing.

[198] Ibid.

[199] Ibid.

8. They were dating boys who were not Muslims.[200] This, in his mind made them Apostates, since such a thing is forbidden to Muslim women under shariah. It brought shame on the family since women are property to Muslims.

This hatred extends to killing those who claim to be Muslims and are not in their view. The charge of blasphemy is a death sentence. Blasphemy charges in countries like Pakistan can even be leveled against American citizens. Tahir Ahmad Naseem moved to America in 1978. He was of the Ammadiya sect of Muslims which is highly persecuted and not accepted by any Muslim group for several reasons. Naseem was sharing his religious views on YouTube in America. People in Pakistan sent him an invitation in 2018 to debate his claims of being a prophet if he would come. He accepted. "The trap" was set, and he went to find himself quickly arrested and charged with Blasphemy. For two years, Tahir Naseem was in jail awaiting his trial. His lawyer was reported to have communicated a likely win because they had no evidence. But on July 29, 2020 the day Naseem was finally going to get his trial and possibly be set free to return to the USA, a 15-year-old boy entered the court room and shot him several times, claiming he killed Naseem in defense of Islam.[201] This hatred of anything non-Muslim can be seen in what happened shortly after. On August 10, 2020, The Wire, out of Indonesia, reported that, "Faisal Khan, a 15-year-

---

[200] Lopez, R. (2019, June 28). *More than a decade after teens killed in suspected honor killing, police believe dad may be in North Texas.* Retrieved August 27, 2020, from WFAA: https://www.wfaa.com/article/news/crime/more-than-a-decade-after-teens-killed-in-suspected-honor-killing-police-believe-dad-may-be-in-north-texas/287-959822c4-85a7-4cf4-af5a-a55f708ef0e9.

[201] Khan, A. (2020, August 19). *Her American father was shot in a blasphemy trial in Pakistan. Now she's fighting for justice.* Retrieved August 22, 2020, from Religion News: https://religionnews.com/2020/08/19/her-father-was-shot-in-a-blasphemy-trial-in-pakistan-now-shes-fighting-for-justice.

old Pakistani, beams for selfies with lawyers and police. Thousands hail him in the streets as a 'holy warrior.'"[202]

One would think that this hatred of all that is not Islamic would surface quietly and be able to be seen easily. Europe is seeing this since the great hijrah in 2015. Numerous churches and synagogues have been attacked and defaced. On August 20, 2020, Sputnik, a Russian news source posted an article on a Muslim migrant from Somalia, having confessed to setting fire to two churches in Norway because someone set fire to a Quran.[203] The result was over $2.2 million in damages!

The culture of hatred is attractive to people who find themselves behind bars and get there with a sense of anger and hatred against the world for whatever injustice they believe exists in the world. In the words of one ex-Muslim, who I will call J, who shared about this attraction posed by the hatred and anger in Islam to those in prison;

It seems it had a special appeal for me, the anger…I've seen a lot of other brothers who were angry, who were Muslim and I felt like I would be a part of something and <by joining them> I would be angry too, and then we would just walk around with our kufis and our prayer rugs, looking tough, ya know, and people would leave us alone…because they were afraid of us.

Patrick Dunleavy, writes about the conversion of men to Islam in the New York State prison system in his book, <u>The Fertile Soil of Jihad: Terrorism's Prison Connection (2011)</u>.

---

[202] Farooq, U., & Ahmad, J. (2020, August 10). *Pakistan: Teen Celebrated, Called 'Holy Warrior' for Killing 'Blasphemous' American.* Retrieved August 22, 2020, from The Wire: https://thewire.in/south-asia/pakistan-teen-celebrated-called-holy-warrior-for-killing-blasphemous-american.

[203] Sputnik News. (2020, August 20). *Somali Man Who Torched Two Norwegian Churches Says It Was Revenge for Quran Burning.* Retrieved August 22, 2020, from Sputnik News: https://sputniknews.com/europe/202008201080223451-somali-man-who-torched-two-norw.

Dunleavy was the Inspector General of the Criminal Intelligence Unit of the New York State Bureau of Correction Services. Dunleavy was a key figure in Operation Hades that exposed elements of an Islamic terror network that utilized prisons.

This is only the tip of the iceberg. Throughout Western Civilization, Islamic organizations such as the Muslim Council of Britain (MCB), in America, The Council of American-Islamic Relations (CAIR), and more are actively working to prevent an equal voice from other religions; worse is that they are preventing factual information from being shared, and in essence, making the public ignorant of what Islam believes and teaches. The previous chapter on Freedom of Speech barely touches on what is happening today in Western Civilization. These two topics, Freedom of Speech and Freedom of Religion are so intertwined.

Chapter 20

Is there an Islamic Social Norm that promotes WAR (Jihad) against Non-Muslims?

Whenever the topic of Jihad, an Islamic war against all non-Muslims comes up, people come out of the woodwork to defend Islam. Nothing you can say or do will allow change in their minds. Worse, is that even if you show them evidence from Islamic scripture, they flat out deny that jihad is an Islamic social norm or worse, an actual essential doctrine of Islam.

Examples of people coming out of the woodwork to defend Islam after an act of terrorism are numerous. Some of the defense of Islam comes from our own politicians.

President George W. Bush (September 20, 2001)
"The terrorists are traitors to their own faith, trying, in effect, to hijack Islam itself. The enemy of America is not our many Muslim friends; it is not our many Arab friends. Our enemy is a radical network of terrorists, and every government that supports them." (Joint Session of Congress and the American People, United States Capitol, Washington, D.C. September 20, 2001.)

This statement alone by Pres. George W. Bush created policy that constrained the Intelligence Community in the United States from truly learning Al Qaeda's threat doctrine. Threat doctrine is essential knowledge for any military professional! Military officials must know their enemy in order to win any battle. In the words of Sun Tzu,

> *If you know the enemy and know yourself, you need not fear the result of a hundred battles. If you know yourself, but not the enemy, for every victory gained you will also suffer a defeat. If you know neither the enemy nor yourself, you will succumb in every battle.*

Steven Coughlin's work "'To Our Great Detriment': Ignoring What Extremists Say About Jihad" (May 2007), revealed that President Bush words on September 20, 2001, essentially forbid a study by members of the Intelligence Community into the Islamic doctrine of Jihad by proclaiming that "Islam was hijacked" and that "the enemy was not Islam." It did not matter whether this was true or not. After that speech, it became off limits to truly discover what jihad is, if it was the threat doctrine of Al Qaeda and how far removed – or not - it was from "mainstream" Islam.

A few years later, other politicians committed the same mistake and in the words of Stephen Coughlin it was indeed "to our great detriment!"

Hillary Clinton (2015) after the attack in Paris and before San Bernardino: "Let's be clear: Islam is not our adversary. Muslims are peaceful and tolerant people and have nothing whatsoever to do with terrorism."[204]

---

[204] Charen, M. (2015, December 4). *'Nothing to Do With Islam'*. Retrieved April 11, 2020, from Real Clear Politics: https://www.realclearpolitics.com/articles/2015/12/04/nothing_to_do_with_islam_128933.html.

Even though Coughlin saw the answer, we still need to ask the question once again. "Were the politicians right? Is Islam not an enemy?" To those, I add my questions:

1) What if there is a social norm that promotes jihad, holy war against non-Muslims?
2) What if Islamic scriptures proclaim jihad against non-Muslims as an active war that will not end until the whole world is Muslim?
3) What if that is true?

The responsible thing would be to look and see what Islamic scriptures, scholars and shariah states about Jihad. Then if Islam indeed does teach jihad as a holy war against non-Muslims, there are two more very important questions that need to be considered.

1) Is this taught in your local mosque?
2) Is this taught in your local madrassa (Islamic school)?

What is in the Islamic scriptures with respect to jihad? Better yet, where should one begin to look for a definition on the concept of jihad? The answer is in their law – Sharia. Sunni Islam has four schools of thought in Shariah, *The International Institute of Islamic Thought,* gave their stamp of approval for the English translation of 'Umdat Al-Salik. In English, the book is called 'Umdat al-Salik aka Reliance of the Traveller. It is extensive and covers everything from daily life to rules about war and more. Shariah's definition of jihad follows:

o9.0 JIHAD
(O: Jihad means to war against the non-Muslims, and is etymologically derived from the word *mujahada,* signifying warfare to establish the religion. And it is the lesser jihad. As for the greater jihad, it is spiritual warfare against the lower self (nafs), which is why the Prophet said, as he was returning from jihad;

"We have returned from the lesser jihad to the greater jihad."

The scriptural basis for jihad, prior to scholarly consensus (def: b7) include Quranic verses such as:

(2) "Fighting is prescribed for you." (Quran 2:216)
(3) **"Slay them wherever you find them."** (Quran 4:89)
(4) "Fight the idolators utterly." (Koran 9:36)

In addition, such hadiths as the one related by Bukhari and Muslim that the Prophet said:

"I have been commanded to fight people until they testify that there is no God but Allah and that Muhammad is the Messenger of Allah, and perform the prayer, and pay zakat. **If they say it, they have saved their blood and possessions from me**, except for the rights of Islam over them. And their final reckoning is with Allah;"

And the hadith reported by Muslim,

"To go forth in the morning or evening to fight in the path of Allah is better than the whole world and everything in it."

WHOA! WAIT! THIS CAN'T BE TRUE! That was what I first thought the moment I read this for myself. Maybe, just maybe it's not for all the believers of Islam. Everything I had learned about Islam was upside down. Had I been lied to? Was I misinformed? How was it possible that just because I read a book for Muslims, I was learning that jihad is not just something for "extremists"? STOP! Extremists are people outside the norm. Jihad is being said here to be the norm! **So, even using the term "extremist" is misinformation.**

Maybe the hadith cited in shariah that states "We have returned from the lesser jihad to the greater jihad," provides an out. When you do a bit of research on this hadith, you learn that it

196

is classified as *da'if,* which means "weak". Credit should go to Stephen Coughlin for being one of the first to reveal that this concept came from a hadith that is labeled WEAK!

Further research on this reveals some very interesting elements about this "hadith." Wiki Islam has an entry labeled, *Lesser vs. Greater Jihad.*[205] It cites several Islamic scholars on the topic. The article states that:

> *It is claimed that this "inner Jihad" essentially refers to all the struggles that a Muslim may go through, in adhering to the religion. For example, a scholarly study of Islam can be an intellectual struggle that some allegedly may refer to as "jihad."*

Origins

During Prophet <u>Muhammad's</u> lifetime, and onward to the present, the word 'Jihad' was, and is, almost always used in a military sense.[1] This idea of a greater and lesser jihad was a later development which originated from the 11th century book, The History of Baghdad, by the Islamic scholar al-Khatib al-Baghdadi, by way of Yahya ibn al 'Ala', who said:

> *We were told by Layth, on the authority of 'Ata', on the authority of Abu Rabah, on the authority of Jabir, who said, 'The Prophet (salallaahu 'alayhee wa sallam) returned from one of his battles, and thereupon, told us, 'You have arrived with an excellent arrival, you have come from the Lesser Jihad to the Greater Jihad - the striving of a servant (of Allah) against his desires.'[2]*

All four schools of Sunni jurisprudence (Fiqh) as well as the Shi'ite tradition, all formulated in the 2nd and 3rd

---

[205]Wiki Islam. (2012). *Lesser vs. Greater Jihad.* Retrieved September 1, 2020, from Wiki Islam:
https://wikiislam.net/wiki/Lesser_vs_Greater_Jihad#Lesser_vs_Greater_Jihad_Concept.

centuries after Muhammad's death, make no reference at all to the "greater" jihad, only the lesser.[206]

(1) Bernard Lewis, "The Crisis of Islam", chapter 2, 2001.
(2) Fayd al-Qadir vol. 4, p. 511

The conclusion drawn by Wiki Islam is that this "hadith" is manufactured. It is made up, a conjecture of someone's imagination; someone who knew next to nothing about Islam, Muhammad or jihad.

This conclusion means that the ads that appeared on buses, and other means of mass transportation for "My jihad is…" was nothing more than a misinformation campaign for the gullible and foolish non-Muslims to swallow.

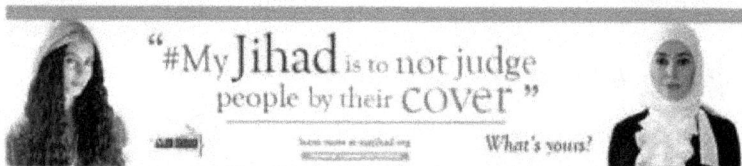

But there is more in shariah on jihad. The law book of Shariah 'Umdat al-Salik aka Reliance of the Traveller talked about the obligation character of jihad.

THE OBLIGATORY CHARACTER OF JIHAD

---

[206] Ibid

o.9.1 Jihad is a communal obligation. (def. c3.2). When enough people perform it to successfully accomplish it, it is no longer obligatory upon others (O: the evidence for which is the Prophet's saying

"He who provides the equipment for a soldier in jihad has performed jihad.").

The lights came on the moment I read this. I now understood why we find so many Muslims involved in raising money for what we call terrorism. But is "terrorism" the right word? After all, isn't what they do murder? Is the label terrorism a crime less severe than murder? Believe it or not, in most countries, murder is a capital offense when it is intentional, resulting in either a death penalty or life imprisonment. But terrorism? You get 20 years as a penalty then get out early for good behavior.

But think about this. If hatred against all that is not Islamic is a social norm, then how does Jihad not fit in as part of their social norms? Hatred against even their own children is approved of if they are not Islamic enough, so what would make us think that they would not have a social norm to wage war against all who are not Islamic?

Remember the topic of Abrogation discussed in Chapter 4. Abrogation is used to nullify passages where there is a disagreement between verses. These verses came earlier in the Quran, before Muhammad had political strength.

Jasser Auda's bio states he is the "Al-Shatibi Chair of Maqasid Studies at the International Peace College South Africa, a Visiting Professor for the Study of Islam at **Carleton University in Canada**, Founding Director of the Maqasid Center in the Philosophy of Islamic Law in London, and a professor at the University of Waterloo, Alexandria University, Islamic University of Novi Pazar, Qatar Faculty of Islamic Studies, and the **American University** of Sharjah in the UAE."[207] Dr. Auda is the author of Maqāsid al-Sharī`ah: A Beginner᾽s Guide. Note that he teaches at the "International Peace College in South Africa. Yet, in this book, he states that the "Verse of the Sword," Surah 9:5 contradicts more than 200 other verses in the Quran; peaceful verses. But because of the law of abrogation, "most exegetes concluded that this verse (9:5), which was revealed towards the end of the Prophet's life, abrogated each and every 'contradicting' verse that was revealed before it."[208] This reveals the importance of lying and deceit in Islam also mentioned in Chapter 4.

After thinking about this and reviewing Shariah, I went back to see what one of the most respected Islamic scholars Ibn Kathir wrote on the alleged "verse of the sword," Surah 9:5.

This is the Āyah of the Sword

Mujahid, 'Amr bin Shu'ayb, Muhammad bin Ishaq, Qatdah, As-Suddi and 'Abdur-Rahman bin Zayd bin Aslam said that the four months mentioned in this Ayah are the four months grace period mentioned in the earlier Ayah.

So, travel freely for four months throughout the land. Allah said next.

So when the sacred months have passed .... meaning, 'Upon the end of the four months during which We prohibited you from fighting the idolators, and which is the grace period We gave them, the fight and kill the idolators wherever you may find them.' Allah's statement next,

---

[207] Universiti Brunei Darussalam. (2015). *Prof. Dr. Jasser Auda.* Retrieved August 24, 2020, from Universiti Brunei Darussalam: https://expert.ubd.edu.bn/jasser.auda.

[208] Auda, J. (2008). *Maqāsid al-Sharī`ah: A Beginner's Guide.* Washington, DC: The International Institute of Islamic Thought, p. 29.

Then fight the Mushrikin wherever you find them, means on the earth in general, except for the Sacred Area, for Allah said,

And fight not with them at Al-Masjid Al-Haram, unless they fight you there, but if they attack you, then fight them. [2:191]

Allah said here,

and capture them, executing some and keeping some as prisoners,

and besiege them, and lie in wait for them in each and every ambush,

do not wait until you find them. Rather, seek and besiege them in their areas and forts, gather intelligence about them in the various roads and fairways that what is made wide looks ever smaller to them. This way they will have no choice, but to die or embrace Islam,

But if they repent and perform the Salah, and give the Zakah, then leave their way free. Verily, Allah is Oft-Forgiving, Most Merciful.

Abu Bakr As-Saddiq used this and other honorable Ayat as proof for fighting those who refrained from paying Zakah. These Ayat allowed fighting people unless, and until, they embrace Islam and implement its rulings and obligations. Allah mentioned the most important aspects of Islam here, including what is less important. Surely, the highest elements of Islam, after the Two testimonials, are the prayer, which is the right of Allah, the Exalted and Ever High, then the Zakah, which benefits the poor and needy. These are the most honorable acts that creatures perform, and this is why Allah often mentions the prayer and Zakah together. In the Two Sahihs, it is that Ibn 'Umar said that the messenger of Allah said,

I have been commanded to fight the people until they testify that there is no deity worthy of worship except Allah and that

*Muhammad is the Messenger of Allah, establish the prayer and pay the Zakah. (*Fath Al-Bari 1:*95 and Muslim 1:53)*

This honorable Ayah (9:5) was called the Ayah of the Sword, about which Ad-Dahhak bin Muzahim said, "it abrogated every treaty, and every term." Al 'Awfi said that ibn 'Abbas commented: "No idolator had any more treaty or promise of safety ever since *Surah Bara'ah* was revealed. The four months in addition to, all peace treaties conducted before *Bara'ah* was revealed and announced had ended by the tenth of the month of Rabi Al-Akhir. (At-Tabari 14:133) [209]

If this is what adults learn about jihad, what are they teaching children in Islamic schools about jihad?

What is said in a 7th grade history textbook for Muslims will shock you even more. What Islam is all About, addresses jihad in a chapter titled: The Three Duties. Jihad is listed as the SECOND DUTY!

This section states that the 1995 attack on the federal building in Oklahoma City, OK was done by a Christian terrorist, and that afterwards, "several majids <mosques> were burnt down, Muslim homes were vandalized and the FBI and news media were fingering Muslims as the responsible party."[210] Timothy McVeigh was not a Christian. The FBI never said that it was an act of Islamic terrorism. In fact, they were pretty silent until they knew what happened! No mosques were burned down and Muslim homes were not vandalized. But why was this said if it was not true in a kid's history book? The purpose was to create the belief that there are "Christians who are terrorists." On the next page, the book states that Islam is against random violence and senseless killing.

---

[209] Kathir, I. (2003). *Tafsir Ibn Kathir, Volume 4.* New York, NY: Darussalam, p. 374-377.

[210] Emerick, Y. (1997). *What Islam Is All About.* Long Island City, NY: International Books and Tapes Supply, p. 163.

According to the Qur'an, *"If you kill a life, it is as if you killed all life."* Of course, the life in question is of an innocent person. (Quran 2:190, 2:229, 16:90) [211]

There are three problems with this quote. The verses cited are indeed of interest also.

Surah 2:190 - And fight in the Way of Allah those who fight you, but transgress not the limits. Truly, Allah likes not the transgressors. [This Verse is the first one that was revealed in connection with Jihad, but it was supplemented by another (V.9:36)].

Surah 2:229 – Has to do with divorce! How this fits makes no sense. **Surah 16:90** is also strangely vague.

Why did they cite verse that do not connect to the topic? Because they teach Muslims you cannot read the Quran unless you know Arabic (See Chapter 7).

The third part of this is the sentence, "Of course the life in question is of an **innocent person**."[212] The word innocent is code to believers in Islam. It means, "Muslim." The verse quoted comes from Surah 5:32. Why is it not cited? Read and find out:

Because of that, **We ordained for the Children of Israel** *that if anyone killed a person not in retaliation of murder, or (and) to spread mischief in the land - it would be as if he killed all mankind,* and if anyone saved a life, it would be as if he saved the life of all mankind. And indeed, there came to them Our Messengers with clear proofs, evidences, and signs; even then, after that, many of them continued to exceed the limits (e.g. by

---

[211] Emerick p. 164.

[212] BBC News. (2013). *Hard Talk with Anjem Chaudary (8/5/2005).* Retrieved September 1, 2020, from YouTube: https://www.youtube.com/watch?v=223gLcfCj_c.

doing oppression unjustly, and exceeding beyond the limits set by Allah by committing the major sins) in the land!

Think of this reference now, they are talking about Jews doing the killing. On top of this, the 7th Grade textbook tells the Muslim children that this references killing Muslims. One paragraph later, it states:

However, the word jihad is most often associated with the act of physically confronting evil and wrong-doing, hence, it can be applied to the act of fighting as well (3:110). But the goal of jihad is not to have a big war, gain riches or kill people, it is to further the Cause of Allah and to create justice on earth (5:8). Then when the evil is removed of the other side wants peace, we are to make peace as well (8:61). ...[213]

A person who engages in jihad is called a **Mujahid,** or struggler for Allah. Allah also explained to us why fighting is sometimes a part of jihad. He said,

"Let those fight in the Cause of Allah who sell the life of this world for the next life. To the one who fights in the cause of Allah whether he is killed or achieves victory, we shall soon give him a great reward. And why shouldn't you fight in the Cause of Allah and those who, being weak, are mistreated, the men women and children, whose only cry is,

'Our Lord, save us from this land whose people are oppressors and bring to us from You someone who will protect us and bring us from You someone who will help.'

---

[213] Emerick, p. 164.

Those who believe in the Cause of Allah and those who reject faith fight in the cause of evil. So fight against the friends of Shaytan (4:74-76)."[214]

The duty of Muslims here is communicated to be one where physical fighting is permitted against unbelievers.

Not stated anywhere is why there is a statement that Jihad is not "for the gain riches or killing people." In Western civilization war is seen as a last resort after talks have failed, or what happens when someone attacks without reason. The thought of getting rich never enters your thoughts. But before the time of Muhammad according to Sayyid A'la Maududi in Jihad in Islam, one of the causes of pre-Islamic warfare was a love of booty (p. 125). Maududi claimed that Arabs before Islam found regular work demeaning, but loved battling to steal the wealth of others.

Maududi also wrote of hadiths where Muhammad claimed that the purpose of jihad is not for money, it is not for honor and it is not for war's sake alone, rather it is for the Cause of Allah. Jihad under these hadiths is not self-defensive. Its purpose is the spreading of Islam alone. Here is one such example:

*A person said to the Prophet that there were those who undertook wars for gathering spoils, some for making gains in respect and power, and others, to establish their reputation for bravery. After stating this, he inquired of the Prophet, as to which of these was in the cause of Allah. **The Prophet replied that, only war alone was in the cause of Allah, which was to spread His word.** " (Narrated by Abu Musa Al-Ashari)* [215]

If Maududi is correct here, and this hadith and others like it are accurate, the purpose of jihad is not defensive at all. Its sole purpose is for the "Cause of Allah". This statement could be equated to spreading Islam through the sword. But then, Maududi

---

[214] Emerick, p. 164-165
[215] Sahih Muslim Book #020, Hadith 4684.

believes he is writing only to Muslims, so his communication is more direct...

Mohshin Khan's translation of 3:110 is revealing also about who they, the jihadis intend to battle;

> *You [true believers in Islamic Monotheism, and real followers of Prophet Muhammad SAW and his Sunnah (legal ways, etc.)] are the best of peoples ever raised up for mankind; you enjoin Al-Ma'ruf (i.e. Islamic Monotheism and all that Islam has ordained) and forbid Al-Munkar (**polytheism, disbelief and all that Islam has forbidden**), and you believe in Allah. And **had the people of the Scripture (Jews and Christians) believed, it would have been better for them**; among them are some who have faith, but most of them are Al-Fasiqun (disobedient to Allah - and rebellious against Allah's Command).*

So, let's look at one of the verses they skipped in Surah 2. Verse 98 is on the topic.

Sahih International: Whoever is an enemy to Allah and His angels and His messengers and Gabriel and Michael - then indeed, Allah is an enemy to the disbelievers.

Muhammad Sarwar: And as a confirmation of (original) Scripture and whoever is the enemy of God, His angels, His Messenger, Gabriel and Michael, should know that God is the enemy of those who hide the Truth...

Mohsin Khan: "Whoever is an enemy to Allah, His Angels, His Messengers, Jibrael (Gabriel) and Mikael (Michael), then verily, Allah is an enemy to the disbelievers."

Is Physical Jihad the only Jihad?

Perhaps one of the most important pieces of knowledge on Jihad and Islam was hidden from the public by the American government from 1915 until the 1960s. In 1915, Ambassador

Morgenthau sent a copy of a Fatwa, issued by the Caliph that led to a genocide of the Armenian people and much more. Morgenthau communicated the violence in his autobiography, <u>Dr. Morgenthau's Story</u>, which is now available for free on the Internet. Dr. Andrew Bostom, revealed this long hidden fatwa in his book, <u>The Legacy Of Jihad: Islamic Holy War And The Fate Of Non-Muslims</u>, published in 2005.[216]

This fatwa proclaims extremely important information that many refuse to acknowledge. Namely, that jihad is not only a physical battle, but the other levels of jihad are indeed extremely dangerous and can at times be seen as more dangerous than an actual bloody confrontation.

> 1) **Jihad in secret**. This is the easiest and simplest. In this case, it is to suppose that every unbeliever is an enemy to persecute and exterminate from the face of the earth. There is not a Muslim in the world who is not inspired by this idea. However, in the Quran, it said: "That such a war is not enough for a Muslim whether young or old, and must also participate in the other parts of the Holy War."

> 2) **Jihad by word of mouth**. That is to say fighting by writing and speaking. This kind of war for example should pertain to the Muslims of the Caucasus. They should have commenced this war three or four months ago, because their actual position does not permit them to, but the carrying on of such warfare. Every Muslim is in duty, bound to write and speak against the unbelievers when actual circumstances do not permit him to assume more stringent measures, as for instances in the Caucasus. Therefore, every writer must use his pen in favor of such a war.

> 3) **Physical Jihad.** This means actual fighting in the fullest sense of the word. This kind of war is also subdivided into two parts, viz: The lesser and greater war.

---

[216] The 1915 fatwa can be found in Appendix B of this book.

Even today, several Imams in what some would call moderate Islamic countries openly state that jihad cannot be ended. Their reference is to a violent jihad. The Middle East Media Research Institute translated a YouTube of Kuwaiti Imam Sheikh Naji Al-Kharas, which was uploaded on August 21, 2020. His sermon that told the world that all the Arab peace agreements with Israel and the Jews, including the Camp David Accords, the Oslo Accords, and the Jordan-Israel peace agreement, are null and void because they "abolish the Jihad." He elaborated that it is impermissible to sign a permanent peace agreement with the enemy. Because Jihad cannot be ended.[217]

Conclusion

In today's world, we often refer to people on jihad as "terrorists." When we talk about 9/11 in America, we talk about terrorism. When people in Great Britain discuss 7/7, they talk about terrorism. Almost every attack that has been labeled a terrorist event, is in truth related to jihad. Under President Barak Hussein Obama, an attack on an American Consulate in Benghazi, Libya resulted in the death of three good men, one of whom was the Ambassador. These actions have all been called acts of terrorism. Laws have even been written to create a class of crime labeled terrorism. The vast majority of those charged under these laws around the world are what Islam calls Mujahedeen, Islamic warriors on jihad.

There has been little discussion, particularly in the open, on the topic of jihad as it relates to terrorism. Professionals who interview terrorists such as Dr. Anne Speckhard, with ISCVE refuse to accept that Islam cannot be peaceful. Groups like ISCVE engage in the creation of "de-radicalization programs" and videos to influence new jihadis from joining specific groups such as the Islamic State (aka ISIS), without an understanding that jihad is a

---

[217] MEMRI. (2020, August 21). *Kuwaiti Imam Sheikh Naji Al-Kharas: All Arab Peace Agreements With The Jews Are Null And Void Because You Cannot Abolish Jihad; Permanent Peace Agreements Are Impermissible.* Retrieved September 1, 2020, from MEMRI: https://www.memri.org/tv/kuwaiti-imam-naji-kharas-permanent-agreements-jews-null-void-abolish-jihad.

part of Islam that cannot be removed. These "professionals" who claim to be concerned about ideology separate "extremist Islam" from Islam by claiming extremist Islam is "violent Islam." This definition was given in the Interior Ministry of France whose head of a de-radicalization program presented to a group sponsored by the Middle East Forum.

No attempt at an academic discussion seems to be allowed to determine if Islamic jihad is indeed tied to three different levels of actions towards bringing about the conversion of nations to Islam. Who is stopping this? That is the question that must be asked and addressed! Who indeed? Why? If organizations that are Islamic are preventing these academic discussions, could it not be evidence of purposeful deception to allow their work to continue?

Appendix A

Where is Hatred and Violence in the Quran?

The passages below come from a translation of the Quran by
ABDULAH YOUSIF ALI – 1934 Lahore Pakistan. While this list is
extensive, it still is not inclusive of all the passages that are filled with
hatred and violence.

02:90   **...as for the disbeliever is a humiliating punishment.**

02:98   ... Lo! Allah is an enemy of those who reject faith.

02:99   ... none reject faith but those who are perverse.

02:154   and do not say about those who are killed in the way of God,
           "They are dead". They are alive but you perceive it not.

02:191   ... Slay them wherever you catch them.

02:216   Fighting is prescribed for you and you dislike it...But Allah
           knows what is good for you.

02:223   Your wives are a tilth unto you, approach your tilth how and
           when you will.

03:07   The Koran in it are verses basic of established meaning.

03:10   Those who reject faith are but fuel for the fire.

03:50   Those who reject faith, I will punish them with a terrible
           agony in this world and in the Hereafter.

03:83   Willing or unwilling, they will bow to his will.

03:85   If any desire a religion other than Islam, never will it be
           accepted of him.

03:86   Those who reject faith after they have accepted: on them is
           the curse of Allah, his Angels and all mankind.

03:151   Soon WE will cast terror into the hearts of the Unbelievers.

04:56   Those who reject our signs, We will cast into the fire as
           often as their skins are roasted through.

04:91   ... seize them and slay them wherever you get them.

04:92   Never should a believer kill a believer...

04:95   Not equal are those believers who sit at home and receive no
           hurt.

04:105   Indeed, We have revealed to you, O Mohamad, the book in
           truth, so you may judge between the people...

04:150   those who wish to adopt a way in-between are equally
           Unbelievers.

04:151	We have prepared for the Unbelievers a humiliating punishment.
05:33	... for mischief is; Execution or crucifixion or cutting the hand and feet off for opposite sides.
05:51	O, you who believe, take not Jews or Christians as friends...
05:54	Whoever of you should revert from his religion, Allah will bring forth a new people.
06:06	Don't they see how many of those before them We destroyed? ... We destroyed them, and in their wake raised fresh generations.
06:43	When the suffering reached them from Us, why did they not learn humility?
06:45	The people who did wrong were completely eliminated.
06:65	or cover you in party strife, giving you each a taste of mutual vengeance – each from the other.
07:04	How many towns have We destroyed? Our punishments took them a sudden by night or while they slept for their afternoon rest.
07:94	... We caused them a pain and suffering in order that they may learn humility.
07:97	Did the people of the town feel secure against the coming of Our wrath while they were asleep?
07:98	Or else in broad day light while they played.
07:182	Those who reject our signs, We shall gradually visit with punishments in ways they perceive not.
08:01	They ask concerning the spoils of war, say "Such spoils are at the disposal of Allah and the Prophet.
08:12	... I will instill terror into the heart of the Unbeliever: You cut of their heads and their fingertips.
08:13	This is because they contended against Allah.
08:17	It was not you that slew them, it was Allah.
08:41	1/5th of all war booty belongs to Allah and his Messenger.
08:65	O Messenger rouse the Believers to fight.
08:67	It is not fitting for a Messenger to have prisoners of war till he has thoroughly subdued the land.
08:69	But enjoy what you took in war...
09:02	... but that Allah will cover with shame those that reject him.
09:05	... then kill the polytheists wherever you find them.
09:14	Fight then and Allah will punish them at your hands.

09:33	... the religion of truth to manifest it over all other religion even though they dislike it.
09:68	Allah has promised the Hypocrites and rejecters of Faith the Fire of Hell.... For them is the curse of Allah and an enduring punishment.
09:110	... suspicion and shakiness in their hearts, until their hearts are cut to pieces.
10:04	Those that reject him will have boiling water to drink.
10:13	We destroyed generations before you who did not believe.
10:14	Then We made you heirs in the land after them to see how you would behave!
11:01	This is a book with verses basic of fundamental of established meaning.
11:08	If We delay the penalty for them for a definite term...
11:10	If We give him a taste of our favors...
11:15	Those that desire a life of the present...
11:82	When our decree issued, We turned the city upside down.
11:109	...but verily WE shall pay them back in full their portion without the least abatement.
11:117	Nor would your Lord be the One to destroy communities for a single wrong – doing ...
13:34	For them is a penalty in the life of this world but harder in the Hereafter.
13:41	Don't they see that We gradually reduced the land in their control.
14:02	... But alas for the Unbelievers for a terrible penalty their Unfaith will bring them.
14:14	"and verily We shall cause you to abide in the land and succeed them"
14:17	In gulps will he sip it, but never will he be near, swallowing it down his throat: death will come to him from every **quarter, yet, he will not die: in front of him is a chastisement unrelenting.**
15:04	We never destroyed a population that had not a term decreed assigned beforehand.
15:23	Verily it is We that give life and We who give death...
16:94	Do not takes oaths to practice deception among yourselves.
16:107	This is because they love this world more than the Hereafter.

17:04	We gave warning to the children of Israel... twice would they be punished.
17:05	...Our servants given to terrible warfare: they entered the very inmost part of your homes; and it was a warning completely fulfilled.
17:08	It may be that your Lord may yet show you mercy; but if you revert to your sin We shall revert to Our punishments: and We have made hell a prison on earth.
17:10	And those who do not believe in the Hereafter; We have prepared a penalty grievous indeed!
17:16	When We decide to destroy a population; We first send a definitive order... then We destroy them utterly.
17:75	In that case, We should have made you taste an equal portion of punishment in this life and in death: ...
18:102	... Verily We have prepared Hell for the Unbelievers.
19:69	Then We shall drag out of every sect all those who were in obstinate rebellion against the party of Allah.
19:98	But how many countless generations before them We have destroyed? Can you find a single one of them now, or hear so much as a whisper of them?
21:06	As to those before them, not one of the populations We destroyed believed; will these believe?
21:11	How many were the populations We utterly destroyed, setting up in their place other people?
21:12	Yet, when they felt our punishment coming, behold they tried to flee from it.
21:15	And that cry of theirs did not cease till We made as a field that is mown, as ashes silent and quenched.
21:95	But there is a ban on any population We have destroyed: they shall not return.
22:19	... but those that deny their lord - for them will be cut a garment of fire: over their heads will be poured boiling water...
22:21	In addition, there will be maces of iron to punish them.
22:22	Every time they wish to get away from the anguish, they will be forced back in. It will be said, "you, taste the punishment of burning."
23:44	... so We made them as a tale that is told: so away with the people that will not believe.

23:75	If We had mercy on them and removed the distress... they would obstinately persist.
24:02	... found guilty of sexual intercourse – lash each of them with one hundred lashes and let not compassion move you. Let a party of four Believers witness their punishment.
25:13	And when they are cast into a constricting place therein, they will plead for destruction there and then.
25:36	And We command "You, go to the people who have rejected our signs," and those people We destroyed utterly.
26:02	These are the verses of a book that makes things clear.
26:201	They will not believe till they see the painful punishment.
27:01	... the Koran, a book that makes things clear.
28:58	And how many populations have We destroyed...
28:59	Nor was your Lord one to destroy a population until...
30:16	And those who have rejected Faith and falsely denied Our signs... such shall be brought forth to punishment.
31:24	We grant them pleasure for a little while: in the end We shall force them to an unrelenting punishment.
32:26	Does it not teach them a lesson, how many generations We destroyed before them...?
33:27	And He made you heirs of their land and houses and goods, and of a land which you had not frequented before.
33:38	The command of Allah is a decree determined.
33:50	...the woman your right hand possess out of the prisoners of war.
33:57	Those who annoy Allah and his Messenger – Allah has cursed them in this world and ...
33:58	And those who annoy believing men and women...
33:61	They shall have a curse on them wherever they are found, they shall be seized and slain without mercy.
36:08	Indeed! We have put shackles on their necks...
36:31	Don't they see how many generations before them We destroyed? Not to them will they return.
36:69	We have not instructed the prophet in poetry.
37:148	And they; so We permitted them to enjoy their life, for a while.
38:08	How many generations before them did We destroy? In the end, they cried for mercy- ...no longer time for being saved.

40:35	They who dispute the signs of Allah are greatly hated by Allah and the Believers.
40:70	Those who deny the book... they are going to know...
40:71	When the shackles are on their necks.
40:72	In boiling water, then the fire.
41:16	So We sent against them a furious wind through days of disaster; that We might give them a taste, of a penalty of humiliation in this life; but the penalty of the hereafter will be more humiliating.
41:27	But We will certainly give the Unbelievers a taste of a Severe punishment...
42:16	But those who dispute concerning Allah after He has accepted, on them is wrath and a terrible penalty.
42:35	But let those know, who dispute about Our signs, that there is no way of escape.
43:08	So We destroyed them...
43:25	... now see what was the end of those that deny the Truth.
43:48	... We seized them with punishments in order that they might turn to Us.
44:15	Indeed, We will remove the torment for a little. Indeed, you disbelievers will return to disbelief.
44:16	One day, We will seize you with a mighty onslaught.
44:37	...We destroyed them because they were guilty of sin.
44:47	"You, seize him and drag him into the Blazing Fire."
44:48	"Then pour over his head the penalty of boiling water."
45:09	And when he learns of something of Our signs, he takes them in jest: For him, there will be a humiliating punishment.
46:27	We have destroyed populations round about you: ...
46:34	... the Unbelievers will be placed before the fire ...
47:13	And how many cities... We destroyed for their sin?
47:36	The life of this world is but play and amusement: ...
48:29	... and those who are with him against the Unbeliever, but are compassionate among each other.
48:06	And that he may punish those that imagine an evil opinion of Allah. On them is a round of Evil: the wrath of Allah is on them: He has cursed them...
48:13	And if any do not believe in Allah and His messenger, We have prepared for the Unbelievers, a blazing Fire.

48:15   … March and take war booty… They wish to change Allah's decree.

48:16   … you shall be summoned to fight…

50:36   But how many generations did We destroy before them… was there place of escape?

50:43   Verily it is We that give life and death: and to Us is the final Goal.

54:21   Yes how terrible is My penalty and My warning!

54:40   …the Koran is easy to understand and remember.

54:42   The people rejected Our signs so We seized them with such a penalty.

54:44   Or do they say, "We acting together can defend ourselves?"

54:45   Soon, will their multitude be put to the fight and they shall show their backs.

58:20   Those who resist Allah and his Messenger will be most humiliated.

58:21   Allah has decreed "It is I and My Messenger who must prevail;" Allah is full of strength able to enforce His Will.

59:13   Of a truth ye are stronger (than they) because of the terror in their hearts, (sent) by Allah. This is because they are men devoid of understanding.

86:15   They plot and scheme against you, and I plot and scheme against them.

APPENDIX B

1915 Ottoman Fatwa

The holy war of today is obligatory on every Muslim, and this present moment - this moment, is the only opportunity for it. Patience and indifference in these times is a grave mistake. The massacre of unbelievers (and only those who command us) whether they are found in public or private places is now our duty, as it is in Allah's words, "Take them and kill them wherever you find them. Behold, we have delivered them into your hands, and from you, must issue supreme sovereignty." The slaying of one unbeliever (of those who rule over us) in public or private shall be called an additional life for Islamism, and will be recompensed by Allah.

Let every Muslim know that his reward for so doing shall be doubled by our Allah who created heaven and earth. His will accounted him as a great precept, and his recompense will be greater than fasting on "Ramadan." He will be saved from the terrors of the day of Judgment – the day of the resurrection of the dead. Who is the man who refuses to enjoy such a reward? For such a small deed?

The faithful Muslim with warm attachment to his faith and belief in the resurrection of the dead does not approach nor befriend the foes of Islam. Such attitude is not according to common sense. The man who does so is far from the religion of Islam. You are astonished why we are so estranged from the unbelievers? But why are you not surprised at your own conduct towards them? What excuse will you give, not to Allah, but to your brethren? If you believe in Allah, in his faith and apostle, hear the words of our sages recorded by his holy prophet; "You, believer, take not the Jews and Christians as friends unto you, He who loves them shall be called one of them. Allah shall not foster the tyrants." You, believers, accept not unto you friends of these who abuse your faith and mock thereof. They are called unbelievers, and you hearken unto the words of Allah if you believe. Therefore, if after you put to heart to these sacred words, perhaps they have been spoken to you by Allah, not acquired unto us Jewish or

Christian friends. From these holy words, you will realize it is forbidden us to approach those who mock our faith – Jews and Christians, for then Allah forbid, All forbid we shall be deemed by the almighty as of one of them Allah forbid.

After all this how can we believe in the sincerity of your faith when you befriend and love unbelievers, and accept their Government without any rising without attempting to expel them from your country. Therefore arise and purify yourselves of such deeds. Arise to the Jihad {Holy War} no matter what it costs so as to carry into execution this sacred deed. It is furthermore said in the Koran, "if your fathers if children taken unto them friends of the unbelievers, estrange yourselves even from them."

Beloved you have not taken to heart these holy words, and you are following an unrighteous path, and therefore why have you pity on your religion. Arouse, arouse, and let not this opportunity pass. You approach the unbeliever so as to enjoy their greatness and honor, and have forgotten Allah's words. To thee O Allah belongs the strength and honor. Therefore, take to heart out holy aims for realization and honor will ultimately follow. If not we are afraid that your name will not be remembered among Muslims.

The Muslim religion enjoins us to set aside some money for Government expenses and for preparations of a Jihad {Holy War}. The rest of your tithes and contributions you are duty bound to send 2 to the capital of the Caliphatic to help them to glorify the name of Allah, through the medium of the Caliph.

Let all Muslims know that the Jihad {Holy War} is created for the purpose. We trust in Allah that Islamic lands will rise from the humiliation and become faithfully tied to the capital of the Caliphate, so as to be called dar al-Islam {"the lands of Islam"}. This is our hope and God help us to carry through our holy aims to a successfully issue for the sake of our holy Prophet. Dear Brethren!

A Jihad {Holy War} is a sacred duty and for your information let it be known that the armies of the Caliph is ready an in three divisions, as follows: War in secret, war by word of mouth, and physical war.

1) **Jihad in secret**. This is the easiest and simplest. In this case it is to suppose that every unbeliever is an enemy to

persecute and exterminate him from the face of the earth. There is not a Muslim in the world who is not inspired by this idea. However in the Quran, it said: "That such a war is not enough for a Muslim; whether young or old, and must also participate in the other parts of the Holy War."

2) **Jihad by word of mouth**. That is to say fighting by writing and speaking. This kind of war for example should pertain to the Muslims of the Caucasus. They should have commenced this war three or four months ago, because their actual position does not permit them to carrying on of such warfare. Every Muslim is in duty bound to write and speak against the unbelievers when actual circumstances do not permit him to assume more stringent measures, as for instances in the Caucasus. Therefore, every writer must use his pen in favor of such a war.

3) **Physical Jihad**. This means actual fighting in the fullest sense of the word. This kind of war is also subdivided into two parts, viz: The lesser and greater war.

   a. **The lesser jihad**, is when a certain section of Muslims rise to fight against their enemies in combination with their compatriots in the war sphere only, without summoning the aid of Muslims of other lands. For example the Sinoussians war with the Italians in Tripoli. Even in such a case every Muslim should offer material and moral help and not follow the course of the Egyptian Government took in the Italian war when acting under the advice of the unbelieving English Government they declared themselves neutral. This sin shall never be forgiven them. However our Egyptian brethren have helped us to a certain degree financially and morally in the last two wars and in spite of their unbelieving rulers forwarded their collections on our behalf to the Capital of the Caliphate.

Every provincial governor may proclaim a lesser Jihad {Holy War}, nevertheless for prestige sake it is necessary to obtain the permission of the Caliph for so doing, as the late Sheik Vaadi did when he proclaimed a lesser Jihad {Holy War} on the French. A greater Jihad {Holy War}, is that which is proclaimed by the whole of Islam in union with all the Muslims throughout the world, such a war can only be called out by the Caliph himself, and as soon as a Muslim hears this call he must hasten to his brethren's assistance, an example, our proclamation of today. There is no doubt at all that he who shall assist in this great Jihad {Holy War}, shall be doubly recompensed by heaven. He who shall fall in this war shall die a hero's death on the battlefield for sanctifying Allah's name and that of the Prophet. hou O Allah pour out thy mercy to arouse the heats of the Muslim children to his holy proclamation. Give ample reward to the victims that shall fall in glorifying thy name and that if thy prophet, for thou art the hoard of righteousness.

Now let us mention here the means to be adopted in carrying on this Jihad {holy war}, as follows:

Every private individual can fight with deadly weapons, as for example. Here is the following illustration of the late Egyptian Verdani who shot the unbelieving Butros Gal Pacha the friend of the English with a revolver. The murder of one of the English police Commissioner Bavaro in India by one of our Indian brethren. The killing of one of the officials of Kansch on his coming from Mecca by the Prophet's friend"Abu Bazir El Pachbi," peace be unto him! Abdallah ibn Aatickand four colleagues killed "Abu Raafa Ibn El Hakiki." The leader of the Jews so famous for his enmity to Islamism. This was executed by our Prophet's command, so did Avrala Ibn Ravacha and his friends when they killed Ocher Ibn Dawas one of the Jewish dignitaries. There are many instances of similar of cases. Lord of the Universal What fails us now, and should not some of us go forth to fight this sacred war for exalting thy glorious name? What could not happen were some individuals among us, men of courage and stout hearted kill the principal Christian men of the Triple Alliance, the foes of Islam. By so doing they would wipe their names from the face of the earth. Thou O Allah art responsible if you will not inspire every Muslim, with the holy spirit, to in this this jihad {holy war}. The second method is to fight this war secretly and deceitfully. This method is well known to every Muslim. This system has special advantages where the number of Muslims is inferior to that of the unbelievers. When the prophecy of Allah inspired our Prophet, "Fight for Allah with those who fight against you," he began to do in secret, and in this way. At first he sent some of his soldiers accompanied by an officer to fight his enemies. Of course only men of exceptional bravery were chosen by the prophet to carry on these expeditions. They formed secret expeditions which ultimately number fifty or sixty which harassed and fought the enemy. Of the first were the expeditions of Hamsha Ibn Abed El Matlav, Abidu Ibn Cahart, Saad Habas, Gzid ibn Chartah, Abu Maslaam Asham ibn Taabet, Manzur ibn Omar, Abed el Rahman ven Oof and AbouTaleb.

It is also the duty of the Muslim of today to follow this method – to arm small riding parties which we hope will bring as much use and advantage at the present moment particularly in the towns of Caucasus, Turkistan, India, and Java. Perpetually harassing the enemy by such means brings great advantage. To prepare such expeditions in our days there are many facilities, but what is certain to us is that these secret raids bring much benefit. Therefore every individual should endeavor to organize such raids, and perhaps in the same way as our holy Prophet did when he entered "Bachlaf El Fazul."

The third method is actual war in the offensive. The commander in Chief of such a war is to be the Caliph of all Muslims or his substitute as it was in the battles of "Badr" and "Uhud." In thee battles our prophet personally was in command of the forces. As it is well known to you, dear brethren, that the participation in the great Jihad {holy war} is obligatory upon every Muslim, so you should know hot to prosecute it. Therefore, dear brethren arouse and trust in Allah, and choose the method most appropriate for you according to the requirements of your places. Do not delay a moment, the time has ultimately arrived for this matter. As the center of the Caliphate has not the power to send armed forces to help you in your respective places, therefore you yourselves must arm and prepare and unite as one man with some powerful nation if it be necessary, and to commence the Jihad {holy war}. Support yourselves on Allah's mercy, observe and guard over all the precepts of Islamism, and do estrange 4 yourselves from politics. If any political difficulties shall confront you, bring them to the notice of your diplomatic brethren in the capital of the Caliph, from who you will receive the necessary advice. And whereas our Muslim code enjoins and compels us to fight in the jihad {holy war}, it also commands us to distinguish between those who love Islam and the Caliph, for they are virtuous, just, powerful and on good terms with us, and though of a different faith to ours, we are commanded to protect them.

SOURCE: 1915 Ottoman Fatwa cited in Bostom, Andrew G. *The Legacy of Jihad: Islamic Holy War and the Fate of Non-Muslims.* Amherst, NY: Prometheus Books, 2008. **(Italics denote corrections. Mussulman and Mohamadians replaced with Muslim. Holy War has Jihad inserted. God is changed to Allah.**

MISSING: The Fatwa according to Ambassador Morgenthau was over 10,000 words in English. This is a little over 2,000. Left off here are two paragraphs informing Muslims that states they should not kill Germans and Austrians.

(Revisions include: 1) returning the word" Jihad" where it previously stated "War," 2) Changing the archaic term" Mahomedans" to "Muslim." ~P. Sutliff)

Appendix C

An Evangelistic Hug for the

Muslim Reader of this book

A Christian writes to his Muslim friend:

Dear Servant of Allah,

Who is superior? Muhammad or Jesus? Whichever one is superior deserves your time and devotion. Whichever one is better is the one you should learn about endlessly. Why give the inferior one any time the at all? Unless of courses the superior prophet says pay attention to what the inferior says. But why would that happen? The Superior could silence the voice of the other.

Love,

Christian

The Muslim Responds:

Dear believer in the prophet Jesus,

Allah is the same God as the God of the Christian. Muhammad was the last prophet, he was the best of all prophets.

Your Neighbor,

Muslim

The Next Day:

The Christian meets his Muslim neighbor grabs his hand in greeting and excitedly says: "I am so glad you have finally admitted that Yahweh of the Bible and Allah of the Quran are the same God. I am so glad you have finally admitted that Allah is triune, that is God the Father, God the Son, and God the Holy Spirit. I am so glad you have finally admitted that Allah came to earth and walked and talked in the heat and cool of the day. I am so glad that you have admitted that Allah died on the cross and rose again. I am so glad that you have admitted that God has a son.

When you claim that Allah and Christianity have the same God, you make these claims. You may not know this, but this is what you are saying to the Christians. You tell them that Allah is not the "best of deceivers" (Sura Ali Imran (3) 54). You tell them that Allah is not three gods (polytheism-the crime of shirk), but one God (monotheism) in three persons. You tell them that Allah came down to earth in the form of a man, allowing himself to be born of a Jewish woman. That Allah allowed himself to be cared for and loved by those who served as his human parents, while not being any less of who he is – God. He allowed himself to grow and live as a human, having needs like food, water, and sleep.

When you tell the Christian that Allah is the same God as their God, You say that Allah in the form of Isa (Jesus), allowed himself to experience hunger when he fasted. That Allah in the form of Isa understood being physically tired and needing sleep. His human father would have taught him the value of hard work, since his human father was a Jewish carpenter.

When you tell the Christian, that Allah is Isa (Jesus). A Jewish man, who did many miracles and taught many lessons and predicted many things during his 33 years on the earth as a human. You tell the Christian that Isa had the power to call down a heavenly army to do his biddings and yet he chose not to because Isa being Allah loved the Jews and the people of the world, so much so, that he felt it wise to offer himself as a perfect sacrifice for their sins. That they would have the GIFT of eternal life for simply believing in Him and his sacrifice.

What kind of a God offers himself in love for his creation? A God of Love! Is Allah really the same as the God of the Christians? Does Allah love those who do not love him? The God of the Christians first loved them before they even had a clue who He was.

To learn more about Isa, read about how he was superior to Muhammad in Surah Maryam (19) and Surah An-Nisa (4). Then read about Isa in the gospels (Matthew, Mark, Luke or John), which the Quran tells you are good books (Surah Al-Ma'idah (5) 47-48).

(Credit is due to Jay Smith for the much of the work in this tract.)

Bibliography

Bibliography

7 Sur7. 2019. "L'horreur pour une Belge en Italie, enlevée par six hommes et violée pendant deux mois." *7Sur7.be.* January 17. Accessed March 21, 2020. https://www.7sur7.be/monde/l-horreur-pour-une-belge-en-italie-enlevee-par-six-hommes-et-violee-pendant-deux-mois~acc93364/.

ABC News Australia. 2019. "Turkey's Erdogan threatens to send Syrian refugees to Europe." *ABC News Australia.* October 10. Accessed May 30, 2021. https://www.abc.net.au/news/2019-10-10/turkish-president-erdogan-threatens-to-flood-europe-refugees/11591930.

Abdi, Nassim. 2018. "Australian Cleric Nassim Abdi: Women Shouldn't Put Themselves Out There If They Don't Want Their Privacy Invaded Sexually." *MEMRI.* April 20. Accessed March 21, 2020. https://www.memri.org/tv/australian-cleric-nassim-abdi-women-should-not-put-themselves-out-there.

Advice for Paradise. 2019. *Muhammad Saeed al-Qahtani.* Accessed March 28, 2020. https://www.adviceforparadise.com/profiles/12/.

AFP. 2021. "Algerian academic gets 3 years for 'offending Islam'." *Daily Mail.* April 22. Accessed April 25, 2021. https://www.dailymail.co.uk/wires/afp/article-9499693/Algerian-academic-gets-3-years-offending-Islam.html.

—. 2021. "Algerian academic gets 3 years for 'offending Islam'." *Daily Mail.* April 22. Accessed April 25, 2021. https://www.dailmail.co.uk/wires/afp/article-9499693/Algerian-academic-gets-3-years-offending-Islam.html.

—. 2016. "Pakistani clerics block 'un-Islamic' child marriage bill." *Al Arabiya*. January 15. http://english.alarabiya.net/en/News/asia/2016/01/15/Pakist ani-clerics-block-un-Islamic-child-marriage-bill.html.

Agenzia Fides. 2013. "ASIA/PAKISTAN - Christian minor raped and tortured by Muslims." *Fides*. February 4. Accessed March 24, 2020. http://www.fides.org/en/news/33195- ASIA_PAKISTAN_Christian_minor_raped_and_tortured_by_M uslims.

al-Faruqi, Ismail. 1986. *The Path of Da'wah In The West*. London.

Al-Fawzan, Abd Al-Aziz. 2007. "Saudi Cleric Abd Al-Aziz Al-Fawzan: Husbands Should Put Up with Their Wives' Slips and Errors, Because the Twisted Nature of Women Stems from Their Very Creation." *Middle East Media Research Institute*. June 11. Accessed October 4, 2019. https://www.memri.org/tv/saudi- cleric-abd-al-aziz-al-fawzan-husbands-should-put-their-wives- slips-and-errors-because/transcript.

Al-Mteiri, Salwa. 2011. *Kuwaiti Political Activist Salwa Al-Mteiri Calls for a Law Permitting the Purchase of POWs in Order to Turn Them into Slave Girls*. May 25. Accessed August 24, 2019. https://www.memri.org/reports/kuwaiti-political-activist- salwa-al-mteiri-calls-law-permitting-purchase-pows-order- turn.

Al-Munajiid, Muhammad Saalih. 2003. "Can Muslims Settle in Kaffir Countries for the Sake of a Better Life"." *Islamqa.info*. April 29. Accessed March 28, 2020. https://islamqa.info/en/13363.

al-Qahtani, Muhammad Saeed. 1999. *Al-Wala' Wa'l-Bara Part 2*. Vol. 2. 3 vols. New York City: Al-Firdous Publications Ltd. Accessed August 14, 2019. http://tawheednyc.com/aqeedah/al%20walaa%20wal%20bar aa/alwalawalbara2.pdf.

Al-Zawahiri, Ayman. 2019. "Addressing Muslim Women, Al-Qaeda Leader Ayman Al-Zawahiri Deems Western Battle Against

Hijab To Be Part Of War On Islamic Ummah." *Middle East Media Research Institute.* August 13. Accessed October 1, 2019. https://www.memri.org/reports/addressing-muslim-women-al-qaeda-leader-ayman-al-zawahiri-deems-western-battle-against-hijab.

Andrews, Luke. 2020. "Moment Uber driver refuses to give a ride to a blind man's guide dog before driving off - as he is fined £1,700 for breaching the Equality Act." *MailOnline.* March 2. Accessed April 22, 2020. https://www.dailymail.co.uk/news/article-8066065/Moment-Uber-driver-refuses-ride-blind-mans-guide-dog-driving-off.html.

AsiaNews.it. 2020. "Court rules that a girl who's had her first period can marry, thus backing Huma Younus's kidnapper. For girl's lawyer, this is shameful." *AsiaNews.it.* February 5. Accessed February 28, 2020. http://asianews.it/news-en/Court-rules-that-a-girl-whos-had-her-first-period-can-marry,-thus-backing-Huma-Younuss-kidnapper.-For-girls-lawyer,-this-is-shameful-49220.html?fbclid=IwAR3RhQZCEvTFUSz_mNQzYib12uCJg1NCugUnRLE9aVe7rTZDq_hS6pIlq1w.

Askew, Ian. 2016. "It's our job as health workers to 'do no harm'." *World Health Organization.* May 16. Accessed December 11, 2019. https://www.who.int/mediacentre/commentaries/fgm-do-no-harm/en/.

Auda, Jasser. 2008. *Maqāsid al-Sharī`ah: A Beginner's Guide.* Washington, DC: The International Institute of Islamic Thought.

Badran, Sheikh Ahmad. 2019. *Clip No: 7350 Friday Sermon in Jatt, Israel by Sheikh Ahmad Badran: Once Muslims Come to Power, They Will Never Allow Infidels to Rule over Muslims.* June 28. Accessed August 19, 2019. https://www.memri.org/tv/israel-jatt-sheikh-badran-muslims-come-power-never-allow-infidels-exploiting-democracy.

Baka, Faima. 2020. "The majority of sexual offenders are white men – there is no 'Muslim problem' with sexual groomin." *The Metro.* April 2. Accessed April 8, 2020. https://metro.co.uk/2020/04/02/majority-sexual-offenders-white-men-no-muslim-problem-sexual-grooming-12451053/.

Baron, Olivia, and Brett Gibbons. 2019. "Taxi driver escapes punishment over vile video threatening to rape Christians who converted from Islam." *Birminham Live.* September 18. https://www.birminghammail.co.uk/news/midlands-news/taxi-driver-escapes-punishment-over-16939646.

Baron, R. A,, D. Byrne, and J. Suls. 1989. "Attitudes:Evaluating the social world." In *Social Psychology, 3rd Edition*, by R. A, Baron, D. Byrne and J. Suls, 79-101. MA: Allyn and Bacon.

Basch, Michelle. 2017. "5 military dogs honored with K-9 Medal of Courage ." *WTOP.* October 11. Accessed April 17, 2020. https://wtop.com/animals-pets/2017/10/5-military-dogs-honored-k-9-medal-courage-photos/.

Bawer, Bruce. 2009. "Excerpt: 'Surrender'." *New York Times.* July 24. Accessed May 13, 2020. https://www.nytimes.com/2009/07/26/books/excerpt-surrender.html.

BBC News. 2015. "Charlie Hebdo attack: Three days of terro." *BBC News.* January 15. Accessed May 21, 2020. https://www.bbc.com/news/world-europe-30708237.

—. 2016. "Germany shocked by Cologne New Year gang assaults on women." *BBC News.* January 5. Accessed March 21, 2020. https://www.bbc.com/news/world-europe-35231046.

—. 2013. "Hard Talk with Anjem Chaudary (8/5/2005)." *YouTube.* Accessed September 1, 2020. https://www.youtube.com/watch?v=223gLcfCj_c.

—. 2020. "Saudi rapper faces arrest for Mecca Girl music video." *BBC News.* February 22. Accessed July 13, 2020. https://www.bbc.com/news/world-middle-east-51597561.

—. 2018. "Turkish child marriage religious document sparks anger." *BBC News.* January 3. Accessed October 23, 2019. https://www.bbc.com/news/world-europe-42558328.

—. 2009. "What happened to the book burners?" *BBC News.* February 13. Accessed May 13, 2020. http://news.bbc.co.uk/2/hi/uk_news/magazine/7883308.stm.

Bild.de. 2019. "Turkey President Demands Help With The Care Of Syrian Refugees: Erdogan Threatens Eu With Border Opening! "Either That Happens - Or We Open The Gates"." *Bild.de.* September 5. Accessed May 30, 2021. https://www.bild.de/politik/ausland/politik-ausland/erdogan-will-hilfe-fuer-syrische-fluechtlinge-und-droht-eu-mit-grenzoeffnung-64440610.bild.html.

Boztas, Senay. 2015. "Sharia in the UK: The courts in the shadow of British law offering rough justice for Muslim women." *Independent.* December 4. Accessed April 17, 2020. https://www.independent.co.uk/news/uk/home-news/sharia-in-the-uk-the-courts-in-the-shadow-of-british-law-offering-rough-justice-for-muslim-women-a6761221.html.

Bukhari, Mubasher. 2019. "Pakistani man kills wife, two children, six others in alleged honor killing." *Reuters.* July 1. Accessed July 29, 2020. https://www.reuters.com/article/us-pakistan-honourkillings/pakistani-man-kills-wife-two-children-six-others-in-alleged-honor-killing-idUSKCN1TW2CK.

Busby, Mattha, and Frances Perraudin. 2019. "Women forced into marriage overseas asked to repay cost of return to UK." *The Guardian.* January 2. Accessed January 28, 2020. https://www.theguardian.com/society/2019/jan/02/women-forced-into-marriage-overseas-asked-to-repay-cost-of-return-to-uk.

Charen, Mona. 2015. "'Nothing to Do With Islam'." *Real Clear Politics*. December 4. Accessed April 11, 2020. https://www.realclearpolitics.com/articles/2015/12/04/nothi ng_to_do_with_islam_128933.html.

Chesler, Phyllis. 2012. "Arrest mother as accomplice in Texas honor killing." *Fox News*. May 12. Accessed August 27, 2020. https://www.foxnews.com/opinion/arrest-mother-as-accomplice-in-texas-honor-killing.

Chowdhry, Juliet. 2016. "Christian girl killed for shrugging off advances of wealthy Muslim boys." *British Pakistani Christians.org*. January 20. Accessed March 21, 2020. https://www.britishpakistanichristians.org/blog/christian-girl-killed-for-shrugging-off-advances-of-rich-muslim-boys.

Churchwell, Bill, and Jonathan Munson. 2019. "'Yes that's fine. I did it,': Mohammad Sahi makes first court appearance since chilling double homicide." *WTSP.com*. September 13. Accessed August 12, 2020. https://www.wtsp.com/article/news/crime/yes-thats-fine-i-did-it-mohammad-sahi-makes-first-court-appearance-since-chilling-double-homicide/503-b23e1ff3-9a19-4f9a-834b-b0b24018b088.

Cikhi, Ferid. 2019. "State secularism: veil or hijab, the real meanings and their scope." *Huffington Post*. March 28. Accessed October 2, 2019. https://quebec.huffingtonpost.ca/ferid-chikhi/laicite-etat-voile-hijab-veritables-significations-portees-quebec_a_23702059/.

CTV News Ottawa. 2019. "Uber driver who allegedly refused ride to woman with service dog charged." *CTV News*. February 10. Accessed April 22, 2020. https://www.ctvnews.ca/canada/uber-driver-who-allegedly-refused-ride-to-woman-with-service-dog-charged-1.4290370.

Daily NewsEgypt . 2009. "Saudis reel as clerics say movie show must not go on." *The Free Library.com*. July 21. Accessed July 16, 2020.

https://www.thefreelibrary.com/Saudis%20reel%20as%20cler
ics%20say%20movie%20show%20must%20not%20go%20on.-
a0204139040.

Dakdok, Usama. 2019. *Email to Paul Sutliff.* August 26.

Davies, Lizzy. 2010. "France: Senate votes for Muslim face veil ban."
The Guardian. September 14. Accessed October 1, 2019.
https://www.theguardian.com/world/2010/sep/14/france-
senate-muslim-veil-ban.

Demir, Marian. 2019. "A 13-year-old Armenian boy tricked into
converting to Islam on live TV." *Asia News.* May 15. Accessed
December 2, 2019. http://www.asianews.it/news-en/A-13-
year-old-Armenian-boy-tricked-into-converting-to-Islam-on-
live-TV-47021.html.

Dictionary.com. 2019. *Racism.* Accessed August 24, 2019.
https://www.dictionary.com/browse/racism.

Dispatches. 2007. "Dispatches - Undercover Mosque." *New English
Review.* January 15. Accessed May 29, 2021.
https://www.newenglishreview.org/Miscellaneous/Dispatche
s_-_Undercover_Mosque.

—. 2016. *Dispatches: Undercover Mosque | The Return | Real Stories.*
April 23. Accessed March 29, 2020.
https://www.youtube.com/watch?v=3WgVa3VRFb4.

Domanig, Michael. 2019. "Taking dogs in Innsbruck taxis remains an
excitement." *Tiroler Tageszeitung.* August 8. Accessed April
22, 2020. https://www.tt.com/artikel/15929619/mitnahme-
von-hunden-in-innsbrucker-taxis-bleibt-ein-
aufreger?sfns=mo.

Eickelman, Dale F, and James P. Piscatori. 1990. *Muslim Travellers:
Pilgrimage, Migration, and the Religious Imagination.*
Berkeley: University of California.

Elias, Abu Amima. 2014. "Does Islam support female genital
mutilation (FGM)?" *Faith in Allah.* April 24. Accessed

December 16, 2019. https://abuaminaelias.com/islam-female-genital-mutilation/.

El-Mekki, Kamal. 2008. "The End of Music." *YouTube.* June 9. Accessed July 9, 2020. https://www.youtube.com/watch?time_continue=92&v=Rthl UOYkI7M&feature=emb_logo.

Elsharq TV. 2020. "Egyptian Islamic Scholar Salama Abd Al-Qawi Defends FGM on Muslim Brotherhood TV: Drinking Water and Eating Eggplants Can Also Lead to Death." *Middle East Media Research Institute.* February 1. Accessed February 10, 2020. https://www.memri.org/tv/egyptian-islamic-scholar-salama-qawi-defends-fgm-air-travel-drinking-water-eggplants-birth-also-lead-death/transcript.

Emerick, Yahiya. 1997. *What Islam Is All About.* Long Island City, NY: International Books and Tapes Supply.

Emerson, Steven. 2013. "Fatwa Permits Rape of Syrian Women." *Newsmax.* January 10. Accessed March 19, 2020. https://www.newsmax.com/Emerson/fatwa-rape-Syrian-women/2013/01/10/id/470865/.

Encountering Islam. 2018. *Muslim World Facts.* Accessed August 24, 2019. https://www.encounteringislam.org/muslim-world-facts.

Esposito, John. 2004. *The Oxford Dictionary of Islam.* NYC: Oxford University Press .

Evening Standard. 2003. "Extremist Muslims praise the 9/11 killers." *Evening Standard.* September 9. Accessed November 14, 2019. https://www.standard.co.uk/news/extremist-muslims-praise-the-911-killers-6962609.html.

Farooq, Umar, and Jibran Ahmad. 2020. "Pakistan: Teen Celebrated, Called 'Holy Warrior' for Killing 'Blasphemous' American." *The Wire.* August 10. Accessed August 22, 2020.

https://thewire.in/south-asia/pakistan-teen-celebrated-called-holy-warrior-for-killing-blasphemous-american.

Fatah, Tarek. 2019. "FATAH: Why some Canadian Muslims celebrated the Quebec hijab ban." *Toronto Sun.* June 18. Accessed October 2, 2019. https://torontosun.com/opinion/columnists/fatah-why-some-canadian-muslims-celebrated-the-quebec-hijab-ban.

Fayoud, Fouad. 2019. "Retired Egyptian General Fouad Fayoud: MB Founder Hassan Al-Banna Was a Jew." *MEMRI.org.* November 25. Accessed November 26, 2019. https://www.youtube.com/watch?v=FK5gnFHnqJM&feature=emb_title.

Fielding, James. 2013. "Sharia court tells 'abused wife' to stay." *Express.* April 7. Accessed April 17, 2020. https://www.express.co.uk/news/uk/389957/Sharia-court-tells-abused-wife-to-stay.

Girls' Health. 2014. "Timing and stages of puberty." *Girls Health.gov.* May 23. Accessed October 23, 2019. https://www.girlshealth.gov/body/puberty/timing.html.

Glenza, Jessica. 2015. "Texas police widen search but admit: 'This is not going to be a fast investigation'." *Guardian.* May 4. Accessed June 16, 2020. https://www.theguardian.com/us-news/2015/may/04/garland-texas-attack-investigation-gunmen-details.

Global News. 2013. "Fact file: 10 Bouchard-Taylor report recommendation." *Global News.* October 13. Accessed October 1, 2019. https://globalnews.ca/news/880174/fact-file-10-bouchard-taylor-report-recommendations/.

GOUVEIA, ALEXANDRIA. 2019. "Ilhan Omar: "To Me, the Hijab Means Power, Liberation, Beauty, and Resistance"." *Vogue Magazine.* March 28. Accessed October 1, 2019. https://en.vogue.me/culture/ilhan-omar-first-somali-american-hijabi-congresswoman/.

Griff, Kate. 2019. "Ont. woman says Uber driver rejected her guide dog." *CTV News*. February 3. Accessed April 22, 2020. https://www.ctvnews.ca/canada/ont-woman-says-uber-driver-rejected-her-guide-dog-1.4280881.

Grundmann, Melina. 2020. "Female genital mutilation feels 'like living in a dead body'." *DW.com*. February 6. Accessed February 11, 2020. https://www.dw.com/en/female-genital-mutilation-feels-like-living-in-a-dead-body/a-52269987.

Hamdan, Salsabeel H. 2019. "The Suppression of Musical Culture in Gaza." *The Washington Report on Middle East Affairs*. June/July. Accessed July 13, 2020. https://www.wrmea.org/2019-june-july/the-suppression-of-musical-culture-in-gaza.html.

Harrod, Andrew. 2020. "Islam in Focus--Arizona's Scottsdale Community College Sharia Censorship." *Blog Talk Radio.com*. May 8. Accessed June 16, 2020. https://www.blogtalkradio.com/global-patriot-radio/2020/05/08/islam-in-focus-arizonas-scottsdale-community-college-sharia-censorship.

Harvey-Jenner, Catronia. 2016. "Muslim women explain how they feel about wearing a hijab: Mainly it's their choice." *Cosmopolitan*. July 4. https://www.cosmopolitan.com/uk/reports/news/a44416/muslim-women-explain-how-feel-wearing-burqa-hijab/.

Hayward, John. 2019. *Libyan PM: Siege of Tripoli Could Drive 800,000 More Migrants into Europe*. April 16. Accessed 22 2019, August. https://www.breitbart.com/national-security/2019/04/16/libyan-pm-siege-of-tripoli-could-drive-800000-more-migrants-into-europe/.

Heinz, Frank. 2020. " Yaser Said, Taxi Driver Accused of Killing His Teen Daughters in 2008, Caught in North Texas." *NBC - Dallas Fort Worth*. August 26. Accessed August 27, 2020. https://www.nbcdfw.com/news/local/yaser-said-taxi-driver-accused-of-killing-his-teen-daughters-in-2008-caught-in-north-texas/2433246/.

Hill, Ella. 2018. "As a Rotherham grooming gang survivor, I want people to know about the religious extremism which inspired my abusers." *The Independent.* March 18. Accessed March 21, 2020. https://www.independent.co.uk/voices/rotherham-grooming-gang-sexual-abuse-muslim-islamist-racism-white-girls-religious-extremism-a8261831.html.

Hohman, Leo. 2020. "Undercover agent: Michigan mosques promoting child marriage, openly campaigning for Bernie Sanders." *LeoHohman.com.* March 9. Accessed June 10, 2020. https://leohohmann.com/2020/03/09/undercover-agent-michigan-mosques-promoting-child-marriage-openly-campaigning-for-bernie-sanders/.

Hudah. 2019. *The Importance of the Arabic Language in Islam.* June 25. Accessed August 24, 2019. https://www.learnreligions.com/arabic-language-in-islam-2004035.

Hunter, William Wilson. 1871. *The Indian Musulmans.* London: Trübner and Company.

Hussein, Taiseer. 2020. "Taiseer Hussein of Hizb ut-Tahrir America: We Will Conquer Rome and Liberate India and Spai." *MEMRI.* January 19. Accessed February 28, 2020. https://www.memri.org/tv/taiseer-hussein-hizb-ut-tahrir-america-conference-islamic-nation-establish-caliphate-conquer-rome.

Ibrahim, Mansour Jamal. 2017. *Racism in The Muslim Community: Are We Really One?* May 18. Accessed April 2, 2020. https://mvslim.com/racism-in-the-muslim-community-are-we-really-one/.

Ibrahim, Raymond. 2020. ""Hating and Loving" for Islam." *Yonkers Tribune.com.* January 18. Accessed July 28, 2020.

https://www.yonkerstribune.com/2020/01/hating-and-loving-for-islam-by-raymond-ibrahim.

—. 2013. *The Rape and Murder of Pakistan's Christian Children.* November 8. Accessed March 24, 2020. https://www.raymondibrahim.com/2012/11/08/the-rape-and-murder-of-pakistans-christian-children-2/.

—. 2013. "Video: Christian Girls Gang Raped to Screams of "Allahu Akbar" in Egypt." *RaymondIbrahim.com.* April 11. Accessed March 21, 2020. https://www.raymondibrahim.com/2013/04/11/video-christian-girls-gang-raped-to-screams-of-allahu-akbar-in-egypt/.

India TV News. 2020. "Couple burnt alive in suspected honour killing in Uttar Pradesh." *India TV News.* August 6. Accessed August 7, 2020. https://www.indiatvnews.com/crime/couple-burnt-alive-in-suspected-honour-killing-in-uttar-pradesh-639962.

Ishaq, Ibn. 1982. *The Life of Muhammad.* Translated by A Guillaume. Karachi: Oxford University Press.

Islam Question & Answer. 2003. *Can Muslims settle in kaafir countries for the sake of a better life?* April 19. https://islamqa.info/en/answers/13363/can-muslims-settle-in-kaafir-countries-for-the-sake-of-a-better-life.

—. 2003. "Can Muslims settle in kaafir countries for the sake of a better life?" *Islam Question & Answer.* April 19. Accessed April 10, 2020. https://islamqa.info/en/answers/13363/can-muslims-settle-in-kaafir-countries-for-the-sake-of-a-better-life.

Islamic Virtues. 2013. *Superiority of the race of Arabs over non-Arabs.* December 12. Accessed August 25, 2019. https://islamicvirtues.com/2013/12/12/superiority-of-the-race-of-arabs-over-non-arabs/.

Jabarti, Somayya. 2005. *Misyar Marriage -- A Marvel or Misery?* June 5. Accessed March 31, 2020. https://web.archive.org/web/20060526024058/http://www.arabnews.com/?page=9&section=0&article=64891.

Karput, Kemal. 1990. "The hijra from Russia and the Balkans: the process of self-definition in the late Ottoman state." In *Muslim Travellers: Plgrimage, Migration and the Religious Immigration*, by Dale F. Eickelman and James Piscatori, 131-152. Los Angeles: University of California Press.

Kathir, Ibn. n.d. "Tafsir Ibn Kathir- Surah 58. Al-Mujadila , Introduction." *Alim.org*. Accessed July 29, 2020. http://www.alim.org/library/quran/AlQuran-tafsir/TIK/58.

—. 2003. *Tafsir Ibn Kathir, Volume 4.* New York, NY: Darussalam.

Kenyon, Peter. 2009. "Sheik of Al Azhar bans face veil." *IslamiCity.org*. October 28. Accessed November 13, 2019. https://www.islamicity.org/3670/sheik-of-al-azhar-bans-face-veil/.

Kern, Soeren. 2019. *Turkey Threatens to Reignite European Migrant Crisis.* July 21. Accessed August 22, 2019. https://www.gatestoneinstitute.org/14624/turkey-threatens-migrant-crisis.

Kern, Soren. 2017. "Germany: Wave of Muslim Honor Killings." *Gatestone Institute.* May 30. Accessed August 12, 2020. https://www.gatestoneinstitute.org/10441/germany-muslim-honor-killings.

Kettani, M.Ali. 1986. *Muslim Minorities in the World Today.* London: Mansell Publishing.

Khadduri, Majid. 2006. *War and Peace in the Law of Islam.* Clark, NJ: The Lawbook Exchange, Ltd.

Khan, Aysha. 2020. "Her American father was shot in a blasphemy trial in Pakistan. Now she's fighting for justice." *Religion News.* August 19. Accessed August 22, 2020.

https://religionnews.com/2020/08/19/her-father-was-shot-in-a-blasphemy-trial-in-pakistan-now-shes-fighting-for-justice.

Klubes, Felisa Neuringer. 2007. "Obituary: Majid Khadduri, Founder of SAIS Middle East Studies Program, Dies." *John Hopkins University.* February 5. Accessed March 24, 2020. https://pages.jh.edu/~gazette/2007/05feb07/05obit.html.

Kredo, Adam. 2015. "Muslim Leaders to Hold 'Stand With the Prophet' Rally in Texas." *Washington Free Beacon.* January 12. Accessed May 24, 2020. https://freebeacon.com/issues/muslim-leaders-to-hold-stand-with-the-prophet-rally-in-texas/.

Kristoffersson, Simon. 2019. "Finnish municipality prohibits migrants in kindergartens and schools after rape scales." *Samhallsnyt.* February 6. Accessed March 21, 2020. https://samnytt.se/finsk-kommun-forbjuder-migranter-pa-dagis-och-skolor-efter-valdtaktsvag/.

Kronen Zeitung. 2018. "Group rape before disco: 8 perpetrators in custody." *Kronen Zeitung.* October 26. Accessed March 21, 2020. https://www.krone.at/1797029.

Lagace, Patrick. 2020. "Four bottles of wine." *La Presse.* February 9. Accessed February 28, 2020. https://www.lapresse.ca/actualites/202002/08/01-5260172-quatre-bouteilles-de-vin.php.

Lake, Emma. 2018. "HONOUR CRIMES What is an honour killing and how common are the horrific crimes in the UK?" *The Sun.* September 17. Accessed August 12, 2020. https://www.thesun.co.uk/news/4091357/what-is-honour-killing-murder-uk/#:~:text=Data%20from%20the%20HBVAN%20estimates,can%20include%20abductions%20and%20beatings.

Layth, Abu. 2019. "Thoughts on Mutah Marriages." *YouTube.* November 11. Accessed March 12, 2020. https://www.youtube.com/watch?v=NxDu8BU5Mal.

Le Parisien. 2020. "Besancon: shaved and beaten by her family because she is seeing a Christian." *Le Parisien.* August 21. Accessed August 22, 2020. https://www.leparisien.fr/faits-divers/besancon-tondue-et-frappee-par-sa-famille-parce-qu-elle-frequente-un-chretien-21-08-2020-8370981.php.

Lerner, Laura. 2015. "Poster for free-speech forum sets off debate at University of Minnesota." *Star Tribune.* May 5. Accessed July 1, 2020. https://www.startribune.com/poster-for-free-speech-forum-sets-off-debate-at-university-of-minnesota/302689691/?refresh=true.

Lopez, Rebecca. 2019. "More than a decade after teens killed in suspected honor killing, police believe dad may be in North Texas." *WFAA.* June 28. Accessed August 27, 2020. https://www.wfaa.com/article/news/crime/more-than-a-decade-after-teens-killed-in-suspected-honor-killing-police-believe-dad-may-be-in-north-texas/287-959822c4-85a7-4cf4-af5a-a55f708ef0e9.

Lykkegaard, John. 2012. *Kurt Westergaard: The Man Behind the Muhammad Cartoon.* Copenhagen, Denmark.

MacEoin, Denis. 2018. "Britain's Grooming Gangs: Part 1." *Gatestone Institute.* December 20. Accessed March 17, 2020. https://www.gatestoneinstitute.org/13075/britain-grooming-gangs.

Maclean, Ruth. 2019. "Senior Islamic cleric issues fatwa against child marriage." *The Guardian.* June 21. Accessed October 21, 2019. https://www.theguardian.com/global-development/2019/jun/21/senior-islamic-cleric-issues-fatwa-against-child-marriage.

Mawdudi, Sayyid Abul A'la. 2007. *The Islamic Movement: Dynamics of Values, Powe and Change.* London: The Islamic Foundation.

McLeod, Saul. 2008. "Social Roles." *Social Psychology.* Accessed April 19, 2021. https://www.simplypsychology.org/social-roles.html.

MEMRI. January 4, 2007. *A Retrospective Study of the Unfolding of the Muhammad Cartoons Crisis and its Implications.* Inquiry & Analysis Series No. 313, Middle East Media Research Institute. Accessed May 15, 2020. https://www.memri.org/reports/retrospective-study-unfolding-muhammad-cartoons-crisis-and-its-implications.

—. 2020. "Kuwaiti Imam Sheikh Naji Al-Kharas: All Arab Peace Agreements With The Jews Are Null And Void Because You Cannot Abolish Jihad; Permanent Peace Agreements Are Impermissible." *MEMRI.* August 21. Accessed September 1, 2020. https://www.memri.org/tv/kuwaiti-imam-naji-kharas-permanent-agreements-jews-null-void-abolish-jihad.

Merse, James. 2017. *Why Can't We Talk About Muslim Supremacism?* September 27. Accessed August 14, 2019. https://dailycaller.com/2017/09/27/why-cant-we-talk-about-muslim-supremacy/.

Miller, Joshua Rhett. 2010. "Comedy Central Censors 'South Park' Episode After Muslim Site's Threats." *FOX News.* April 22. Accessed May 15, 2020. https://www.foxnews.com/entertainment/comedy-central-censors-south-park-episode-after-muslim-sites-threats.

Muslim Mindano. 2005. "A Primer on the Code of Muslim Personal Laws of the Philippines." *Muslim Mindano.* Accessed October 21, 2019. http://www.muslimmindanao.ph/shari%27a/pesonal_laws.pdf.

2020. "Muslim Music Lessons for Children in France (Sept 2015)." *3Speak.* January 1. Accessed July 13, 2020. https://3speak.online/watch?v=vladtepesblog/zopmwglx&utm_source=studio.

New York Times. 1989. "2 Bookstores in Berkeley Are Firebombed; Rushdie Tie Is Explored." *New York Times.* March 1. Accessed May 13, 2020.

https://www.nytimes.com/1989/03/01/world/2-bookstores-in-berkeley-are-firebombed-rushdie-tie-is-explored.html.

Newsome, Janella. 2014. "Capital Murder Suspect Added to FBI's Ten Most Wanted Fugitives List." *FBI.gov.* December 4. Accessed August 27, 2020. https://www.fbi.gov/contact-us/field-offices/dallas/news/press-releases/capital-murder-suspect-added-to-fbis-ten-most-wanted-fugitives-list.

Ng, Kate. 2019. "US suspends export of sniffer dogs to Jordan and Egypt after series of deaths." *Inependent.* December 24. Accessed April 17, 2020. https://www.independent.co.uk/news/world/americas/us-sniffer-dogs-exports-jordan-egypt-deaths-trump-administration-a9259211.html.

Nsubuga, Jimmy. 2020. "Girl, 12, dies after undergoing female genital mutilation in Egypt." *Metro News.* January 31. Accessed February 5, 2020. https://metro.co.uk/2020/01/31/girl-12-dies-undergoing-female-genital-mutilation-egypt-12161820.

Okiror, Samuel. 2018. "The Ugandan girl who trekked barefoot to escape marriage at 13." *The Guardian.* June 26. Accessed October 24, 2019. https://www.theguardian.com/global-development/2018/jun/26/uganda-girl-trekked-barefoot-escape-marriage-13.

Palestinian Authority TV. 2016. "Palestinian Cleric Sameeh Hajaj Explains Wife-Beating in Islam: Not on the Face, No More than 10 Blows, Avoid Permanent Marks." *MEMRI.* November 24. Accessed April 13, 2020. https://www.memri.org/tv/palestinian-cleric-sameeh-hajaj-explains-wife-beating-islam-not-face-no-more-10-blows-avoid.

Pinto, Barbara. 2007. "Muslim Cab Drivers Refuse to Transport Alcohol, and Dogs." *ABC News.* January 26. Accessed May 8, 2021. https://abcnews.go.com/International/story?id=2827800.

Pipes, Daniel. 2007. "Islamists and Music." *DanielPipes.ortg.* August 3. Accessed July 16, 2020. http://www.danielpipes.org/blog/2007/08/music-and-islamists.

—. 2005. "The Erratic Career of Western Music in Iran." *DanielPipes.org.* December 29. Accessed July 16, 2020. http://www.danielpipes.org/blog/2005/12/ahmadinejad-bans-western-music-in-iran.

Point Blank with Luqman. 2010. *Pakistan TV Debate on Concubines and Slavery in Islam.* June 28. Accessed August 24, 2019. https://www.memri.org/reports/pakistan-tv-debate-concubines-and-slavery-islam.

Potts, Randy R. 2015. "Exclusive: Inside the Texas 'Draw Muhammad' Event as Shots Rang Out." *The Daily Beast.* May 4. Accessed June 11, 2020. https://www.thedailybeast.com/exclusive-inside-the-texas-draw-muhammad-event-as-shots-rang-out.

R., Emma. 2020. "Foreign robbers peed in Swedish teenager's mouth while shouting racist slurs." *Voice of Europe.* February 11. Accessed February 28, 2020. https://voiceofeurope.com/2020/02/foreign-robbers-peed-in-swedish-teenagers-mouth-while-shouting-racist-slurs/.

Rasheed, Shaykh Amjad. 2008. *Arabs preferred over other nations.* Edited by Ustadha Shazia Ahmad. Accessed August 25, 2019. https://web.archive.org/web/20140201113831/http://qa.sun nipath.com/issue_view.asp?HD=7&ID=9427&CATE=1.

Reid, Scott. 2017. "Here are 26 reasons why the M-103 committee's report should condemn anti-Muslim discrimination rather than the undefined term, 'Islamophobia.'." *Scott reid, MP.* November 14. Accessed June 11, 2020. https://scottreid.ca/here-are-26-reasons-why-the-m-103-committees-report-should-condemn-anti-muslim-discrimination-rather-than-the-undefined-term-islamophobia/.

Ripperger, Sabine. 2011. "Study finds thousands of forced marriages in Germany." *DW.com*. November 10. Accessed February 29, 2020. https://www.dw.com/en/study-finds-thousands-of-forced-marriages-in-germany/a-15522401.

Rizvi, Syed. 2007. "Is Music forbidden in Shia Islam?" *ShiaChat.com*. June 28. Accessed July 9, 2020. https://www.shiachat.com/forum/topic/234928794-is-music-forbidden-in-shia-islam/.

Saleem, Dr. Shehzad. 2016. "Punishment for Blasphemy against the Prophet (sws)." *Al-Mawrid*. February 6. Accessed May 18, 2020. http://www.al-mawrid.org/index.php/articles/view/punishment-for-blasphemy-against-the-prophet-sws.

Savage, Mark. 2020. "Mehdi Rajabian was sent to prison for making music - but he says that won't stop him." *BBC*. January 1. Accessed July 13, 2020. https://www.bbc.com/news/entertainment-arts-51188865.

Schleifer, Theodore. 2016. "Donald Trump: 'I think Islam hates us'." *CNN*. March 10. Accessed July 28, 2020. https://www.cnn.com/2016/03/09/politics/donald-trump-islam-hates-us/index.html.

Shafaq, Nasim, Nusrat Parsa, and Abubakar Siddique. 2018. "In Afghan Leader's Home District, Taliban Ban Girls From Education." *Gandhara*. June 20. Accessed October 23, 2019. https://gandhara.rferl.org/a/afghan-leader-home-district-taliban-ban-girls-from-education/29306920.html.

Shultz, Marisa. 2018. "House finally lifting hat ban after 181 years." *New York Post*. November 15. Accessed September 30, 2019. https://nypost.com/2018/11/15/house-finally-lifting-hat-ban-after-181-years/.

Sirajuddin. 2019. "KP govt makes it mandatory for schoolgirls across the province to 'cover up'." *Dawn*. September 16. Accessed September 30, 2019. https://www.dawn.com/news/1505542.

Sommerlad, Nick, and Geraldine McKelvie. 2018. "Britain's 'worst ever' child grooming scandal exposed: Hundreds of young girls raped, beaten, sold for sex and some even KILLE." *The MIrror.* March 12. Accessed March 21, 2020. https://www.mirror.co.uk/news/uk-news/britains-worst-ever-child-grooming-12165527.

Sookhdeo, Dr. Patrick. 2005. *Islam in Britain.* London: The Institute for the Study of Islam and Christianity.

Sookhdeo, Patrick. 2015. *Dawa: The Islamic Strategy for Reshaping the Modern World.* London: Isaac Publishing.

Soylu, Süleyman. 2019. *Interior Minister Soylu: When we open the doors, their government cannot last 6 months.* July 21. Accessed March 28, 2020. https://www.aa.com.tr/tr/politika/icisleri-bakani-soylu-kapilari-actigimizda-hukumetleri-6-ay-dayanamaz/1537340.

Sputnik News. 2020. "Somali Man Who Torched Two Norwegian Churches Says It Was Revenge for Quran Burning." *Sputnik News.* August 20. Accessed August 22, 2020. https://sputniknews.com/europe/202008201080223451-somali-man-who-torched-two-norwegian-churches-says-it-was-revenge-for-quran-burning/.

Stewart, Will. 2020. "Horrifying moment two 'Islamic terrorists' - including an arm-wrestling champion - kill two cops in a knife frenzy after mowing one down in a car in a Russian city." *Daily Mail.* January 1. Accessed July 28, 2020. https://www.dailymail.co.uk/news/article-7842643/Horrifying-moment-two-Islamic-terrorists-kill-two-cops-knife-frenzy-Russia.html.

Storhaug, Hege. 2018. *Islam: Europe Invaded America Warned.* Kolofon.

Sultan, Wafa. 2009. *A God Who Hates.* New York City: St. Martin's Press.

Svihovec, Travis. 2019. "Man accused of abusing stepdaughter with broomstick over religious beliefs." *The Bismark Tribune.* December 6. Accessed March 30, 2020. https://bismarcktribune.com/news/local/bismarck/man-accused-of-abusing-stepdaughter-with-broomstick-over-religious-beliefs/article_4d95d50a-95c1-555f-a2bb-cca8e84dd7d1.html.

Taylor, Carri-Ann. 2017. "HATE SCHOOLS: Inspectors find books in UK Islamic schools that sanction wife-beating and say women can go to hell for cutting their hair." *The Sun.* November 28. Accessed April 13, 2020. https://www.thesun.co.uk/news/5021414/ofsted-finds-books-in-islamic-schools-sanction-wife-beating/.

The United West. 2015. "Islamists Deny Media Access at At Muslim Free Speech Conference." *YouTube.* January 20. Accessed May 21, 2020. https://www.youtube.com/watch?v=FoOCMjc-n_o.

—. 2015. "Over 2,000 Protest Stand with Mohammad event in TX." *YouTube.* January 17. Accessed May 21, 2020. https://www.youtube.com/watch?time_continue=65&v=VQMtNvx_gnw&feature=emb_logo.

Toll, Ian W. 2006. *Six frigates: The Epic History of the Founding of the US Navy.* New York City, NY: W. W. Norton & Co., Inc.

Tribune.pk. 2019. "Morocco TV show censured for guest's boast of 'beating wife'." *Tribune.pk.* September 18. Accessed April 13, 2020. https://tribune.com.pk/story/2059551/3-morocco-tv-show-censured-guests-boast-beating-wife/.

Trifkovic, Srdja. 2002. *The Islamic Conquest of Britain.* December 20. Accessed August 2, 2019. https://web.archive.org/web/20040710081633/chroniclesmagazine.org/news/trifkovic/newsst122002.html.

Trinko, Katrina. 2012. "Obama: 'The Future Must Not Belong To Those Who Slander the Prophet of Islam'." *National Review.* September 25. Accessed April 29, 2020.

https://www.nationalreview.com/corner/obama-future-must-not-belong-those-who-slander-prophet-islam-katrina-trinko/.

ummtaalib. 2015. "Instrument Free Music." *Islamic Teachings.com.* January 29. Accessed July 8, 2020. https://www.islamicteachings.org/forum/topic/22387-instument-free-music/ .

—. 2015. "Instument-free Music." *Islamic Teachings.org.* January 29. Accessed July 2, 2020. https://www.islamicteachings.org/forum/topic/22387-instument-free-music/.

Universiti Brunei Darussalam. 2015. "Prof. Dr. Jasser Auda." *Universiti Brunei Darussalam.* Accessed August 24, 2020. https://expert.ubd.edu.bn/jasser.auda.

US Department of Justice. 2009. "Two Chicago Men Charged in Connection with Alleged Roles in Foreign Terror Plot That Focused on Targets in Denmark." *USA Department of Justice.* October 27. Accessed May 15, 2020. https://www.justice.gov/opa/pr/two-chicago-men-charged-connection-alleged-roles-foreign-terror-plot-focused-targets-denmark.

Uutiset. 2019. "Helsinki city councillor apologises for false story about abusive taxi passenger." *Uutiset.* November 11. Accessed November 14, 2019. https://yle.fi/uutiset/osasto/news/helsinki_city_councillor_apologises_for_false_story_about_abusive_taxi_passenger/11063252.

Ware, Alexis. 2020. "Dog brutally beaten by Ingham County man gets a second chance." *WILX.com.* February 7. Accessed May 8, 2021. https://www.wilx.com/content/news/Dog-brutally-beaten-by-Ingham-county-man-g-567673011.html.

Washington Times. 2009. "Taliban bans education for girls in Swat Valley." *Washington Times.* January 5. Accessed October 4,

2019.
https://www.washingtontimes.com/news/2009/jan/05/taliba
n-bans-education-for-girls-in-pakistans-swat/.

Weisman, Steven R. 1991. "Japanese Translator of Rushdie Book
Found Slain." *New York Times.* July 13. Accessed May 13,
2020.
https://archive.nytimes.com/www.nytimes.com/books/99/04
/18/specials/rushdie-translator.html.

Welt. 2020. "Man kills his wife - in the middle of a bus." *Welt.de.* July
6. Accessed August 12, 2020.
https://www.welt.de/vermischtes/article211129199/Bayern-
Mann-toetet-seine-Ehefrau-mitten-in-einem-Linienbus.html.

Wienand, Lars. 2019. "Koran pages in the toilet: Iraqi caught red-
handed." *t-online.de.* September 12. Accessed November 14,
2019. https://www.t-
online.de/nachrichten/deutschland/gesellschaft/id_86435956
/koran-im-wc-iraker-als-verdaechtiger-in-schleswig-
gefasst.html.

Wiki Islam. 2012. "Lesser vs. Greater Jihad." *Wiki Islam.* Accessed
September 1, 2020.
https://wikiislam.net/wiki/Lesser_vs_Greater_Jihad#Lesser_v
s_Greater_Jihad_Concept.

Wright, Loveday. 2020. "Why do so many girls still face FGM?"
DW.com. February 6. Accessed February 11, 2020.
https://www.dw.com/en/female-genital-mutilation-why-do-
so-many-girls-still-face-fgm-a-52265630/a-52265630.

Yaqeen Institutue. 2019. "Jurisprudence (fiqh) Does Islam call Muslim
men to oppress women with polygamy." *Yaqeen Institute.*
December 20. Accessed April 19, 2021.
https://yaqeeninstitute.org/yaqeen-institute/does-islam-call-
for-muslim-men-to-oppress-women-with-polygamy.

Yuen, Jenny. 2015. "Draw Mohammed drawing in fans, foes." *Toronto
Sun.* May 20. Accessed May 21, 2020.

The Cancer of Civilization Jihad

https://web.archive.org/web/20100524091256/http://www.torontosun.com/news/torontoandgta/2010/05/20/14026241.html.

INDEX